Organs without Bodies

Gu

Organs without Bodies

Bodies

Deleuze and Consequences

Slavoj Žižek

ROUTLEDGE
NEW YORK AND LONDON

Published in 2004 by
Routledge
29 West 35th Street
New York, NY 10001
www.routledge-ny.com

Published in Great Britain by
Routledge
11 New Fetter Lane
London EC4P 4EE
www.routledge.co.uk

Routledge is an imprint of the Taylor & Francis Group.

Library of Congress Cataloging-in-Publication Data

Žižek, Slavoj.
Organs without bodies : Deleuze and consequences / Slavoj Žižek.
        p.   cm.
Includes index.
        ISBN 0-415-96920-4 (alk. paper)—ISBN 0-415-96921-2 (pbk.: alk. paper)
    1. Deleuze, Gilles.   I. Title.
    B2430.D454Z59   2003
    194—dc21

                                                                          2003011948

To Joan Copjec, with the coldness and cruelty of a true friendship

Contents

INTRODUCTION
An Encounter, Not a Dialogue

Gilles Deleuze was well known for his aversion toward debate—he once wrote that when a true philosopher sits in a café and hears somebody say "Let us debate this point a little bit!" he jumps up and runs away as fast as possible. He could have quoted as the proof of his attitude the entire history of philosophy. That Plato, the first true metaphysician, wrote dialogues is perhaps the greatest irony in the history of philosophy, since his dialogues never involve a symmetrical exchange of arguments. In the early dialogues, Socrates occupies the position of the one who "knows that he knows nothing," and, from it, undermines the presumed knowledge of his partners; in the late ones, the main character does all the talking while the partner's contribution is limited to occasional exclamations like "It is so!" "By Zeus, you are right!" and so forth. And, instead of bemoaning this fact, one should fully endorse and assume it. As Alain Badiou put it, philosophy is inherently *axiomatic,* the consequent deployment of a fundamental insight. Hence, all great "dialogues" in the history of philosophy were so many cases of misunderstanding: Aristotle misunderstood Plato, Thomas Aquinas misunderstood Aristotle, Hegel misunderstood Kant and Schelling, Marx misunderstood Hegel, Nietzsche misunderstood Christ, Heidegger misunderstood Hegel.... Precisely when one philosopher exerted a key influence upon another, this influence was without exception grounded in a productive misreading—did not the entirety of analytic philosophy emerge from misreading the early Wittgenstein?

Another complication that pertains to philosophy concerns the fact that, often, other disciplines take over (at least part of) the "normal" role of philosophy: in some of the nineteenth-century nations like Hungary or Poland, it was literature that played the role of philosophy (that of articulating the ultimate horizon of meaning of the nation in the process of its full constitution); in the United States today—in the conditions of the predominance of cognitivism and brain studies in philosophy departments—most of "Continental Philosophy" takes place in Departments of Comparative Literature, Cultural Studies, English, French, and German (as they are now saying, if you analyze a rat's vertebra, you are doing philosophy; if you analyze Hegel, you belong to CompLit); in Slovenia during the 1970s, the "dissident" philosophy took place in sociology departments and institutes. There is also the other extreme of philosophy itself taking over the tasks of other academic (or even nonacademic) practices and disciplines: again, in the former Yugoslavia and some other socialist countries, philosophy was one of the spaces of the first articulation of "dissident" political projects—it effectively was "politics pursued with other means" (as Althusser put it apropos of Lenin). So, where did philosophy play its "normal role"? One usually invokes Germany. However, is it not already a commonplace that the extraordinary role of philosophy in German history was grounded in the belatedness of the realization of the German national political project? As Marx already put it (taking his cue from Heine), Germans had their philosophical revolution (German Idealism) because they missed the political revolution (which took place in France). Is, then, there a norm at all? The closest one comes to it is if one looks upon the anemic established academic philosophy like neo-Kantianism one hundred years ago in Germany or French Cartesian epistemology (Leon Brunschvicg, etc.) of the first half of the twentieth century, which was precisely philosophy at its most stale, academic, irrelevant, and "dead." (No wonder that, in 2002, Luc Ferry, a neo-Kantian, was nominated the minister of education in the new center-right French government.) What if, then, there is no "normal role"? What if it is exceptions themselves that retroactively create the illusion of the "norm" they allegedly violate? What if not only, in philosophy, exception is the rule but also what if philosophy—the need for authentic philosophical thought—arises precisely in those moments when (other) parts-constituents of the social edifice cannot play their "proper role?" What if the "proper" space for philosophy *is* these very gaps and interstices opened up by "pathological" displacements in the social edifice?

For this (and other) reasons, Alain Badiou is right in rejecting Lacan's "anti-philosophy." In fact, when Lacan endlessly varies the motif of how philosophy tries to "fill in the holes," to present a totalizing view of the universe, to cover up all the gaps, ruptures, and inconsistencies (say, in the total self-transparency of self-consciousness)—and how, against philosophy, psychoanalysis asserts the constitutive gap/rupture/inconsistency, and so on and so forth—he simply misses the point of what the most fundamental philosophical gesture is: not to close the gap, but, on the contrary, to open up a radical gap in the very edifice of the universe, the "ontological difference," the gap between the empirical and the transcendental, in which neither of the two levels can be reduced to the other (as we know from Kant, transcendental constitution is a mark of our—human—finitude and has nothing to do with "creating reality"; on the other hand, reality appears to us only within the transcendental horizon, so we cannot generate the emergence of the transcendental horizon from the ontic self-development of reality).[1]

A Lacanian book on Deleuze cannot ignore all these facts. Consequently, *Organs without Bodies* is not a "dialogue" between these two theories but something quite different: an attempt to trace the contours of an *encounter* between two incompatible fields. An encounter cannot be reduced to symbolic exchange: what resonates in it, over and above the symbolic exchange, is the echo of a traumatic impact. While dialogues are commonplace, encounters are rare.

So, why Deleuze? In the past decade, Deleuze emerged as the central reference of contemporary philosophy: notions like "resisting multitude," "nomadic subjectivity," the "anti-Oedipal" critique of psychoanalysis, and so on are the common currency of today's academia—not to mention the fact that Deleuze more and more serves as the theoretical foundation of today's anti-globalist Left and its resistance to capitalism. *Organs without Bodies* here goes "against the current": its starting premise is that, beneath this Deleuze (the popular image of Deleuze based on the reading of the books he coauthored with Felix Guattari), there is another Deleuze, much closer to psychoanalysis and Hegel, a Deleuze whose consequences are much more shattering. This book therefore starts by discerning the inner tension of Deleuze's thought between *Anti-Oedipus* and *The Logic of Sense*, between the Deleuze who celebrated the productive multitude of Becoming against the reified order of being and the Deleuze of the sterility of the incorporeal becoming of the Sense-Event. The consequences of this tension are then deployed with regard to three principal domains: science, art (cinema), and politics (it is not difficult to discern in these three domains the good old triad of the True, the

[1] Perhaps, along these lines, one should even take the risk of proposing that psychoanalysis—the subject's confrontation with its innermost fantasmatic kernel—is no longer to be accepted as the ultimate gesture of subjective authenticity.

Beautiful, and the Good).[2] With regard to science, the possible links
between psychoanalysis, on one side, and cognitivism and the brain
sciences, on the other side, are explored. With regard to cinema, the
analysis of a series of formal procedures in classical and contemporary
Hollywood films (from Hitchcock to *Fight Club*) is used to deploy how
the notion of the "organ without a body" (which inverts the Deleuzian
notion of the body without organs) plays a key role not only in formal analysis but also with regard to the new figures of revolutionary
subjectivity. And, finally, in relation to politics, the deadlock and impotence of the popular "Deleuzian politics" is exposed, and the contours
of a different "Deleuzian politics" are outlined. The target of critique
here involves those aspects of Deleuzianism that, while masquerading as
radical chic, effectively transform Deleuze into an ideologist of today's
"digital capitalism."

*

During the shooting of David Lean's *Doctor Zhivago* in a Madrid suburb
in 1964, a crowd of Spanish statists had to sing the "Internationale" in a
scene involving a mass demonstration. The movie team was astonished
to discover that they all knew the song and were singing it with such
a passion that the Francoist police intervened, thinking that they were
dealing with a real political manifestation. Even more, when, late in the
evening (the scene was to take place in darkness), people living in the
nearby houses heard the echoes of the song, they opened up bottles and
started to dance in the street, wrongly presuming that Franco had died
and the Socialists had taken power.

This book is dedicated to those magic moments of illusory freedom
(which, in a way, were precisely not simply illusory) and to the hopes
thwarted by the return to "normal" reality.

[2] Especially with regard to the philosophical aspect of the book, I would like to thank Adrian
Johnston for many helpful critical suggestions.

Deleuze

The Reality of the Virtual

The measure of the true love for a philosopher is that one recognizes traces of his concepts all around in one's daily experience. Recently, while watching again Sergei Eisenstein's *Ivan the Terrible*, I noticed a wonderful detail in the coronation scene at the beginning of the first part: when the two (for the time being) closest friends of Ivan pour golden coins from the large plates onto his newly anointed head, this veritable rain of gold cannot but surprise the spectator by its magically excessive character— even after we see the two plates almost empty, we cut to Ivan's head on which golden coins "nonrealistically" continue to pour in a continuing flow. Is this excess not very "Deleuzian"? Is it not the excess of the pure flow of becoming over its corporeal cause, of the virtual over the actual?

The first determination that comes to mind apropos of Deleuze is that he is the philosopher of the Virtual—and the first reaction to it should be to oppose Deleuze's notion of the Virtual to the all-pervasive topic of virtual reality: what matters to Deleuze is not virtual reality but *the reality of the virtual* (which, in Lacanian terms, is the Real). Virtual Reality in itself is a rather miserable idea: that of imitating reality, of reproducing its experience in an artificial medium. The reality of the Virtual, on the other hand, stands for the reality of the Virtual as such, for its real effects and consequences. Let us take an attractor in mathematics: all positive lines or points in its sphere of attraction only approach it in an endless fashion, never reaching its form—the existence of this form is purely virtual, being nothing more than the shape toward which lines and points tend. However, precisely as such, the virtual is the Real of this field: the immovable focal point around which all elements circulate. Is not this Virtual ultimately the Symbolic as such? Let us take symbolic authority: to function as an effective authority, it has to remain not-fully-actualized, an eternal threat.

Perhaps, the ontological difference between the Virtual and the Actual is best captured by the shift in the way quantum physics conceives of the relationship between particles and their interactions: in an initial moment, it appears as if first (ontologically, at least) there are particles interacting in the mode of waves, oscillations, and so forth; then, in a second moment, we are forced to enact a radical shift of perspective—the primordial ontological fact are the waves themselves (trajectories, oscillations), and particles are nothing but the nodal points in which different waves intersect.[1] This brings us to the constitutive ambiguity of the relationship between actual and virtual: (1) the human eye *reduces* the perception of light; it actualizes light in a certain way (perceiving certain colors, etc.), a rose in a different way, a bat in a different way. . . . The flow of light "in itself" is nothing actual, but, rather, the pure virtuality of infinite possibilities actualized in a multitude of ways; (2) on the other hand, the human eye expands perception—it inscribes what it "really sees" into the intricate network of memories and anticipations (like Proust with the taste of madeleine), it can develop new perceptions, and so forth.[2]

The genius of Deleuze resides in his notion of "transcendental empiricism": in contrast to the standard notion of the transcendental as the formal conceptual network that structures the rich flow of empirical data, *the Deleuzian "transcendental" is infinitely RICHER than reality*—it is the infinite potential field of virtualities out of which reality is actualized. The term "transcendental" is used here in the strict philosophical sense of the a priori conditions of possibility of our experience of constituted reality. The paradoxical coupling of opposites (transcendental + empirical) points toward a field of experience beyond (or, rather, beneath) the

---

[1] The genealogy of Deleuze's concepts is often strange and unexpected—say, his assertion of the Anglo-Saxon notion of external relations is clearly indebted to the religious problematic of grace. The missing link here is Alfred Hitchcock, the English Catholic, in whose films a change in relations between persons, in no way rooted in their characters, totally external to them, changes everything, deeply affects them (say, when, at the beginning of *North-by-Northwest,* Thornhill is wrongly identified as Kaplan). Chabrol and Rohmer's Catholic reading of Hitchcock (in their *Hitchcock,* 1954) deeply influenced Deleuze since, in the Jansenist tradition, it focuses precisely on "grace" as a contingent divine intervention that has nothing to do with the inherent virtues and qualities of the affected characters.

[2] And is this ambiguity not homologous to the ontological paradox of quantum physics? The very "hard reality" that emerges out of the fluctuation through the collapse of the wave-function, is the outcome of observation, that is, of the intervention of consciousness. Consciousness is thus not the domain of potentiality, multiple options, and so forth, as opposed to hard single reality—reality *previous* to its perception is fluid-multiple-open, and conscious perception reduces this spectral, preontological multiplicity to one ontologically, fully constituted, reality.

experience of constituted or perceived reality. We remain here within the field of consciousness: Deleuze defines the field of transcendental empiricism as "a pure a-subjective current of consciousness, an impersonal prereflexive consciousness, a qualitative duration of consciousness without self."[3] No wonder that (one of) his reference(s) here is the late Fichte, who tried to think the absolute process of self-positing as a flow of Life beyond the opposites of subject and object: "A life is the immanence of immanence, absolute immanence: it is sheer power, utter beatitude. Insofar as he overcomes the aporias of the subject and the object Fichte, in his later philosophy, presents the transcendental field as a life which does not depend on a Being and is not subjected to an Act: an absolute immediate consciousness whose very activity no longer refers back to a being but ceaselessly posits itself in a life."[4]

Perhaps Jackson Pollock is the ultimate "Deleuzian painter": does his action-painting not directly render this flow of pure becoming, the impersonal-unconscious life energy, the encompassing field of virtuality out of which determinate paintings can actualize themselves, this field of pure intensities with no meaning to be unearthed by interpretation? The cult of Pollock's personality (heavy-drinking American macho) is secondary with regard to this fundamental feature: far from "expressing" his personality, his works "sublate" or cancel it.[5] The first example that comes to mind in the domain of cinema is Sergei Eisenstein: if his early silent films are remembered primarily on account of their practice of montage in its different guises, from the "montage of attractions" to "intellectual montage" (i.e., if their accent is on cuts), then his "mature" sound films shift the focus onto the continuous proliferation of what Lacan called *sinthomes,* of the traces of affective intensities. Recall, throughout both parts of *Ivan the Terrible* the motif of the thunderous explosion of rage that is continuously morphed and thus assumes different guises, from the thunderstorm itself to the explosions of uncontrolled fury. Although it may at first appear to be an expression of Ivan's psyche, its sound detaches itself from Ivan and starts to float around, passing from one to another person or to a state not attributable to any diegetic person. This motif should be interpreted not as an "allegory" with a fixed "deeper meaning" but as a pure "mechanic" intensity beyond meaning (this is what

---

[3] Gilles Deleuze, "Immanence: une vie . . . ," quoted from John Marks, *Gilles Deleuze* (London: Pluto Press, 1998), p. 29.

[4] Deleuze, op. cit., p. 30. One is tempted to oppose to this Deleuzian absolute immanence of the flow of Life, as the *presubjective consciousness,* the Freudo-Lacanian *unconscious subject* ($) as the agency of the death drive.

[5] So what about the opposition Pollock-Rothko? Does it not correspond to the opposition of Deleuze versus Freud/Lacan? The virtual field of potentialities versus the minimal difference, the gap between background and figure?

Eisenstein aimed at in his idiosyncratic use of the term "operational"). Other such motives echo and reverse each other, or, in what Eisenstein called "naked transfer," jump from one to another expressive medium (say, when an intensity gets too strong in the visual medium of mere shapes, it jumps and explodes in movement—then in sound, or in color...). For example, Kirstin Thompson points out how the motif of a single eye in *Ivan* is a "floating motif," in itself strictly meaningless, but a repeated element that can, according to context, acquire a range of expressive implications (joy, suspicion, surveillance, quasi-godlike omniscience).[6] And the most interesting moments in *Ivan* occur when such motifs seem to explode their preordained space. Not only do they acquire a multitude of ambiguous meanings no longer covered by an encompassing thematic or ideological agenda but also, in the most excessive moments, such a motif seems even to have no meaning at all, instead just floating there as a provocation, as a challenge to find the meaning that would tame its sheer provocative power.

Among contemporary filmmakers, the one who lends himself ideally to a Deleuzian reading is Robert Altman, whose universe, best exemplified by his masterpiece *Short Cuts,* is effectively that of contingent encounters between a multitude of series, a universe in which different series communicate and resonate at the level of what Altman himself refers to as "subliminal reality" (meaningless mechanic shocks, encounters, and impersonal intensities that precede the level of social meaning).[7] So, in *Nashville,* when violence explodes at the end (the murder of Barbara Jean at the concert), this explosion, although unprepared and unaccounted for at the level of the explicit narrative line, is nonetheless experienced as fully justified, since the ground for it was laid at the level of signs circulating in the film's "subliminal reality." And is it not that, when we hear the songs in *Nashville,* Altman directly mobilizes what Brian Massumi calls the "autonomy of affect"?[8] That is to say, we totally misread *Nashville* if we locate the songs within the global horizon of the ironico-critical depiction of the vacuity and ritualized commercial alienation of the universe of American country music: on the contrary, we are allowed to—even seduced into—enjoy fully the music on its own, in its affective intensity, independent of Altman's obvious critico-ideological project. (Incidentally, the same goes for the songs from Brecht's great

---

[6] See Kirstin Thompson, *Eisenstein's "Ivan the Terrible": A Neoformalist Analysis* (Princeton, N.J.: Princeton University Press, 1981).

[7] See Robert T. Self, *Robert Altman's Subliminal Reality* (Minneapolis: University of Minnesota Press, 2002).

[8] See Brian Massumi, "The Autonomy of Affect," in *Deleuze: A Critical Reader,* edited by Paul Patton (Oxford: Blackwell, 1996).

pieces—their musical pleasure is independent of their ideological message.) What this means is that one should also avoid the temptation of reducing Altman to a poet of American alienation, rendering the silent despair of everyday lives. There is another Altman, namely, the one of opening oneself to joyful contigent encounters. Along the same lines as Deleuze and Guattari's reading of Kafka's universe of the Absence of the inaccessible and elusive transcendent Center (Castle, Court, God) as the Presence of multiple passages and transformations, one is tempted to read the Altmanian "despair and anxiety" as the deceiving obverse of the more affirmative immersion into the multitude of subliminal intensities. Of course, this underlying plane can also contain the obscene superego subtext of the "official" ideological message—recall the notorious "Uncle Sam" recruiting poster for the U.S. Army:

> This is an image whose demands, if not desires, seem absolutely clear, focussed on a determinate object: it wants "you," that is, the young men of the proper age for military service. The immediate aim of the picture looks like a version of the Medusa effect: that is, it "hails" the viewer, verbally, and tries to transfix him with the directness of its gaze and (its most wonderful pictorial feature) the foreshortened pointing hand and finger that single out the viewer, accusing, designating, and commanding the viewer. But the desire to transfix is only a transitory and momentary goal. The longer-range motive is to move and mobilize the viewer, to send the beholder on to "the nearest recruiting station," and ultimately overseas to fight and possibly die for his country.
>
> . . . Here the contrast with the German and Italian posters is clarifying. These are posters in which young soldiers hail their brothers, call them to the brotherhood of honorable death in battle. *Uncle* Sam, as his name indicates, has a more tenuous, indirect relation to the potential recruit. He is an older man who lacks the youthful vigor for combat, and perhaps even more important, lacks the direct blood connection that a figure of the fatherland would evoke. He asks young men to go fight and die in a war in which neither he nor his sons will participate. There are no "sons" of Uncle Sam. . . . Uncle Sam himself is sterile, a kind of abstract, pasteboard figure who has no body, no blood, but who impersonates the nation and calls for other men's sons to donate their bodies and their blood.
>
> So what does this picture want? A full analysis would take us deep into the political unconscious of a nation that is nominally imagined as a disembodied abstraction, an Enlightenment polity of laws and not men, principles and not blood relationships, and actually embodied as a place where old white men send young men and women of all races (including a disproportionately high number of colored people) to fight their wars. What this real and imagined nation lacks is meat—bodies and blood—and what it sends to obtain them is a hollow man, a meat supplier, or perhaps just an artist.[9]

---

[9] Tom Mitchell, "What Do Pictures *Really* Want?" *October*, no. 77 (summer 1996): 64–66.

The first thing to do here is to add to this series the famous Soviet poster "Motherland is calling you," in which the interpellator is a mature strong woman. We thus move from the American imperialist Uncle through European Brothers to the Communist Mother—here we have the split, constitutive of interpellation, between law and superego (or want and desire). What a picture like this *wants* is not the same as what it *desires:* while it wants us to participate in the noble struggle for freedom, it desires blood, the proverbial pound of our flesh (no wonder the elder sterile "Uncle [not Father] Sam" can be deciphered as a Jewish figure, along the lines of the Nazi reading of American military interventions: "the Jewish plutocracy wants the blood of the innocent Americans to feed their interests"). In short, it would be ridiculous to say that "Uncle Sam desires you": Uncle Sam wants you, but he desires the partial object in you, your pound of flesh. When a superego call WANTS (and enjoins) you to do it, to gather the strength and succeed, the secret message of DESIRE is "I know you will not be able to achieve it, so I desire you to fail and to gloat in your failure!" This superego character, confirmed by the Yankee Doodle association (recall the fact that superego figures inextricably mix obscene ferocity and clownish comedy), is further sustained by the contradictory character of its call: it first wants to arrest our movement and fixate our gaze, so that, surprised, we stare at it; in a second moment, it wants us to follow its call and go to the nearest conscription office—as if, after stopping us, it mockingly addresses us: "Why do you stare at me like an idiot? Didn't you get my point? Go to the nearest conscription post!" In the arrogant gesture typical of the mocking characteristics of the superego, it laughs at our very act of taking seriously its first call.[10]

When Eric Santner told me about a game his father played with him when he was a small boy (the father showed, opened up in front of him, his palm, in which there were a dozen or so different coins; the father then closed his palm after a couple of seconds and asked the boy how much money there was in his palm—if the small Eric guessed the exact sum, the father gave him the money), this anecdote provoked in me an explosion of deep and uncontrollable anti-Semitic satisfaction expressed in wild laughter: "You see, this is how Jews really teach their children! Is this not a perfect case of your own theory of a proto-history which accompanies the explicit symbolic history? At the level of explicit history, your father was probably telling you noble stories about Jewish suffering and the universal horizon of humanity, but his true secret teaching was

---

[10] What, then, more generally, does a picture want? One is tempted to apply here the good old Lacanian triad of ISR: at the level of the Imaginary, it is a lure that wants to seduce us into aesthetic pleasure; at the level of the Symbolic, it calls for its interpretation; at the level of the Real, it endeavors to shock us, to cause us to avert our eyes or to fixate our gaze.

contained in those practical jokes about how to quickly deal with money."
Anti-Semitism effectively *is* part of the ideologocal obscene underside of
most of us.

And one finds a similar obscene subtext even where one would not
expect it—in some texts that are commonly perceived as feminist. To
confront this obscene "plague of fantasies" that persists at the level of
"subliminal reality" at its most radical, suffice it to (re)read Margaret
Atwood's *The Handmaid's Tale,* the distopia about the "Republic of
Gilead," a new state on the East Coast of the United States that emerged
when the Moral Majority took over. The ambiguity of the novel is radical:
its "official" aim is, of course, to present as actually realized the darkest
conservative tendencies in order to warn us about the threats of Christian
fundamentalism—the evoked vision is expected to give rise to horror in
us. However, what strikes the eye is the utter *fascination* with this imagined universe and its invented rules. Fertile woman are allocated to those
privileged members of the new nomenklatura whose wives cannot bear
children—forbidden to read, deprived of their names (they are called
after the man to whom they belong: the heroine is Offred—"of Fred"),
they serve as receptacles of insemination. The more we read the novel,
the more it becomes clear that the fantasy we are reading is not that of the
Moral Majority but that of feminist liberalism itself: an exact mirror image of the fantasies about the sexual degeneration in our megalopolises
that haunt members of the Moral Majority. So, what the novel displays
is desire—not of the Moral Majority but the hidden desire of feminist
liberalism itself.

Becoming versus History

The ontological opposition between Being and Becoming that underpins
Deleuze's notion of the virtual is a radical one in that its ultimate reference
is *pure becoming without being* (as opposed to the metaphysical notion of
pure being without becoming). This pure becoming is not a particular
becoming *of* some corporeal entity, a passage of this entity from one
to another state, but a becoming-it-itself, thoroughly extracted from
its corporeal base. Since the predominant temporality of Being is that
of the present (with past and future as its deficient modes), the pure
becoming-without-being means that one should sidestep the present—
it never "actually occurs," it is "always forthcoming and already past."[11] As
such, pure becoming suspends sequentiality and directionality: say, in an
actual process of becoming, the critical point of temperature (0 degrees
Celsius) always has a direction (water either freezes or melts), whereas,

[11] Gilles Deleuze, *The Logic of Sense* (New York: Columbia University Press, 1990), p. 80.

considered as pure becoming extracted from its corporeality, this point of passage is not a passage from one to another state but a "pure" passage, neutral as to its directionality, perfectly symmetric—for instance, a thing is simultaneously getting larger (that it was) and smaller (than it will be). And is not the ultimate example of the poetry of pure becoming the Zen poems that aim merely to render the fragility of the pure event extracted from its causal context?

The Foucault closest to Deleuze is therefore the Foucault of *The Archeology of Knowledge,* his underrated key work delineating the ontology of utterances as pure language events: not elements of a structure, not attributes of subjects who utter them, but events that emerge, function within a field, and disappear. To put it in Stoic terms, Foucault's discourse analysis studies *lekta,* utterances as pure events, focusing on the inherent conditions of their emergence (as the concatenation of events themselves) and not on their inclusion in the context of historical reality. This is why the Foucault of *The Archeology of Knowledge* is as far as possible from any form of historicism, of locating events in their historical context—on the contrary, Foucault *abstracts* them from their reality and its historical causality and studies the *immanent* rules of their emergence. What one should bear in mind here is that Deleuze is *not* an evolutionary historicist; his opposition of Being and Becoming should not deceive us. He is not simply arguing that all stable, fixed entities are just coagulations of the all-encompassing flux of Life—why not? The reference to the notion of *time* is crucial here. Let us recall how Deleuze (with Guattari), in his description of becoming in/of philosophy, explicitly opposes becoming and history:

> Philosophical time is thus a grandiose time of coexistence that does not exclude the before and after but *superimposes* them in a stratigraphic order. It is an infinite becoming of philosophy that crosscuts its history without being confused with it. The life of philosophers, and what is most external to their work, conforms to the ordinary laws of succession; but their proper names coexist and shine as luminous points that take us through the components of a concept once more or as the cardinal points of a stratum or layer that continually come back to us, like dead stars whose light is brighter than ever.[12]

The paradox is thus that transcendental becoming inscribes itself into the order of positive being, of constituted reality, *in the guise of its very opposite,* of a static superimposition, of a crystallized freeze of historical development. This Deleuzian eternity is, of course, not simply outside

---

[12] Gilles Deleuze and Felix Guattari, *What Is Philosophy?* (New York: Columbia University Press, 1994), p. 59.

time; rather, in the "stratigraphic" superimposition, in this moment of stasis, it is *time itself* that we experience, time as opposed to the evolutionary flow of things *within* time. It was Schelling who, following Plato, wrote that time is the image of eternity—a statement more paradoxical than it may appear. Is time, temporal existence, not the very opposite of eternity, the domain of decay, of generation and corruption? How then can time be the image of eternity? Does this not involve two contradictory claims, namely, that time is the fall from eternity into corruption *and* its very opposite, the striving for eternity? The only solution is to bring this paradox to its radical conclusion: *time is the striving of eternity to REACH ITSELF.* What this means is that eternity is not outside time but the pure structure of time "as such": as Deleuze put it, the moment of stratigraphic superimposition that suspends temporal succession is time as such. In short, one should oppose here development *within time* to the explosion of *time itself*: time itself (the infinite virtuality of the transcendental field of Becoming) appears *within* the intra-temporal evolution in the guise of *eternity*. The moments of the emergence of the New are precisely the moments of Eternity in time. The emergence of the New occurs when a work overcomes its historical context. And, on the opposite side, if there is a true image of fundamental ontological immobility, it is the evolutionary image of the universe as a complex network of endless transformations and developments in which *plus que ça change, plus ça reste le même:*

> I became more and more aware of the possibility of distinguishing between becoming and history. It was Nietzsche who said that nothing important is ever free from a "nonhistorical cloud." . . . What history grasps in an event is the way it's actualized in particular circumstances; the event's becoming is beyond the scope of history. . . . Becoming isn't part of history; history amounts only to the set of preconditions, however recent, that one leaves behind in order to "become," that is, to create something new.[13]

To designate this process, one is tempted to use a term strictly prohibited by Deleuze, that of TRANSCENDENCE: is Deleuze here not arguing that a certain process can transcend its historical conditions by way of giving rise to an Event? It was Sartre (one of Deleuze's secret points of reference) who already used the term in this sense when he discussed how, in the act of synthesis, the subject can transcend its conditions. Examples abound here from cinema (Deleuze's reference to the birth of the Italian neorealism: of course it arose out of circumstances—the shock of World War II, and so on—but the neorealist Event is not reducible to these historical causes) to politics. In politics (and, in a way, reminiscent of Badiou),

---

[13] Gilles Deleuze, *Negotiations* (New York: Columbia University Press, 1995), pp. 170–71.

Deleuze's basic reproach to conservative critics who denounce the miserable and even terrifying actual results of a revolutionary upheaval is that they remain blind to the dimension of becoming:

> It is fashionable these days to condemn the horrors of revolution. It's nothing new; English Romanticism is permeated by reflections on Cromwell very similar to present-day reflections on Stalin. They say revolutions turn out badly. But they're constantly confusing two different things, the way revolutions turn out historically and people's revolutionary becoming. These relate to two different sets of people. Men's only hope lies in a revolutionary becoming: the only way of casting off their shame or responding to what is intolerable.[14]

Becoming is thus strictly correlative to the concept of REPETITION: far from being opposed to the emergence of the New, the proper Deleuzian paradox is that something truly New can *only* emerge through repetition. What repetition repeats is not the way the past "effectively was" but the *virtuality* inherent to the past and betrayed by its past actualization. In this precise sense, the emergence of the New changes the past itself, that is, it retroactively changes not the actual past—we are not in science fiction—but the balance between actuality and virtuality in the past.[15] Recall the old example provided by Walter Benjamin: the October Revolution repeated the French Revolution, redeeming its failure, unearthing and repeating the same impulse. Already for Kierkegaard, repetition is "inverted memory," a movement forward, the production of the New and not the reproduction of the Old. "There is nothing new under the sun" is the strongest contrast to the movement of repetition. So, it is not only that repetition is (one of the modes of) the emergence of the New— *the New can ONLY emerge through repetition.* The key to this paradox is, of course, what Deleuze designates as the difference between the Virtual and the Actual (and which—why not?—one can also determine as the difference between Spirit and Letter).

Let us take a great philosopher like Kant. There are two modes to repeat him. Either one sticks to his letter and further elaborates or changes his system, as neo-Kantians (up to Habermas and Luc Ferry) are doing, or one tries to regain the creative impulse that Kant himself betrayed in

---

[14] Deleuze, op. cit., p. 171.

[15] When, in 1953, Chou En Lai, the Chinese prime minister, was in Geneva for the peace negotiations to end the Korean War, a French journalist asked him what he thought about the French Revolution, and Chou replied, "It is still too early to tell." In a way, he was right. With the disintegration of socialist states, the struggle for the historical place of the French Revolution flared up again. The liberal Rightist revisionists try to impose the notion that the demise of communism in 1989 occurred at exactly the right moment: it marked the end of the era that began in 1789. In short, what effectively vanished from history was the revolutionary model that first entered the scene with the Jacobins. François Furet and others thus try to deprive the French Revolution of its status as the founding event of modern democracy, relegating it to a historical anomaly.

the actualization of his system (i.e., to connect to what was already "in Kant more than Kant himself," more than his explicit system, its excessive core). There are, accordingly, two modes of betraying the past. The true betrayal is an ethico-theoretical act of the highest fidelity: one has to betray the letter of Kant to remain faithful to (and repeat) the "spirit" of his thought. It is precisely when one remains faithful to the letter of Kant that one really betrays the core of his thought, the creative impulse underlying it. One should bring this paradox to its conclusion. It is not only that one can remain really faithful to an author by way of betraying him (the actual letter of his thought); at a more radical level, the inverse statement holds even more, namely, one can only truly betray an author by way of repeating him, by way of remaining faithful to the core of his thought. If one does not repeat an author (in the authentic Kierkegaardian sense of the term), but merely "criticizes" him, moves elsewhere, turns him around, and so forth, this effectively means that one unknowingly remains within his horizon, his conceptual field.[16] When G. K. Chesterton describes his conversion to Christianity, he claims that he "tried to be some ten minutes in advance of the truth. And I found that I was eighteen years behind it."[17] Does the same not hold even more for those who, today, desperately try to catch up with the New by way of following the latest "post" fashion and are thus condemned to remain forever eighteen years behind the truly New?

And, this brings us to the complex topic of the relationship between Hegel and Kierkegaard. Against the "official" notion of Kierkegaard as *the* "anti-Hegel," one should assert that Kierkegaard is arguably the one who, through his very "betrayal" of Hegel, effectively remained faithful to him. He effectively *repeated* Hegel, in contrast to Hegel's pupils, who "developed" his system further. For Kierkegaard, the Hegelian *Aufhebung* is to be opposed to repetition. Hegel is the ultimate Socratic philosopher of rememorization, of reflectively returning to what the thing always-already was, so that what Hegel lacks is simultaneously repetition and the emergence of the New—the emergence of the New *as* repetition. The

---

[16] Authentic fidelity is the fidelity to the void itself—to the very act of loss, of abandoning or erasing the object. Why should the dead be the object of attachment in the first place? The name for this fidelity is death drive. In the terms of dealing with the dead, one should, perhaps, against the work of mourning as well as against the melancholic attachment to the dead who return as ghosts, assert the Christian motto "let the dead bury their dead." The obvious reproach to this motto is, What are we to do when, precisely, the dead do not accept to stay dead, but continue to live in us, haunting us by their spectral presence? One is tempted here to claim that the most radical dimension of the Freudian death drive provides the key to how are we to read the Christian "let the dead bury their dead": what death drive tries to obliterate is not the biological life but the very afterlife—it endeavors to kill the lost object the second time, not in the sense of mourning (accepting the loss through symbolization) but in a more radical sense of obliterating the very symbolic texture, the letter in which the spirit of the dead survives.

[17] G. K. Chesterton, *Orthodoxy* (San Francisco: Ignatius Press, 1995), p. 16.

Hegelian dialectical process/progress is, in this precise Kierkegaardian sense, the very model of a pseudo-development in which nothing effectively New ever emerges. That is to say, the standard (Kierkegaardian) reproach to Hegel is that his system is a closed circle of rememoration that does not allow for anything New to emerge. All that happens is just the passage from In-itself to For-itself, that is, in the course of the dialectical process, things just actualize their potentials, explicitly posit their implicit content, become what (in themselves) they always-already are. The first enigma apropos of this reproach is that it is usually accompanied with the *opposite* reproach: Hegel deploys how "the One divides into Two," the explosion of a split, loss, negativity, antagonism, which affects an organic unity; but, then, the reversal of *Aufhebung* intervenes as a kind of deux ex machina, always guaranteeing that the antagonism will be magically resolved, the opposites reconciled in a higher synthesis, the loss recuperated without a remainder, the wound healed without a scar remaining. The two reproaches thus point in the opposite directions: the first one claims that nothing new emerges under the Hegelian sun, whereas the second one claims that the deadlock is resolved by an imposed solution that emerges as deux ex machina, from outside, not as the outcome of the inherent dynamic of the preceding tension.

The mistake of the second reproach is that it misses the point—or, rather, the temporality—of the Hegelian "reconciliation." It is not that the tension is magically resolved and the opposites are reconciled. The only shift that effectively occurs is subjective, the shift of our perspective (i.e., all of a sudden, we become aware that what previously appeared as conflict *already is* reconciliation). This temporal move backward is crucial: the contradiction is not resolved; we just establish that it always-already *was* resolved. (In theological terms, Redemption does not follow the Fall; it occurs when we become aware of how what we previously (mis)perceived as Fall "in itself" already was Redemption.)[18] And, paradoxically, although this temporality may seem to confirm the first reproach (that nothing new emerges in the Hegelian process), it effectively enables us to refute it. The truly New is not simply a new content but the very shift of perspective by means of which the Old appears in a new light.

Deleuze is right in his magnificent attack on historicist "contextualization": becoming means transcending the context of historical conditions out of which a phenomenon emerges. This is what is missing in historicist antiuniversalist multiculturalism: the explosion of the eternally New in/as the process of becoming. The standard opposition of the abstract

---

[18] For a more detailed account of this move, see chapter 3 of Slavoj Žižek, *The Puppet and the Dwarf* (Cambridge, Mass.: MIT Press, 2003).

Universal (say, Human Rights) and particular identities is to be replaced by a new tension between Singular and Universal: the Event of the New as a universal singularity.[19] What Deleuze renders here is the (properly Hegelian) link between true historicity and eternity: a truly New emerges as eternity in time, transcending its material conditions. To perceive a past phenomenon in becoming (as Kierkegaard would have put it) is to perceive the virtual potential in it, the spark of eternity, of virtual potentiality that is there forever. A truly new work *stays new forever*—its newness is not exhausted when its "shocking value" passes away. For example, in philosophy, the great breakthroughs—from Kant's transcendental turn to Kripke's invention of the "rigid designator"—forever retain their "surprising" character of invention.

One often hears that to understand a work of art one needs to know its historical context. Against this historicist commonplace, a Deleuzian counterclaim would be not only that too much of a historical context can blur the proper contact with a work of art (i.e., that to enact this contact one should abstract from the work's context), but also that it is, rather, the work of art itself that provides a context enabling us to understand properly a given historical situation. If someone were to visit Serbia today, the direct contact with raw data there would leave him confused. If, however, he were to read a couple of literary works and see a couple of representative movies, they would definitely provide the context that would enable him to locate the raw data of his experience. There is thus an unexpected truth in the old cynical wisdom from the Stalinist Soviet Union: "he lies as an eyewitness!"

"Becoming-Machine"

Perhaps the core of Deleuze's concept of repetition is the idea that, in contrast to the mechanical (not machinic!) repetition of linear causality, in a proper instance of repetition, the repeated event is re-created in a radical sense: it (re)emerges every time as New (say, to "repeat" Kant is to rediscover the radical novelty of his breakthrough, of his problematic, not to repeat the statements that provide his solutions). One is tempted to establish here a link with Chesterton's Christian ontology, in which repetition of the same is the greatest miracle. There is nothing "mechanical" in the fact that the sun rises again every morning; this fact, on the contrary, displays the highest miracle of God's creativity.[20]

---

[19] This holds even if we reformulate the Universal in the Laclauian sense of empty signifier caught in the struggle for hegemony: the universal singularity is not the empty universal signifier filled in—hegemonized by—some particular content. It is almost its obverse: a singularity that explodes the given contours of the universality in question and opens it up to a radically new content.

[20] See Chesterton, *Orthodoxy*, p. 65.

What Deleuze calls "desiring machines" concerns something wholly different from the mechanical: the "becoming-machine." In what does this becoming consist? To many an obsessional neurotic, his or her fear of flying has a very concrete image: one is haunted by the thought of how many parts of such an immensely complicated machine as a modern plane have to function smoothly for the plane to remain in the air—one small lever breaks somewhere, and the plane may very well spiral downward. One often relates in the same way toward one's own body: how many small things have to run smoothly for me to stay alive?—a tiny clot of blood in a vein and I die. When one starts to think how many things can go wrong, one cannot but experience total and overwhelming panic. The Deleuzian "schizo," on the other hand, merrily identifies with this infinitely complex machine that is our body: he experiences this impersonal machine as his highest assertion, rejoicing in its constant tickling. As Deleuze emphasizes, what we get here is not the relationship of a *metaphor* (the old boring topic of "machines replacing humans") but that of *metamorphosis,* of the "becoming-machine" of a man. It is here that the "reductionist" project goes wrong: the problem is not how to reduce mind to neuronal "material" processes (to replace the language of mind by the language of brain processes, to translate the first one into the second one) but, rather, to grasp how mind can emerge only by being embedded in the network of social relations and material supplements. In other words, the true problem is not "How, if at all, could machines *imitate* the human mind?" but "How does the very identity of human mind rely on external mechanical supplements? How does it incorporate machines?"

Instead of bemoaning how the progressive externalization of our mental capacities in "objective" instruments (from writing on paper to relying on a computer) deprives us of human potentials, one should therefore focus on the liberating dimension of this externalization: the more our capacities are transposed onto external machines, the more we emerge as "pure" subjects, since this emptying equals the rise of substanceless subjectivity. It is only when we will be able to rely fully on "thinking machines" that we will be confronted with the void of subjectivity. In March 2002, the media reported that Kevin Warwick from London became the first cyberman: in a hospital in Oxford, his neuronal system was directly connected to a computer network. He is thus the first man to whom data will be fed directly, bypassing the five senses. *This* is the future: the combination of the human mind with the computer (rather than the replacement of the former by the latter).

We got another taste of this future in May 2002 when it was reported that scientists at New York University had attached a computer chip able to receive signals directly to a rat's brain so that one can control the rat (determine the direction in which it will run) by means of a steering mechanism (in the same way one runs a remote-controlled toy car). This is not the first case of the direct link between a brain and a computer network. There already are such links that enable blind people to get elementary visual information about their surroundings directly fed into their brain, bypassing the apparatus of visual perception (eyes, etc.). What is new in the case of the rat is that, for the first time, the "will" of a living animal agent, its "spontaneous" decisions about the movements it will make, are taken over by an external machine. Of course, the big philosophical question here is, How did the unfortunate rat "experience" its movement that was effectively decided from outside? Did it continue to "experience" it as something spontaneous (i.e., was it totally unaware that its movements are steered?) or was it aware that "something is wrong," that another external power is deciding its movements? Even more crucial is to apply the same reasoning to an identical experiment performed with humans (which, ethical questions notwithstanding, shouldn't be much more complicated, technically speaking, than in the case of the rat). In the case of the rat, one can argue that one should not apply to it the human category of "experience," while, in the case of a human being, one cannot avoid asking this question. So, again, will a steered human being continue to "experience" his movements as something spontaneous? Will he remain totally unaware that his movements are steered, or will he become aware that "something is wrong," that another external power is deciding his movements? And, how, precisely, will this "external power" appear—as something "inside me," an unstoppable inner drive, or as a simple external coercion?[21] Perhaps the situation will be the one described in Benjamin Libet's famous experiment:[22] the steered human being will continue to experience the urge to move as his "spontaneous" decision, but due to the famous half-a-second delay he or she will retain the minimal freedom to *block* this decision.

It is also interesting to note which applications of this mechanism were mentioned by the scientists and the reporting journalists. The first uses mentioned related to the couple of humanitarian aid and the

[21] Cognitivists often advise us to rely on commonsense evidence: of course we can indulge in speculations about how we are not the causal agents of our acts, of how our bodily movements are steered by a mysterious evil spirit, so that it just appears that we freely decide what movements to make. In the absence of good reasons, such skepticism is nonetheless simply unwarranted. However, does the experiment with the steered rat not provide a pertinent reason for entertaining such hypotheses?

[22] See Benjamin Libet, "Unconscious Cerebral Initiative and the Role of Conscious Will in Voluntary Action," in *The Behavioral and Brain Sciences* (Cambridge: Cambridge University Press, 1985), vol. 8, pp. 529–39, and Benjamin Libet, "Do We Have Free Will?" *Journal of Consciousness Studies* (Charlottesville: Imprint Academic) 1 (1999): 47–57.

antiterrorist campaign (one could use the steered rats or other animals to contact victims of an earthquake under the rubble as well as to approach terrorists without risking human lives). The crucial thing one has to bear in mind here is that this uncanny experience of the human mind directly integrated into a machine is not the vision of a future or of something new but the insight into something that is always-already going on, which was here from the very beginning since it is co-substantial with the symbolic order. What changes is that, confronted with the direct materialization of the machine, its direct integration into the neuronal network, one can no longer sustain the illusion of the autonomy of personhood. It is well known that the patients who need dialysis at first experience a shattering feeling of helplessness: it is difficult to accept the fact that one's very survival hinges on the mechanical device that I see out there in front of me. Yet, the same goes for all of us. To put it in somewhat exaggerated terms, we are all in the need of a mental-symbolic apparatus of dialysis.

The trend in the development of computers is toward their invisibility. The large humming machines with mysterious blinking ligthts will be more and more replaced by tiny bits fitting imperceptibly into our "normal" environs, enabling them to function more smoothly. Computers will become so small that they will be invisible, everywhere and nowhere—so powerful that they will disappear from view. One should only recall today's car, in which many functions run smoothly because of small computers we are mostly unaware of (opening windows, heating, etc.). In the near future, we will have computerized kitchens or even dresses, glasses, and shoes. Far from being a matter for the distant future, this invisibility is already here. Philips soon plans to offer on the market a phone and music player that will be interwoven into the texture of a jacket to such an extent that it will be possible not only to wear the jacket in an ordinary way (without worrying what will happen to the digital machinery) but even to launder it without damaging the electronic hardware. This disappearance from the field of our sensual (visual) experience is not as innocent as it may appear. The very feature that will make the Philips jacket easy to deal with (as no longer a cumbersome and fragile machine but a quasi-organic prothesis to our body) will confer on it the phantomlike character of an all-powerful, invisible Master. The machinic prothesis will be less an external apparatus with which we interact and more part of our direct self-experience as a living organism—thus decentering us from within. For this reason, the parallel between computers' growing invisibility and the well-known fact that when people learn something sufficiently well they cease to be aware of it is misleading. The sign that we learned a language is that we no longer need to focus on its rules: we not only speak it "spontaneously" but an active focus on the rules even prevents us from fluently speaking it. However, in the case of language, we previously had to learn it (we "have it in our mind"), whereas invisible computers in our environs are out there, not acting "spontaneously" but simply blindly.

One should accomplish here a step further: Bo Dahlbom is right, in his critique of Dennett,[23] in which he insists on the *social* character of "mind"—not only are theories of mind obviously conditioned by their historical, social context (does Dennett's theory of competing multiple drafts not display its roots in "postindustrial" late capitalism, with its motifs of competition, decentralization, etc.?—a notion also developed by Fredric Jameson, who proposed a reading of *Consciousness Explained* as an allegory of today's capitalism). Much more important, Dennett's insistence on how tools—externalized intelligence on which humans rely—are an inherent part of human identity (it is meaningless to imagine a human being as a biological entity *without* the complex network of his or her tools—such a notion is the same as, say, a goose without its feathers) opens up a path that should be taken much further than Dennett goes himself. Since, to put it in good old Marxist terms, man is the totality of his social relations, why does Dennett not take the next logical step and directly analyze this network of social relations? This domain of "externalized intelligence," from tools to, especially, language itself forms a domain of its own, that of what Hegel called "objective spirit," the domain of artificial substance as opposed to natural substance. The formula proposed by Dahlbom is thus: from "Society of Minds" (the notion, developed by Minsky, Dennett, and others) to "Minds of Society" (i.e., the human mind as something that can only emerge and function within a complex network of social relations and artificial mechanic supplements which "objectivize" intelligence).

Un jour, peut-être, le siècle sera empiriomoniste?

The elementary coordinates of Deleuze's ontology are thus provided by the "Schellingian" opposition between the Virtual and the Actual: the space of the actual (real acts in the present, experienced reality, and persons as formed individuals) accompanied by its virtual shadow (the field of proto-reality, of multiple singularities, impersonal elements later synthetized into our experience of reality). This is the Deleuze of "transcendental empiricism," the Deleuze giving to Kant's transcendental his unique twist: the proper transcendental space is the virtual space of the

---

[23] See Bo Dahlbom, "Mind Is Artificial," in *Dennett and His Critics*, edited by Bo Dahlbom (Oxford: Blackwell, 1993).

multiple singular potentialities, of "pure" impersonal singular gestures, affects, and perceptions that are not yet the gestures-affects-perceptions *of* a preexisting, stable, and self-identical subject. This is why, for example, Deleuze celebrates the art of cinema: it "liberates" gaze, images, movements, and, ultimately, time itself from their attribution to a given subject. When we watch a movie, we see the flow of images from the perspective of the "mechanical" camera, a perspective that does not belong to any subject; through the art of montage, movement is also abstracted or liberated from its attribution to a given subject or object—it is an impersonal movement that is only secondarily, afterward, attributed to some positive entities.

Here, however, the first crack in this edifice appears. In a move that is far from self-evident, Deleuze links this conceptual space to the traditional opposition between production and representation. The virtual field is (re)interpreted as that of generative, productive forces, opposed to the space of representations. Here we get all the standard topics of the molecular multiple sites of productivity constrained by the molar totalizing organizations, and so on and so forth. Under the heading of the opposition between becoming and being, Deleuze thus seems to identify these two logics, although they are fundamentally incompatible (one is tempted to attribute the "bad" influence, which pushed him toward the second logic to Felix Guattari).[24] The proper site of production is *not* the virtual space as such, but, rather, the very *passage* from it to constituted reality, the collapse of the multitude and its oscillations into one reality—production is fundamentally a limitation of the open space of virtualities, the determination and negation of the virtual multitude (this is how Deleuze reads Spinoza's *omni determinatio est negatio* against Hegel).

The line of Deleuze proper is that of the great early monographs (the key ones being *Difference and Repetition* and *The Logic of Sense*) as well as some of the shorter introductory writings (like *Proust and Signs* and the *Introduction to Sacher-Masoch*). In his late work, it is the two cinema books that mark the return to the topics of *The Logic of Sense*. This series is to be distinguished from the books Deleuze and Guattari cowrote, and one can only regret that the Anglo-Saxon reception of Deleuze (and, also, the politicial impact of Deleuze) is predominantly that of a "guattarized" Deleuze. It is crucial to note that *not a single one* of Deleuze's own texts is in any way directly political; Deleuze "in himself" is a highly elitist author, indifferent toward politics. The only serious philosophical question is thus: what inherent impasse caused Deleuze to turn toward Guattari? Is

---

[24] I follow here Alain Badiou, on whose reading of Deleuze I rely extensively; see Badiou, *Deleuze: The Clamour of Being* (Minneapolis: University of Minnesota Press, 2000).

Anti-Oedipus, arguably Deleuze's worst book, not the result of escaping the full confrontation of a deadlock *via* a simplified "flat" solution, homologous to Schelling escaping the deadlock of his *Weltalter* project *via* his shift to the duality of "positive" and "negative" philosophy or Habermas escaping the deadlock of the "dialectic of Enlightenment" via his shift to the duality of instrumental and communicational reason? Our task is to confront again this deadlock. Therefore, was Deleuze not pushed toward Guattari because Guattari presented an alibi, an easy escape from the deadlock of his previous position? Does Deleuze's conceptual edifice not rely on *two* logics, on *two* conceptual oppositions, that coexist in his work? This insight seems so obvious, stating it seems so close to what the French call a *lapalissade,* that one is surprised how it has not yet been generally perceived:

(1) on the one hand, the logic of sense, of the immaterial becoming as the sense-event, as the EFFECT of bodily-material processes-causes, the logic of the radical gap between generative process and its immaterial sense-effect: "multiplicities, being incorporeal effects of material causes, are impassible or causally sterile entities. The time of a pure becoming, always already passed and eternally yet to come, forms the temporal dimension of this impassibility or sterility of multiplicities."[25] And is cinema not the ultimate case of the sterile flow of surface becoming? The cinema image is inherently sterile and impassive, the pure effect of corporeal causes, although nonetheless acquiring its pseudo-autonomy.

(2) on the other hand, the logic of becoming as PRODUCTION of Beings: "the emergence of metric or extensive properties should be treated as a single process in which a continuous *virtual spacetime* progressively differentiates itself into actual discontinuous spatio-temporal structures."[26]

Say, in his analyses of films and literature, Deleuze emphasizes the de-substantialization of affects: in a work of art, an affect (boredom, for instance) is no longer attributable to actual persons but becomes a free-floating event. How, then, does this impersonal intensity of an affect-event relate to bodies or persons? Here we encounter the same ambiguity: either this immaterial affect is generated by interacting bodies as a sterile surface of pure Becoming or it is part of the virtual intensities out of which bodies emerge through actualization (the passage from Becoming to Being).

And, is this opposition not, yet again, that of materialism versus idealism? In Deleuze, this means *The Logic of Sense* versus *Anti-Oedipus.*

[25] Manuel DeLanda, *Intensive Science and Virtual Philosophy* (New York: Continuum, 2002), pp. 107–108.
[26] DeLanda, op. cit., p. 102.

Either the Sense-Event, the flow of pure Becoming, is the immaterial effect (neutral, neither active nor passive) of the intrication of bodily-material causes *or* the positive bodily entities are themselves the product of the pure flow of Becoming. Either the infinite field of virtuality is an immaterial effect of the interacting bodies or the bodies themselves emerge, actualize themselves, from this field of virtuality. In *The Logic of Sense,* Deleuze himself develops this opposition in the guise of two possible modes of the genesis of reality: the formal genesis (the emergence of reality out of the immanence of impersonal consciousness as the pure flow of Becoming) is supplemented by the real genesis, the latter accounting for the emergence of the immaterial event-surface itself out of bodily interaction. Sometimes, when he follows the first path, Deleuze comes dangerously close to "empiriocriticist" formulas: the primordial fact is the pure flow of experience, attributable to no subject, neither subjective nor objective—subject and object are, as all fixed entities, just secondary "coagulations" of this flow. This cannot but recall the basic philosophical position of Bogdanov, the main representative of Russian "empiriocriticism," who is best known as the target of Lenin's critique in his *Materialism and Empiriocriticism* from 1908:

> If . . . we assume that the ultimate elements of experience are sensations, it is obvious that what we ordinarily think of as the world of experience would not have arisen without a process of organization. . . . What we regard as the material world, nature, the common world, is the product of collectively organized experience, having a social basis. That is to say, the common world as experienced has been progressively formed in the course of human history out of the raw material of sensation. . . . In addition to the world which is basically the same for all, there are, so to speak, private worlds. That is to say, in addition to collectively organized experience there is organization in the form of ideas or concepts which differ from person to person or from group to group. There are different points of view, different theories, different ideologies.[27]

Bogdanov emphasized that the flow of sensations *precedes* the subject. It is not a subjective flow but neutral with regard to the opposition between subject and objective reality—they both emerge out of this flow (Is empiriomonism," one of the self-designations of the empiriocriticists—is this term not also an adequate designation of Deleuze's "transcendental empiricism?"—not to mention Bogdanov's "mechanism," his "machinic" notion of development? Lacan *versus* Deleuze: again, dialectical materialism versus empriocriticism? Deleuze—a new Bogdanov? In a proto-Deleuzian way, Bogdanov accused the defenders of Matter as an

---

[27] Frederick Copleston, *Philosophy in Russia* (Notre Dame, Ind.: University of Notre Dame Press, 1986), p. 286.

objectively existing Thing-in-itself to commit the cardinal metaphysical sin of explaining the known in terms of the unknown, the experienced in terms of the nonexperienced—exactly like Deleuze's rejection of any form of transcendence. Furthermore, Bogdanov was also a radical Leftist, keen on machinic experiments. His basic attitude was precisely that of uniting the "vitalism" of the flow of sensations with the machinic *combinatoire.* Although Bogdanov supported the Bolsheviks against reformist opportunism, his political stance was that of the radical Leftist striving for organizations that form themselves "from below," and are not imposed from above by some central authority.[28]

When, in *The Logic of Sense,* Deleuze deploys the two geneses, transcendental and real, does he not thereby follow in the steps of Fichte and Schelling? Fichte's starting point is that one can practice philosophy in two basic ways, Spinozan and idealist. One either starts from objective reality and tries to develop from it the genesis of free subjectivity or starts from the pure spontaneity of the absolute Subject and tries to develop the entirety of reality as the result of the Subject's self-positing. The early Schelling of the *System of Transcendental Idealism* goes a step further by claiming that, in this alternative, we are not dealing with a choice: the two options are complementary, not exclusive. Absolute idealism, its claim of the identity of Subject and Object (Spirit and Nature), can be demonstrated in two ways: one either develops Nature out of Spirit (transcendental idealism, à la Kant and Fichte) or develops the gradual emergence of Spirit out of the immanent movement of Nature (Schelling's own *Naturphilosophie*). However, what about the crucial new advance achieved by Schelling in his *Weltalter* fragments, in which he introduces a *third* term into this alternative, namely, that of the genesis of Spirit (logos) not out of nature as such—as a constituted realm of natural reality—but out of the nature of/in God himself as that which is "in God himself not yet God," the abyss of the preontological Real in God, the blind rotary movement of "irrational" passions? As Schelling makes clear, this realm is not yet ontological but, in a sense, more "spiritual" than natural reality: a shadowy realm of obscene ghosts that return again and again as "living dead" because they *failed* to actualize themselves in full reality.[29] To risk an anachronistic parallel, is this genesis, the

---

[28] It is easy to ridicule Lenin's *Materialism and Empiriocriticism,* its utter philosophical worthlessness, yet the book's "political instinct" for the class struggle in theory is unerring and 100 percent right. We all recall Lenin's remarks on the edge of Hegel's *Logic,* apropos of Hegel's statements such as "the immanent deployment of the concrete wealth of the universal as the self-development of the eternal divine Idea," in the style of "the first line profound and true, the second line theological rubbish!"—one is tempted to jot a similar remark on the edge of *Materialism and Empiriocriticism:* "the deployment of the political overdetermination of philosophy—profound and true, the inherent philosophical value of the book—rubbish!"

[29] See F. W. J. Schelling, *The Ages of the World* (Albany: State University of New York Press, 2000).

prehistory of what went on in God before he fully became God (the divine logos), not effectively close to the quantum physics notion of the state of virtual quantum oscillation preceding constituted reality?

And, effectively, what about the results of quantum physics? What if matter *is* just a reified wave oscillation? What if, instead of conceiving waves as oscillations between elements, elements are just knots, contact points, between different waves and their oscillations? Does this not give some kind of scientific credibility to Deleuze's "idealist" project of generating bodily reality from virtual intensities? There is a way to conceptualize the emergence of Something out of Nothing in a materialist way: when we succeed in conceiving this emergence not as a mysterious excess but as a RELEASE—a LOSS—of energy. Does not the so-called Higgs field in contemporary physics point precisely in this direction? Generally, when we take something away from a given system, we lower its energy. However, the hypothesis is that there is some substance, a "something," that we cannot take away from a given system without *raising* that system's energy: when the "Higgs field" appears in an empty space, its energy is *lowered further.*[30] Does not the biological insight that living systems are perhaps best characterized as systems that dynamically avoid attractors (i.e., that the processes of life are being maintained at or near phase transitions) point in the same direction, which is toward the Freudian death drive in its radical opposition to any notion of the tendency of all life toward nirvana? Death drive means precisely that the most radical tendency of a living organism is to maintain a state of tension, to avoid final "relaxation" in obtaining a state of full homeostasis. "Death drive" as "beyond the pleasure principle" is this very insistence of an organism on endlessly repeating the state of tension.

One should thus get rid of the fear that once we ascertain that reality is the infinitely divisible, substanceless void within a void, "matter will disappear." What the digital informational revolution, the biogenetic revolution, and the quantum revolution in physics all share is that they mark the reemergence of what, for want of a better term, one is tempted to call a *post-metaphysical idealism.* Recall Chesterton's insight into how the materialist struggle for the full assertion of reality, against its subordination to any "higher" metaphysical order, culminates in the loss of reality itself: what began as the assertion of material reality ended up as the realm of pure formulas of quantum physics. Is, however, this really a form of idealism? Since the radical materialist stance asserts that there is no World, that the World in its Whole is Nothing, materialism has nothing to do with the presence of damp, dense matter—its proper figures are,

[30] For a more detailed reference to "Higgs field," see chapter 3 of Slavoj Žižek, *The Puppet and the Dwarf.* For a popular scientific explanation, see Gordon Kane, *Supersymmetry* (Cambridge: Helix Books, 2001).

rather, constellations in which matter seems to "disappear," like the pure oscillations of the superstrings or quantum vibrations. On the contrary, if we see in raw, inert matter more than an imaginary screen, we always secretly endorse some kind of spiritualism, as in Tarkovsky's *Solaris,* in which the dense plastic matter of the planet directly embodies Mind. This "spectral materialism" has three different forms: in the informational revolution, matter is reduced to the medium of purely digitalized information; in biogenetics, the biological body is reduced to the medium of the reproduction of the genetic code; in quantum physics, reality itself, the density of matter, is reduced to the collapse of the virtuality of wave oscillations (or, in the general theory of relativity, matter is reduced to an effect of space's curvature). Here we encounter *another* crucial aspect of the opposition idealism/materialism. Materialism is not the assertion of inert material density in its humid heaviness—*such* a "materialism" can always serve as a support for gnostic spiritualist obscurantism. In contrast to it, a true materialism joyously assumes the "disappearance of matter," the fact that there is only void.

With biogenetics, the Nietzschean program of the emphatic and ecstatic assertion of the body is thus over. Far from serving as the ultimate reference, the body loses its mysterious impenetrable density and turns into something technologically manageable, something we can generate and transform through intervening into its genetic formula—in short, something the "truth" of which is this abstract genetic formula. And it is crucial to conceive the two apparently opposite "reductions" discernible in today's science (the "materialist" reduction of our experience to neuronal processes in neurosciences and the virtualization of reality itself in quantum physics) as two sides of the same coin, as two reductions to the same third level. The old Popperian idea of the "Third World" is here brought to its extreme: what we get at the end is neither the "objective" materiality nor the "subjective" experience but rather the reduction of *both* to the scientific Real of mathematized "immaterial" processes.

The issue of materialism versus idealism thus gets more complex. If we accept the claim of quantum physics that the reality we experience as constituted emerges out of a preceding field of virtual intensities that are, in a way, "immaterial" (quantum oscillations), then embodied reality is the result of the "actualization" of pure eventlike virtualities. What if, then, there is a double movement here? First, positive reality itself is constituted through the actualization of the virtual field of "immaterial" potentialities; then, in a second move, the emergence of thought and sense signals the moment when the constituted reality, as it were, *reconnects with its virtual genesis.* Was Schelling not already pursuing something similar when he claimed that, in the explosion of consciousness, of human thought, the primordial abyss of pure potentiality explodes, acquires existence, in the middle of created positive reality—man is the unique creature that is directly (re)connected with the primordial abyss out of which all things emerged?[31] Perhaps Roger Penrose is right in believing there is a link between quantum oscillations and human thought.[32]

Quasi-Cause

So, on one hand, Manuel DeLanda, in his excellent compte-rendu of Deleuze's ontology, affirms the logic of the "disappearance of process under product," the logic that relies on a long (also Hegelian-Marxist!) tradition of "reification": "This theme of the disguising of process under product is key to Deleuze's philosophy since his philosophical method is, at least in part, designed to overcome the objective illusion fostered by this concealment."[33] And the proper level of production is also *unambiguously* designated as that of virtualities. In and beneath the constituted reality, "the extensive and qualitative properties of the final product,"[34] one should discover the traces of the intensive process of virtualities—Being and Becoming relate as Actual and Virtual. How, then, are we to combine this unambiguous affirmation of the Virtual as the site of production that generates constituted reality with the no less unambiguous statement that "*the virtual is produced* out of the actual"?

> Multiplicities should not be conceived as possessing the capacity to actively interact with one another through these series. Deleuze thinks about them as endowed with only a mere capacity to be affected, since they are, in his words, "impassive entities—impassive results." The neutrality or sterility of multiplicities may be explained in the following way. Although their divergent universality makes them independent of any particular mechanism (the same multiplicity may be actualized by several causal mechanisms) *they do depend on the empirical fact that some causal mechanism or another actually exists. . . .* They are not transcendent but immanent entities. . . . Deleuze views multiplicities as *incorporeal effects of corporeal causes,* that is, as historical results of actual causes possessing no causal powers of their own. On the other hand, as he writes, "to the extent that they differ in nature from these causes, they enter, with one another, into relations of *quasi-causality*. Together they enter into a relation with a *quasi-cause* which is itself incorporeal and assures them a very special independence.". . . Unlike actual capacities, which are always capacities to affect and be affected, virtual affects are sharply divided into a pure capacity to be affected (displayed by impassible multiplicities) and a *pure capacity to affect.*[35]

---

[31] See Schelling, op. cit.
[32] See Roger Penrose, *Shadows of the Mind* (Oxford: Oxford University Press, 1994).
[33] DeLanda, op. cit., p. 73.
[34] DeLanda, op. cit., p. 74.
[35] DeLanda, op. cit., p. 75.

The concept of quasi cause is that which prevents a regression into simple reductionism: it designates the pure agency of transcendental causality. Let us take Deleuze's own example from his *Time-Image*, namely, the emergence of cinematic neorealism. One can, of course, explain neorealism by a set of historical circumstances (the trauma of World War II, etc.). However, there is an excess in the emergence of the New: neorealism is an Event that cannot simply be reduced to its material/historical causes, and the "quasi cause" is the cause of this excess, the cause of that which makes an Event (an emergence of the New) irreducible to its historical circumstances. One can also say that the quasi cause is the second level cause, the metacause of the very excess of the effect over its (corporeal) causes. This is how one should understand what Deleuze says about being affected. Insofar as the incorporeal Event is a pure affect (an impassive-neutral-sterile result), and insofar as something New (a new Event, an Event of/as the New) can emerge only if the chain of its corporeal causes is not complete, *one should postulate, over and above the network of corporeal causes, a pure, transcendental, capacity to affect.* This is also why Lacan appreciated so much *The Logic of Sense:* is the Deleuzian quasi cause not the exact equivalent of Lacan's *objet petit a,* this pure, immaterial, spectral entity that serves as the object-cause of desire?

One should be very precise here not to miss the point. Deleuze is not affirming a simple psycho-physical dualism in the sense of someone like John Searle; he is not offering two different "descriptions" of the same event. It is not that the same process (say, a speech activity) can be described in a strictly naturalistic way, as a neuronal and bodily process embedded in its actual causality, or, as it were, "from within," at the level of meaning, in which the causality ("I answer your question because I understand it") is pseudo causality. In such an approach, the material-corporeal causality remains complete, whereas the basic premise of Deleuze's ontology is precisely that corporeal causality is *not* complete. In the emergence of the New, something occurs that *cannot* be properly described at the level of corporeal causes and effects. Quasi cause is not the illusory theater of shadows, like a child who thinks he is magically making a toy run, unaware of the mechanic causality that effectively does the work—on the contrary, the quasi cause *fills in the gap of corporeal causality.* In this strict sense, and insofar as the Event is the Sense-Event, quasi cause is non-sense as inherent to Sense: if a speech could have been reduced to its sense, then it would fall into reality—the relationship between Sense and its designated reality would have been simply that of objects in the world. Nonsense is that which maintains the autonomy of the level of sense, of its surface flow of pure becoming, with regard to the designated reality ("referent"). And, does this not bring us back to the unfortunate "phallic signifier" as the "pure" signifier without signified? Is the Lacanian phallus not precisely the point of non-sense sustaining the flow of sense?

One should therefore problematize the very basic *duality* of Deleuze's thought, that of Becoming versus Being, which appears in different versions (the Nomadic versus the State, the molecular versus the molar, the schizo versus the paranoiac, etc.). This duality is ultimately overdetermined as "the Good versus the Bad": the aim of Deleuze is to liberate the immanent force of Becoming from its self-enslavement to the order of Being. Perhaps the first step in this problematizing is to confront this duality with the duality of Being and Event, emphasizing their ultimate incompatibility: Event cannot be simply identified with the virtual field of Becoming that generates the order of Being—quite the contrary, in *The Logic of Sense*, Event is emphatically asserted as "sterile," capable only of pseudo-causality. So, what if, at the level of Being, we have the irreducible multitude of interacting particularities, and it is the Event that acts as the elementary form of totalization/unification?

Deleuze's remobilization of the old humanist-idealist topic of regressing from the "reified" result to its process of production is telltale here. Is Deleuze's oscillation between the two models (becoming as the impassive effect; becoming as the generative process) not homologous to the oscillation, in the Marxist tradition, between the two models of "reification"? First, there is the model according to which reification/fetishization misperceives properties belonging to an object insofar as this object is part of a sociosymbolic link, as its immediate "natural" properties (as if products are "in themselves" commodities); then, there is the more radical young Lukacs (et al.) notion according to which *"objective" reality as such is something "reified," a fetishized outcome of some concealed subjective process of production.* So, in exact parallel to Deleuze, at the first level, we should not confuse an object's social properties with its immediate natural properties (in the case of a commodity, its exchange value with its material properties that satisfy our needs). In the same way, we should not perceive (or reduce) an immaterial virtual affect linked to a bodily cause to one of the body's material properties. Then, at the second level, we should conceive objective reality itself as the result of the social productive process—in the same way that, for Deleuze, actual being is the result of the virtual process of becoming.

Perhaps the limit of Deleuze resides in his vitalism, in his elevation of the notion of Life to a new name for Becoming as the only true encompassing Whole, the One-ness, of Being itself. When Deleuze describes the gradual self-differentiation of the pure flux of Becoming, its gradual "reification" into distinct entities, does he not effectively render a kind of Plotinian process of emanation? Against this "idealist" stance, one should stick to Badiou's thesis on mathematics as the only adequate ontology, the only science of pure Being: the meaningless Real of the pure multitude, the vast infinite coldness of the Void. In Deleuze, Difference refers to the multiple singularities that express the One of infinite Life, whereas, with Badiou, we get multitude(s) without any underlying Oneness. In Deleuze, Life is still the answer to "Why is there Something and not Nothing?" whereas Badiou's answer is a more sober one, closer to Buddhism *and* Hegel: *there IS only Nothing,* and all processes take place "from Nothing through Nothing to Nothing," as Hegel put it.

In his notional determination of the constituted reality to be undermined by the shift toward the virtual space of becoming, Deleuze condenses the two levels that, for Heidegger in *Sein und Zeit,* form the most elementary ontological opposition, that of *Vorhandene* (present-at-hand) and *Zuhandene* (ready-at-hand). For Deleuze, this standard attitude *simultaneously* considers objects as isolated positive entities occupying a particular location in abstract geometric space, as objects of contemplative representation, *and* as objects perceived through the standpoint of the subject's existential engagement, reduced to their potential use within the horizon of the subject's interests, projects, desires, and so on. (For Heidegger, as well as for the late Husserl, the elementary metaphysical gesture is precisely the withdrawal from the immersion into a concrete life-world to the position of abstract observer.) The fact of this condensation does not imply any direct criticism of Deleuze. It can easily be shown that what he defines as the proper conceptual work of philosophy (or, at a different level, the work of art) undermines *both* our immersion into the life-world *and* our position of abstract observers of reality. When a philosopher produces a new concept, or when an artist renders an affect in a new way, liberated from the closed circle of a subjectivity situated in a given positive reality, he shatters our immersion in the habitual life-world as well as our safe position as the observer of reality. We lose our position of abstract observers; we are forced to admit that new concepts or works of art are the outcome of our engaged production. Yet, in the same gesture, philosophy or art also undermines our immersion in the habitus of a particular life-world.[36]

---

[36] What is a concept? It is not only that, often, we are dealing with pseudo-concepts, with mere representations (*Vorstellungen*) posing as concepts; sometimes, much more interestingly, a concept can reside in what appears to be a mere common expression, even a vulgar one. In 1922, Lenin dismissed "the intellectuals, the lackeys of capital, who think they're the brains of the nation. In fact, they're not its brains, they're its shit." (Quoted in Helene Carrere D'Encausse, *Lenin* [New York: Holmes and Meier, 2001], p. 308.) As Badiou did apropos of Sartre's (in)famous claim that "anti-communists are dogs," one should, instead of shamefully ignoring this statement, take the risk and elaborate the underlying *concept* of shit.

Is this opposition of the virtual as the site of productive Becoming and the virtual as the site of the sterile Sense-Event not, at the same time, the opposition of the "body without organs" (BwO) and "organs without body" (OwB)? Is, on one hand, the productive flux of pure Becoming not the BwO, the body not yet structured or determined as functional organs? And, on the other hand, is the OwB not the virtuality of the pure affect extracted from its embeddedness in a body, like the smile in *Alice in Wonderland* that persists alone, even when the Cheshire cat's body is no longer present? "'All right,' said the Cat; and this time it vanished quite slowly, beginning with the end of the tail, and ending with the grin, which remained some time after the rest of it had gone. 'Well! I've often seen a cat without a grin,' thought Alice; 'but a grin without a cat! It's the most curious thing I ever saw in my life!'" This notion of an extracted OwB reemerges forcefully in *The Time-Image,* in the guise of the *gaze* itself as such an autonomous organ no longer attached to a body.[37] These two logics (Event as the power that generates reality; Event as the sterile, pure effect of bodily interactions) also involve two privileged psychological stances: the generative Event of Becoming relies on the productive force of the "schizo," this explosion of the unified subject in the impersonal multitude of desiring intensities, intensities that are subsequently constrained by the Oedipal matrix; the Event as sterile, immaterial effect relies on the figure of the masochist who finds satisfaction in the tedious, repetitive game of staged rituals whose function is to postpone forever the sexual *passage à l'acte.* Can one effectively imagine a stronger contrast than that of the schizo throwing himself without any reservation into the flux of multiple passions and of the masochist clinging to the theater of shadows in which his meticulously staged performances repeat again and again the same sterile gesture?

So, what if we conceive of Deleuze's opposition of the intermixing of material bodies and the immaterial effect of sense along the lines of the Marxist opposition of infrastructure and superstructure? Is not the flow of becoming superstructure par excellence the sterile theater of shadows ontologically cut off from the site of material production, and precisely as such the only possible space of the Event? In his ironic comments

---

[37] One of the metaphors for the way mind relates to body, that of a magnetic field, seems to point in the same direction: "*as a magnet generates its magnetic field, so the brain generates its field of consciousness*" (William Hasker, *The Emergent Self* [Ithaca, N.Y.: Cornell University Press, 1999], p. 190). The field thus has a logic and consistency of its own, although it can persist only as long as its corporeal ground is here. Does this mean that mind cannot survive the body's disintegration? Even here, another analogy from physics leaves the gate partially open. When Roger Penrose claims that, after a body collapses into a black hole, one can conceive the black hole as a kind of self-sustaining gravitational field, so even within physics, one considers the possibility that a field generated by a material object could persist in the object's absence. (See Hasker, op. cit., p. 232).

on the French Revolution, Marx opposes the revolutionary enthusiasm to the sobering effect of the "morning after": the actual result of the sublime revolutionary explosion, of the Event of freedom, equality, and brotherhood, is the miserable utilitarian/egotistic universe of market calculations. (And, incidentally, is not this gap even wider in the case of the October Revolution?) However, one should not simplify Marx. His point is not the rather commonsensical insight into how the vulgar reality of commerce is the "truth" of the theater of revolutionary enthusiasm, "what all the fuss really was about." In the revolutionary explosion as an Event, another utopian dimension shines through, the dimension of universal emancipation, which, precisely, is the excess betrayed by the market reality that takes over "the day after"—as such, this excess is not simply abolished, dismissed as irrelevant, but, as it were, *transposed into the virtual state*, continuing to haunt the emancipatory imaginary as a dream waiting to be realized. The excess of revolutionary enthusiasm over its own "actual social base" or substance is thus literally that of an attribute-effect over its own substantial cause, a ghostlike Event waiting for its proper embodiment. It was none other than G. K. Chesterton who, apropos of his critique of aristocracy, provided the most succinct Leftist egalitarian rebuttal of those who, under the guise of respect for traditions, endorse existing injustice and inequalities: "Aristocracy is not an institution: aristocracy is a sin; generally a very venial one."[38]

Here, we can discern in what precise sense Deleuze wants to be a materialist. One is almost tempted to put it in classic Stalinist terms: in opposition to the mechanical materialism which simply reduces the flow of sense to its material causes, dialectical materialism is able to think this flow in its relative autonomy. That is to say, the whole point of Deleuze is that, although sense is an impassive sterile effect of material causes, it does have an autonomy and efficiecy of its own. Yes, the flow of sense is a theater of shadows, but this does not mean that we should neglect it and focus on "real struggle"—in a way, this very theater of shadows is the *crucial* site of the struggle; *everything* is ultimately decided here.

William Hasker perspicuously drew attention to the strange fact that critics of reductionism are very reluctant to admit that the arguments against radical reductionism are false: "Why are so many non-eliminativists strongly resistant to the idea that eliminativism has been conclusively refuted?"[39] Their resistance betrays a fear of the prospect that, if their position fails, they will need reductionism as the last resort. So, although they consider eliminativism false, they nonetheless strangely hold onto it as a kind of reserve ("fall-back") position, thereby betraying

---

[38] Chesterton, *Orthodoxy*, p. 127.
[39] Hasker, op. cit., p. 24.

a secret disbelief in their own nonreductionist materialist account of consciousness—this being a nice example of a disavowed theoretical position, of the fetishist split in theory. (Is their position not homologous to that of enlightened rational theologians who nonetheless secretly want to keep open the more "fundamentalist" theological position they constantly criticize? And, do we not encounter a similar split attitude in those Leftists who condemn the suicide-bomber attacks on the Israelis, but not wholeheartedly, with an inner reservation—as if, if "democratic" politics fails, one should nonetheless leave the door open for the "terrorist" option?) Here, one should return to Badiou and Deleuze, since they really and thoroughly reject reductionism. The assertion of the "autonomy" of the level of Sense-Event is for them not a compromise with idealism, but a *necessary* thesis of a true materialism.[40]

And, what is crucial is that this tension between the two ontologies in Deleuze clearly translates into two different political logics and practices. The ontology of productive Becoming clearly leads to the Leftist topic of the self-organization of the multitude of molecular groups that resist and undermine the molar, totalizing systems of power—the old notion of the spontaneous, nonhierarchical, living multitude opposing the oppressive, reified System, the exemplary case of Leftist radicalism linked to philosophical idealist subjectivism. The problem is that this is the only model of the politicization of Deleuze's thought available. The other ontology, that of the sterility of the Sense-Event, appears "apolitical." However, what if this other ontology also involves a political logic and practice of its own, of which Deleuze himself was unaware? Should we not, then, proceed like Lenin in 1915 when, to ground anew revolutionary practice, he returned to Hegel—not to his directly political writings, but, primarily, to his *Logic?* What if, in the same way, there is another Deleuzian politics to be discovered here? The first hint in this direction may be provided by the already mentioned parallel between the couple *corporeal causes/immaterial flow of becoming* and the old Marxist couple *infrastructure/superstructure:* such a politics would take into account the irreducible duality of "objective" material/socioeconomic processes taking place in reality and the explosion of revolutionary Events, of the political logic proper. What if the domain of politics is inherently "sterile," the domain of pseudo causes, a theater of shadows, but nonetheless crucial in transforming reality?

---

[40] There is nonetheless a specific seductive charm in a position like that of Patricia and Paul Churchland (similar to Dennett concerning qualia), the position of blatantly *denying* our most "immediate" experience. Is this not the ultimate paradox, that the materialists whose standard starting point is the defense of immediate material reality against all transcendent claims end up denying our most immediate experience of reality?

Is It Possible Not to Love Spinoza?

Perhaps, a return to the philosopher who is Deleuze's unsurpassable point of reference will help us to unravel this ambiguity in Deleuze's ontological edifice: Spinoza. Deleuze is far from alone in his unconditional admiration for Spinoza. One of the unwritten rules of today's academia, from France to America, is the injunction to love Spinoza. Everyone loves him, from the Althusserian strict "scientific materialists" to Deleuzean schizo-anarchists, from rationalist critics of religion to the partisans of liberal freedoms and tolerances, not to mention feminists like Genevieve Lloyd, who propose to decipher a mysterious third type of knowledge in the *Ethics* as feminine intuitive knowledge (a knowledge surpassing the male analytic understanding). Is it, then, possible at all *not* to love Spinoza? Who can be against a lone Jew who, on top of it, was excommunicated by the "official" Jewish community itself? One of the most touching expressions of this love is how one often attributes to him almost divine capacities—like Pierre Macherey, who, in his otherwise admirable *Hegel ou Spinoza* (arguing against the Hegelian critique of Spinoza), claims that one cannot avoid the impression that Spinoza had already read Hegel and, in advance, answered his reproaches. Perhaps the most appropriate first step in rendering problematic this status of Spinoza is to draw attention to the fact that it is totally incompatible with what is arguably the hegemonic stance in today's Cultural Studies, that of the ethicotheological "Judaic" turn of deconstruction best exemplified by the couple Derrida/Levinas—is there a philosopher more foreign to this orientation than Spinoza, more foreign to the Jewish universe, which, precisely, is the universe of God as radical Otherness, of the enigma of the divine, of the God of negative prohibitions instead of positive injunctions? Were, then, the Jewish priests in a way not *right* to excommunicate Spinoza?

However, instead of engaging in this rather boring academic exercise of opposing Spinoza and Levinas, one should rather risk a consciously old-fashioned Hegelian reading of Spinoza—what both Spinozans and Levinasians share is a radical anti-Hegelianism. In the history of modern thought, the triad of paganism-Judaism-Christianity repeats itself twice, first as Spinoza-Kant-Hegel, then as Deleuze–Derrida-Lacan. Deleuze deploys the One-Substance as the indifferent medium of multitude; Derrida inverts it into the radical Otherness that differs from itself; finally, in a kind of "negation of negation," Lacan brings back the cut, the gap, into the One itself. The point is not so much to play Spinoza and Kant against each other, thus securing the triumph of Hegel; rather, it is, to present the three philosophical positions in all their unheard-of radicality—in a way, the triad Spinoza-Kant-Hegel *does* encompass the whole of philosophy.

So, what is Spinoza? He is, effectively, the philosopher of Substance, and this at a precise historical moment: *after* Descartes. For that reason, he is able to draw all (unexpected, for most of us) consequences from it. Substance means, first of all, that there is no mediation between attributes: each attribute (thoughts, bodies, etc.) is infinite in itself; it has no outer limit in which it would touch another attribute. "Substance" is the very name for this absolutely neutral medium of the multitude of attributes. This lack of mediation is the same as the lack of subjectivity, because subject *is* such a mediation. It ex-sists in/through what Deleuze, in *The Logic of Sense,* called the "dark precursor," the mediator between the two different series, the point of suture between them. Thus, what is missing in Spinoza is the elementary "twist" of dialectical inversion characterizing negativity, the inversion by means of which the very renunciation of desire turns into desire of renunciation, and so on. What is unthinkable for him is what Freud terms "death drive": the idea that *conatus* is based on a fundamental act of self-sabotaging. Spinoza, with his assertion of *conatus,* of every entity's striving to persist and strengthen its being and, in this way, striving for happiness, remains within the Aristotelian frame of what a good life is. What is outside his scope is what Kant refers to as the "categorical imperative," an unconditional thrust that parasitizes upon a human subject without any regard for its well-being, "beyond the pleasure principle"—and this, for Lacan, is the name of desire at its purest.

The first philosophical consequence of this notion of Substance is the motif on which Deleuze insists so much: the univocity of being. Among other things, this univocity means that the mechanisms of establishing the ontological links described by Spinoza are thoroughly *neutral* with regard to their "good" or "bad" effects. Spinoza thus avoids both traps of the standard approach: he neither dismisses the mechanism that constitutes a multitude as the source of the irrational destructive mob nor does he celebrate it as the source of altruistic self-overcoming and solidarity. Of course, he was deeply and painfully aware of the destructive potential of the "multitude"—recall *the* big political trauma of his life, a wild mob lynching the de Witt brothers, his political allies. However, he was aware that the noblest collective acts are generated by exactly the same mechanism—in short, democracy and a lynching mob have the same source. It is with regard to this neutrality that the gap that separates Negri and Hardt from Spinoza becomes palpable. In *The Empire,* we find a celebration of multitude as the force of resistance, whereas, in Spinoza, the concept of multitude qua crowd is fundamentally ambiguous: multitude is resistance to the imposing One, but, at the same time, it designates what we call "mob," a wild, "irrational" explosion of violence that, through *imitatio afecti,* feeds on and propels itself. This profound insight of Spinoza gets lost in today's ideology of multitude. The "undecidability" of the crowd goes all the way down: "crowd" designates a certain mechanism that engenders social links, and *this very same* mechanism that supports, say, the enthusiastic formation of social solidarity also supports the explosive spread of racist violence. What the "imitation of affects" introduces is the notion of transindividual circulation and communication. As Deleuze later developed in a Spinozan vein, affects are not something that belong to a subject and are then passed over to another subject; affects function at the preindividual level, as free-floating intensities that belong to no one and circulate at a level "beneath" intersubjectivity. This is what is so new about *imitatio afecti:* the idea that affects circulate *directly,* as what psychoanalysis calls "partial objects."

The next philosophical consequence is the thorough rejection of negativity. Each entity strives toward its full actualization—every obstacle comes *from outside.* In short, since every entity endeavors to persist in its own being, nothing can be destroyed from within, for all change must come from without. What Spinoza excludes with his rejection of negativity is the very symbolic order, since, as we have learned already from Saussure, the minimal definition of the symbolic order is that every identity is reducible to a bundle (*faisceau*—the same root as in fascism!) of differences: the identity of the signifier resides solely in its difference(s) from other signifier(s). What this amounts to is that absence can exert a positive causal influence—only within a symbolic universe is the fact that the dog did not bark an event. This is what Spinoza wants to dispense with—all that he admits is a purely positive network of causes and effects in which, by definition, an absence cannot play any positive role. Or, to put it in yet another way: Spinoza is not ready to admit into the order of ontology what he himself, in his critique of the anthropomorphic notion of god, describes as a false notion that merely fills in the lacunae within our knowledge—say, an object that, in its very positive existence, just gives body to a lack. For him, any negativity is "imaginary," the result of our anthropomorphic, limited, false knowledge that fails to grasp the actual causal chain. What remains outside his scope is a notion of negativity that would be precisely obfuscated by our imaginary (mis)cognition. While the imaginary (mis)cognition is, of course, focused on lacks, these are always lacks *with regard to some positive measure* (from our imperfection with regard to god to our incomplete knowledge of nature). What eludes it is a *positive* notion of lack, a "generative" absence.

It is this assertion of the positivity of Being that grounds Spinoza's radical equation of power and right. Justice means that every entity is allowed to freely deploy its inherent power-potentials, that is, the amount of justice owed to me equals my power. Spinoza's ultimate thrust is here antilegalistic: the model of political impotence is for him the reference to an abstract law that ignores the concrete differential network and relationship of forces. A "right" is, for Spinoza, always a right to "do," to act upon things according to one's nature, not the (judicial) right to "have," to possess things. It is precisely this equation of power and right that, in the very last page of his *Tractatus Politicus,* Spinoza evokes as the key argument for the "natural" inferiority of women:

> If by nature women were equal to men, and were equally distinguished by force of character and ability, in which human power and therefore human right chiefly consist; surely among nations so many and different some would be found, where both sexes rule alike, and others, where men are ruled by women, and so brought up, that they can make less use of their abilities. And since this is nowhere the case, one may assert with perfect propriety, that women have not by nature equal right with men.[41]

However, rather than score easy points with such passages, one should here oppose Spinoza to the standard bourgeois liberal ideology, which would publicly guarantee to women the same legal status as to men, relegating their inferiority to a legally irrelevant "pathological" fact (and, in fact, all great bourgeois antifeminists from Fichte up to Otto Weininger were always careful to emphasize that, "of course," they do not mean that the inequality of the sexes should be translated into inequality in the eyes of the law). Furthermore, one should read this Spinozan equation of power and right against the background of Pascal's famous *pensée:* "Equality of possessions is no doubt right, but, as men could not make might obey right, they have made right obey might. As they could not fortify justice they have justified force, so that right and might live together and peace reigns, the sovereign good."[42] Crucial in this passage is the underlying *formalist* logic: the *form* of justice matters more than its content—the form of justice should be maintained even if it is, as to its content, the form of its opposite, of injustice. And, one might add, this discrepancy between form and content is not just the result of particular unfortunate circumstances but constitutive of the very notion of justice: justice is "in itself," in its very notion, the form of injustice, namely, a "justified force." Usually, when we are dealing with a fake trial in which the outcome is fixed in advance by political and power interests, we speak of a "travesty of justice"—it pretends to be justice, whereas it

[41] Benedict de Spinoza, *A Theologico-Political Treatise and a Political Treatise* (New York: Dover Publications, 1951), p. 387.
[42] Blaise Pascal, *Pensées* (Harmondsworth, England: Penguin Books, 1965), p. 51.

is merely a display of raw power or corruption posing as justice. What, however, if justice is "as such," in its very notion, a travesty? Is this not what Pascal implies when he concludes, in a resigned way, that if power cannot come to justice, then justice should come to power?

Is the ultimate status of Justice not that of *fantasy* at its purest and most radical? Even in deconstruction, even in the late Frankfurt School, Justice functions as the ultimate horizon, "indeconstructible," as Derrida put it. Although Justice comes neither from reasoning nor from experience, it is absolutely inner to our experience and has to be intuitively presupposed ("there has to be justice"), otherwise everything is meaningless, our entire universe falls apart (Kant was on the trace of this status of Justice with his notion of the "postulates" of pure practical reason). As such, Justice is the pure construct-presupposition—true or not, it *has* to be presupposed. In other words, it is the ultimate "je sais bien, mais quand même . . . ": although we know it may be an illusion, we *have* to rely on it. Justice provides the secret link between ethics and ontology: there *has* to be justice in the universe, as its hidden underlying principle. Since even the "deconstruction" remains within this theological horizon, one can see why it is so difficult to be an atheist.

Kant gets involved in a similar predicament when he distinguishes between "ordinary" evil (the violation of morality on behalf of some "pathological" motivation, such as greed, lust, ambition, etc.), "radical" evil, and "diabolical" evil. It may seem that we are dealing with a simple linear gradation: "normal" evil, more "radical" evil, and, finally, the unthinkable "diabolical" evil. However, on closer inspection, it becomes clear that the three species are not at the same level. In other words, Kant confuses different principles of classification.[43] "Radical" evil does not designate a specific type of evil act but designates an a priori propensity of human nature (to act egotistically, to give preference to pathological motivations over universal ethical duty) that opens up the very space for "normal" evil acts, which roots them in human nature. In contrast to it, "diabolical" evil does indeed designate a specific type of evil act: acts that are not motivated by any pathological motivation but are done "just for the sake of it," elevating evil itself into an a priori *nonpathological* motivation—something akin to Poe's "imp of perversity." While Kant claims that "diabolical evil" cannot actually occur (it is impossible for a human being to elevate evil itself into a universal ethical norm), he nonetheless asserts that one should posit it as an abstract possibility. Interestingly enough, the concrete case he mentions (in Part I of his *Metaphysics of Morals*) is that of judicial regicide, the murder of a

---

[43] I rely here on Alenka Zupancic, *The Ethics of the Real* (London: Verso, 2000).

king carried out as a punishment pronounced by a court. Kant's claim is that, in contrast to a simple rebellion in which the mob kills only the person of a king, the judicial process that condemns the king to death (qua embodiment of the rule of law) destroys from within the very form of the (rule of) law, turning it into a terrifying travesty, which is why, as Kant put it, such an act is an "indelible crime" that cannot ever be pardoned. However, in a second step, Kant desperately argues that in the two historical cases of such an act (under Cromwell and in 1793 France), we were dealing just with a mob taking revenge. Why is there this oscillation and classificatory confusion in Kant? Because, if he were to assert the actual possibility of "diabolical evil," he would be utterly unable to distinguish it from the Good: since both acts would be nonpathologically motivated, the travesty of justice would become indistinguishable from justice itself. And, the shift from Kant to Hegel is simply the shift from this Kantian inconsistency to Hegel's reckless assumption of the identity of "diabolical" evil with the Good itself. Far from involving a clear classification, the distinction between "radical" and "diabolical" evil is thus the distinction between the general irreducible propensity of human nature and a series of particular acts (which, although impossible, are thinkable). Why, then, does Kant need this excess over the "normal" pathological evil? Because, without it, his theory would amount to no more than the traditional notion of the conflict between good and evil as the conflict between two tendencies in human nature: the tendency to act freely and autonomously and the tendency to act out of pathological, egotistic motivations.[44] From this perspective, the choice between good and evil is not itself a free choice since we only act in a truly free way when we act autonomously for the sake of duty (when we follow pathological motivations, we are enslaved to our nature). However, this goes against the fundamental thrust of Kantian ethics, according to which *the very choice of evil is an autonomous free decision.*

Back to Pascal. Is his version of the unity of right and might not homologous to Nietzsche's *amor fati* and eternal return of the same?

[44] According to Kant, if one finds oneself alone on the sea with another survivor of a sunken ship near a floating piece of wood that can keep only one person afloat, moral considerations are no longer valid. There is no moral law preventing me from fighting to death with the other survivor for the place on the raft; I can engage in it with moral impunity. It is here that, perhaps, one encounters the limit of Kantian ethics: what about someone who would willingly sacrifice himself to give the other person a chance to survive, and, furthermore, is ready to do it for no pathological reasons? Since there is no moral law commanding me to do this, does this mean that such an act has no ethical status proper? Does this strange exception not demonstrate that ruthless egotism, the care for personal survival and gain, is the silent "pathological" presupposition of Kantian ethics, namely, that the Kantian ethical edifice can maintain itself only if we silently presuppose the "pathological" image of man as a ruthless utilitarian egotist?

Since, in this unique life of mine, I am constrained by the burden of the past weighing on me, the assertion of my unconditional will to power is always thwarted by that which, in the finitude of being thrown into a particular situation, I was forced to assume as given. Consequently, the only way to assert effectively my will to power is to transpose myself into a state in which I am able to will freely, assert as the outcome of my will, what I otherwise experience as imposed on me by external fate; and, the only way to accomplish this is to imagine that, in the *future* "returns of the same," repetitions of my present predicament, I am fully ready to assume it freely. However, does this reasoning not also conceal the same formalism as that of Pascal? Is its hidden premise not "if I cannot freely choose my reality and thus overcome the necessity which determines me, I should formally elevate this necessity itself into something freely assumed by me?" Or, as Wagner, Nietzsche's great nemesis, put it in *The Twilight of Gods:* "Fear of the gods' downfall grieves me not, / since now I will it so! / What once I resolved in despair, / in the wild anguish of dissension, / now I will freely perform, gladly and gaily." And does the Spinozan position not rely on the same resigned identification? Is Spinoza, therefore, not diametrically opposed to the Jewish-Levinasian-Derridean-Adornian hope of the final Redemption, of the idea that this world of ours cannot be "all there is" as the last and ultimate Truth, of the insistence that we should stick to the promise of some Messianic Otherness? This Derridean "messianicity, stripped of everything"[45] is effectively close to the attitude toward religion in the late Frankfurt School, best encapsulated by Max Horkheimer's formula of fetishist disavowal he resorted to when he wrote about the Critical Theory itself: "It knows there is no God, and it nevertheless believes in him."[46]

The final feature in which all the previous ones culminate is Spinoza's radical suspension of any "deontological" dimension, that is, of what we usually understand by the term "ethical" (norms that proscribe us how we should act when we have a choice)—and this in a book called *Ethics,* which is an achievement in itself. In his famous reading of the Fall, Spinoza claims that God had to utter the prohibition "You should not eat the apple from the Tree of Knowledge!" because our capacity to know the true causal connection was limited. For those who know, one should say: "Eating from the Tree of Knowledge is dangerous for your health." This complete translation of injunction into cognitive statements again desubjectivizes the universe, implying that true freedom is not the

---

[45] Jacques Derrida, "Faith and Knowledge," in *Religion,* edited by J. Derrida and G. Vattimo (Cambridge: Polity Press, 1998), p. 18.
[46] Max Horkheimer, *Gesammelte Schriften,* vol. 14 (Frankfurt: Suhrkamp Verlag, 1994), p. 508.

freedom of choice but the accurate insight into the necessities that determine us. Here is the key passage from his *Theologico-Political Treatise:*

> [T]he affirmations and the negations of God always involve necessity or truth; so that, for example, if God said to Adam that He did not wish him to eat of the tree of knowledge of good and evil, it would have involved a contradiction that Adam should have been able to eat of it, and would therefore have been impossible that he should have so eaten, for the Divine command would have involved an eternal necessity and truth. But since Scripture nevertheless narrates that God did give this command to Adam, and yet that none the less Adam ate of the tree, we must perforce say that God revealed to Adam the evil which would surely follow if he should eat of the tree, but did not disclose that such evil would of necessity come to pass. Thus it was that Adam took the revelation to be not an eternal and necessary truth, but a law—that is, an ordinance followed by gain or loss, not depending necessarily on the nature of the act performed, but solely on the will and absolute power of some potentate, so that the revelation in question was solely in relation to Adam, and *solely through his lack of knowledge* a law, and God was, as it were, a lawgiver and potentate. From the same cause, namely, from lack of knowledge, the Decalogue in relation to the Hebrews was a law. . . . We conclude, therefore, that God is described as a lawgiver or prince, and styled just, merciful, etc., merely in concession to popular understanding, and the imperfection of popular knowledge; that in reality God acts and directs all things simply by the necessity of His nature and perfection, and that His decrees and volitions are eternal truths, and always involve necessity.[47]

Two levels are opposed here, that of imagination and opinions and that of true knowledge. The level of imagination is anthropomorphic: we are dealing with a narrative about agents giving orders that we are free to obey or disobey, and so forth; God himself is here the highest prince who dispenses mercy. The true knowledge, on the contrary, delivers the totally nonanthropomorphic causal nexus of impersonal truths. One is tempted to say that Spinoza here out-Jews Jews themselves. He extends iconoclasm to man himself—not only "do not paint god in man's image" but also "do not paint man himself in man's image." In other words, Spinoza here moves a step beyond the standard warning not to project onto nature human notions like goal, mercy, good and evil, and so on— we should not use them to conceive man himself. The key words in the quoted passage are *"solely through the lack of knowledge"*—the whole "anthropomorphic" domain of law, injunction, moral command, and so forth, is based on our ignorance. What Spinoza thus rejects is the necessity of what Lacan calls "Master Signifier," the reflexive signifier

---

[47] Spinoza, op. cit., pp. 63–65.

that fills in the very lack of the signifier. Spinoza's own supreme example of "God" is crucial here: when conceived as a mighty person, god merely embodies our ignorance of true causality. One should recall here notions like "flogiston" or Marx's "Asiatic mode of production" or, as a matter of fact, today's popular "postindustrial society"—notions that, while they appear to designate a positive content, merely signal our ignorance. Spinoza's unheard-of endeavor is to think ethics itself outside the "anthropomorphic" moral categories of intentions, commandments, and the like. What he proposes is stricto sensu an *ontological ethics,* an ethics deprived of the deontological dimension, an ethics of "is" without "ought." What, then, is the price paid for this suspension of the ethical dimension of commandment, of the Master Signifier? The psychoanalytic answer is clear: superego. Superego is on the side of knowledge; like Kafka's law, it wants nothing from you—it is just there if you come to it. This is the command operative in the warning we see everywhere today: "Smoking may be dangerous to your health." Nothing is prohibited; you are just informed of a causal link. Along the same lines, the injunction "Only have sex if you really want to enjoy it!" is the best way to sabotage enjoyment. This conclusion may appear strange. In a first approach, if there ever was a philosopher foreign to superego, it is Spinoza. Does his thought not display a unique attitude of almost saintly indifference, of the elevation not only above ordinary human passions and interests but also above all feelings of guilt and moral outrage? Is his universe not that of pure positivity of forces with no life-denying negativity? Is his attitude not one of the joyful assertion of life? However, what if superego is the hidden name of this very indifference and pure assertion of life?

Kant, Hegel

It is at this precise point that Kant—the Kantian break—sets in. What Spinoza and Kant share is the idea that virtue is its own reward and needs no other. They both reject with contempt the popular idea that our good deeds will be remunerated and our bad deeds punished in the afterlife. However, Kant's thesis is that the Spinozan position of knowledge without the deontological dimension of an unconditional Ought is impossible to sustain: there is an irreducible crack in the edifice of Being and it is through this crack that the "deontological" dimension of "Ought" intervenes—the "Ought" fills in the incompleteness of "Is," of Being. When Kant says that he reduced the domain of knowledge to make space for religious faith, he is to be taken quite literally, in a radically anti-Spinozist way: from the Kantian perspective, Spinoza's position appears as a nightmarish vision of subjects reduced to marionettes. What, exactly, does a marionette stand for—as a subjective stance? In Kant, we find the term "Marionette" in a mysterious subchapter of his *Critique of Practical Reason* titled "Of the Wise Adaptation of Man's Cognitive Faculties to His Practical Vocation," in which he endeavors to answer the question of what would happen to us if we were to gain access to the noumenal domain, to the *Ding an sich:*

> [I]nstead of the conflict which now the moral disposition has to wage with inclinations and in which, after some defeats, moral strength of mind may be gradually won, God and eternity in their awful majesty would stand unceasingly before our eyes.... Thus most actions conforming to the law would be done from fear, few would be done from hope, none from duty. The moral worth of actions, on which alone the worth of the person and even of the world depends in the eyes of supreme wisdom, would not exist at all. The conduct of man, so long as his nature remained as it is now, would be changed into mere mechanism, where, as in a puppet show, everything would gesticulate well but no life would be found in the figures.[48]

So, for Kant, the direct access to the noumenal domain would deprive us of the very "spontaneity" that forms the kernel of transcendental freedom: it would turn us into lifeless automata, or, to put it in today's terms, into "thinking machines." The implication of this passage is much more radical and paradoxical than it may appear. If we discard its inconsistency (how could fear and lifeless gesticulation coexist?), the conclusion it imposes is that, at the level of phenomena as well as at the noumenal level, we—humans—are a "mere mechanism" with no autonomy and freedom. As phenomena, we are not free, we are a part of nature, a "mere mechanism," totally submitted to causal links, a part of the nexus of causes and effects, and, as noumena, we are again not free but reduced to a "mere mechanism." (Is what Kant describes as a person who directly knows the noumenal domain not strictly homologous to the utilitarian subject whose acts are fully determined by the calculus of pleasures and pains?) *Our freedom persists only in a space IN BETWEEN the phenomenal and the noumenal.* It is therefore not that Kant simply limited causality to the phenomenal domain to be able to assert that, at the noumenal level, we are free autonomous agents: we are only free insofar as our horizon is that of the phenomenal, insofar as the noumenal domain remains inaccessible to us. What we encounter here is again the tension between the two notions of the Real, the Real of the inaccessible noumenal Thing and the Real as the pure gap, the interstice between the repetition of the same: the Kantian Real is the noumenal Thing beyond phenomena whereas the Hegelian Real is the gap itself between the phenomenal and the noumenal, the gap that sustains freedom.

48 Immanuel Kant, *Critique of Practical Reason* (New York: Macmillan, 1956), pp. 152–53.

Is the way out of this predicament to assert that we are free insofar as we *are* noumenally autonomous, *but* our cognitive perspective remains constrained to the phenomenal level? In this case, we *are* "really free" at the noumenal level, but our freedom would be meaningless in we were also to have the cognitive insight into the noumenal domain, since that insight would always determine our choices—who *would* choose evil, when confronted with the fact that the price of doing evil will be the divine punishment? However, does this imagined case not provide us with the only consequent answer to the question "what would a truly free act be," a free act for a noumenal entity, an act of true *noumenal* freedom? It would be to *know* all the inexorable horrible consequences of choosing the evil *and nonetheless to choose it.* This would have been a truly "nonpathological" act, an act of acting with no regard for one's pathological interests.

The basic gesture of Kant's transcendental turn is thus to invert the obstacle into a positive condition. In the standard Leibnizean ontology, we, finite subjects, can act freely *in spite of* our finitude, since freedom is the spark that unites us with the infinite God; in Kant, this finitude, our separation from the Absolute, is the POSITIVE condition of our freedom. In short, the condition of impossibility is the condition of possibility. In this sense, Susan Neiman is right to remark that "the worry that fueled debates about the difference between appearance and reality was *not* the fear that the world might not turn out to be the way it seems to us—but rather the fear that it would."[49] This fear is ultimately ethical: the closure of the gap between appearance and reality would deprive us of our freedom and thus of our ethical dignity. What this means is that the gap between noumenal reality and appearance is redoubled: one has to distinguish between noumenal reality "in itself" and the way noumenal reality *appears* within the domain of appearance (say, in our experience of freedom and the moral Law). This tiny edge distinguishing the two is the edge between the sublime and the horrible. God is sublime for us, from our finite perspective—experienced in itself, God would turn into a mortifying horror.

However, one should be very careful not to miss what Kant is aiming at. In a first approach, it may appear that he merely assumes a certain place prefigured by Spinoza: unable to sustain the nonanthropomorphic position of true knowledge, he proclaims the substantial order of Being inaccessible, out of bounds for our reason, and thus opens up the space for morality. (And, incidentally, is the same stance not clearly discernible in today's neo-Kantian reactions to biogenetics? Basically, Habermas is saying that, although we now know that our dispositions

---

[49] Susan Neiman, *Evil in Modern Thought* (Princeton, N.J.: Princeton University Press, 2002), p. 11.

depend on meaningless genetic contingencies, let us pretend and act as if this is not the case so that we can maintain our sense of dignity and autonomy—the paradox here is that autonomy can only be maintained by prohibiting access to the blind natural contingency which determines us. That is to say, we maintain our autonomy, paradoxically, by *limiting* our freedom of scientific intervention.) However, things are more complex. In his *Les mots et les choses*, Foucault introduced the notion of the "empirico-transcendental doublet": in the modern philosophy of subjectivity, the subject is, by definition, split between an inner-worldly entity (as the empirical person, the object of the positive sciences and political administration) and the transcendental subject, the constitutive agent of the world itself—the problematic enigma is the umbilical cord that links the two in an irreducible way. And, it is against this background that one can measure Heidegger's achievement: he grounded the "transcendental" dimension (*Dasein* as the site of the opening of the world) in the very finitude of man. Mortality is no longer a stain, an index of factual limitation, of the otherwise ideal-eternal Subject; it is the very source of its unique place. There is no longer any place here for the neo-Kantian (Cassirer) assertion of man as inhabiting two realms, the eternal realm of ideal values and the empirical realm of nature; there is no longer any place even for Husserl's morbid imagine of the whole of humanity succumbing to a pestilence and the transcendental ego surviving it. One should insist here on the split between this doublet and the pre-Kantian metaphysical problematic of particular/sensual/animal and universal/rational/divine aspect of man. The Kantian transcendental is irreducibly rooted in the empirical/temporal/finite—it is the transphenomenal *as it appears within the finite horizon of temporality.* And this dimension of the transcendental (specifically as opposed to the noumenal) is what is missing in Spinoza.

Consequently, do we not find the distinction between how things appear to me and how things *effectively* appear to me in the very heart of Kant's transcendental turn? Phenomenal reality is not simply the way things appear to me. It designates the way things "really" appear to me, the way they constitute phenomenal reality, as opposed to a mere subjective/illusory appearance. Consequently, when I misperceive some object in my phenomenal reality, when I mistake it for a different object, what is wrong is not that I am unaware of how things "really are in themselves" but of how they "really appear" to me. One cannot overestimate the importance of this Kantian move. Ultimately, philosophy as such is Kantian, and it should be read from the vantage point of the Kantian revolution, namely, not as a naive attempt at "absolute knowledge," at a total description of the entirety of reality, but as the work of deploying the horizon of preunderstanding presupposed in every engagement with entities in the world. It is only with Kant (with his notion of the transcendental) that true philosophy begins. What we had before was a simple global ontology, the knowledge about All, and not yet the notion of the transcendental-hermeneutic horizon of the World. Consequently, the basic task of post-Kantian thought was "only" to think Kant through to the end. This is what, among others, Heidegger's intention was in *Being and Time,* namely, to read the history of ontology (Descartes, Aristotle) backward from Kant—say, to interpret Aristotle's physics as the hermeneutic deployment of what being, life, and so forth meant for the Greeks. (Later, unfortunately, Heidegger renounced this idea of pursuing to the end the Kantian breakthrough, dismissing Kant's transcendental turn as a further step in the course of the subjectivist forgetting of Being.) And, the ultimate irony is that Deleuze was, in a way, fully aware of this fact. In his 1978 lectures on Kant, he claims that, for Kant, "there is no longer an essence behind appearance, there is rather the sense or non-sense of what appears"; what this bears witness to is "a radically new atmosphere of thought, to the point where I can say that in this respect we are all Kantians."[50]

What does Hegel bring to this constellation? He is not any kind of "mediator" between the two extremes of Spinoza and Kant. On the contrary, from a truly Hegelian perspective, the problem with Kant is that *he remains all too Spinozan:* the crackless, seamless positivity of Being is merely transposed onto the inaccessible In-Itself. In other words, from the Hegelian standpoint, this very fascination with the horrible Noumenon in itself is the ultimate lure. The thing to do here is not to rehabilitate the old Leibnizean metaphysics, even in the guise of heroically forcing one's way into the noumenal "heart of darkness" and confronting its horror, but to transpose this absolute gap that separates us from the noumenal Absolute into the Absolute itself. So, when Kant asserts the limitation of our knowledge, Hegel does not answer him by claiming that he can overcome the Kantian gap and thereby gain access to Absolute Knowledge in the style of a precritical metaphysics. What he claims is that the Kantian gap already *is* the solution: Being itself is incomplete. *This* is what Hegel's motto "one should conceive the Absolute not only as Substance, but also as Subject" means: "subject" is the name for a crack in the edifice of Being.

Hegel 1: Taking Deleuze from Behind

In his autobiography, Somerset Maugham reports how he was always an avid reader of great philosophers and found in all of them something interesting to learn, a way to get in contact with them—in all of them

---

[50] Gilles Deleuze, Seminar 1, available on the Internet at www.deleuze.fr.st.

except Hegel, who remained totally foreign and impenetrable to him. The same figure of Hegel as the absolute Otherness, the philosopher from whom one has to differentiate oneself ("whatever this means, it is clear that it is incompatible with Hegelian absolute knowledge"), persists in contemporary philosophy up to Deleuze. Besides Hegel, there are three other philosophers who are obviously hated by Deleuze: Plato, Descartes, and Kant. However, with the last three, he nonetheless finds a way to read them "against the grain," to discover in their very theoretical practice procedures (of conceptual invention, of "staging" concepts) that offer a way to undermine their "official" position. Suffice it to recall the reading of Plato in the appendix to *The Logic of Sense,* which almost makes out of Plato the first anti-Platonist, the detailed reconstruction of the process of "montage" and staging that Descartes enacts in his construction of the concept of *cogito,* or the reading of Kant's multitude of the faculties of reason as opposed to the transcendental unity of the subject. In all three cases, Deleuze tries to enter the enemy's territory and twist, for his own ends, the very philosopher who should be his greatest enemy. However, there is no such operation with Hegel; Hegel is "thoroughly bad," unredeemable. Deleuze characterizes his reading of philosophers as guided by the tendency

> to see the history of philosophy as a sort of buggery or (it comes to the same thing) immaculate conception. I saw myself as taking an author from behind and giving him a child that would be his own offspring, yet monstrous. It was really important for it to be his own child, because the author had to actually say all I had him saying. But the child was bound to be monstrous too, because it resulted from all sorts of shifting, slipping, dislocations, and hidden emissions that I really enjoyed.[51]

Perhaps this unexpected reference to the *philosophical* practice of buggery provides the best exemplification of what Deleuze is effectively aiming at through his insistence on the univocity of Being: an attitude of perceiving disparate and incompatible events or propositions ("immaculate conception," "buggery," "philosophical interpretation") as occurring at the same ontological level. It is therefore crucial to perceive how the proper attitude toward propositions like "taking a philosopher from behind" is not one of an obscene, condescending, and dismissive sneer but one of completely naive seriousness: Deleuze is not trying to amuse us by way of generating a shocking effect. And the same goes for Foucault who, in his genealogy, locates at the same level of univocity philosophical statements, economic debates, legal theories, pedagogical injunctions, sexual advice. This practice of buggery is also what distinguishes Deleuze from

---

[51] Deleuze, *Negotiations,* p. 6.

the field of deconstruction; perhaps the most obvious sign of the gap that separates Deleuze from deconstruction is his fierce opposition to the latter's "hermeneutics of suspicion." He advised his students to

> trust the author you are studying. Proceed by feeling your way. . . . You must silence the voices of objection within you. You must let him speak for himself, analyze the frequency of his words, the style of his own obsessions.[52]

(It would just be good if Deleuze were to display some readiness to follow this approach also in his reading of Hegel.) Linked to this is the second feature separating Deleuze from deconstruction, which concerns his style of philosophical "indirect free speech." Both Deleuze and Derrida deploy their theories through a detailed reading of other philosophers, that is to say, they both reject the pre-Kantian, uncritical, direct deployment of philosophical systems. For both of them, philosophy today can be practiced only in the mode of metaphilosophy, as a reading of (other) philosophers. But, while Derrida proceeds in the mode of critical de-construction, of undermining the interpreted text or author, Deleuze, in his buggery, imputes to the interpreted philosopher his own inner-most position and endeavors to extract it from him. So, while Derrida engages in a "hermeneutics of suspicion," Deleuze practices an excessive benevolence toward the interpreted philosopher. At the immediate material level, Derrida has to resort to quotation marks all the time, signalling that the employed concept is not really his, whereas Deleuze endorses everything, directly speaking through the interpreted author in an indirect free speech *without* quotation marks. And, of course, it is easy to demonstrate that Deleuze's "benevolence" is much more violent and subversive than the Derridean reading: his buggery produces true monsters.

One should resist the temptation to submit Deleuzian notions of immanence and "pure presence" of the flux of becoming to a direct Derridean critique (deconstructive reading), reproaching Deleuze with "metaphysics of presence." It is not that such critique is simply wrong but, rather, that it misses the point by being too much "up to the point," by hitting its target all too directly. *Of course* Deleuze asserts presence against representation, and so forth, but precisely this "obvious" fact renders palpable that we are dealing here with a radical misunderstanding. What gets lost in such a critique is the fact that Derrida and Deleuze speak different, totally incompatible, languages, with no shared ground between them.

---

[52] Quoted from André-Pierre Colombat, "Three Powers of Literature and Philosophy," in *A Deleuzian Century?* edited by Ian Buchanan (Durham, N.C.: Duke University Press, 1999), p. 204.

Deleuze is here deeply Lacanian: does Lacan not do the same in his reading of Kant "with Sade"? Jacques-Alain Miller once characterized this reading with the same words as Deleuze. The aim of Lacan is to "take Kant from behind," to produce the Sadean monster as Kant's own offspring. (And, incidentally, does the same not go also for Heidegger's reading of pre-Socratic fragments? Is he also not taking from behind Parmenides and Heraclitus? Is his extensive explanation of Parmenides' "Being and thought are the same" not one of the greatest buggeries in the history of philosophy?) The term "immaculate conception" is to be linked to the notion, from *The Logic of Sense*, of the flow of sense as infertile, without a proper causal power. Deleuzian reading does not move at the level of the actual imbrication of causes and effects; it stands to "realistic" interpretations as anal penetration does with regard to "proper" vaginal penetration. This is the "truth" of Deleuze's indirect free speech: a procedure of philosophical buggery. Deleuze even introduces variations into this topic of taking a philosopher from behind. He claims that, in his book on Nietzsche, things got turned around so that it was Nietzsche who took him from behind; Spinoza resisted being taken from behind, and so forth. However, Hegel is the absolute exception—as if this exception is constitutive, a kind of prohibition of incest in this field of taking philosophers from behind, opening up the multitude of other philosophers available for buggery. And what if we are effectively dealing here with the prohibition of incest? This would mean that, in an unacknowledged way, Hegel is uncannily *close* to Deleuze.

So, in short, why should we not risk the act of taking from behind Deleuze himself and engage in the practice of the *Hegelian buggery of Deleuze?* Therein resides the ultimate aim of the present booklet. What monster would have emerged if we were to stage the ghastly scene of the spectre of Hegel taking Deleuze from behind? How would the offspring of *this* immaculate conception look? Is Hegel really the one philosopher who is "unbuggerable," who cannot be taken from behind? What if, on the contrary, Hegel is the greatest and unique self-buggerer in the history of philosophy? What if the "dialectical method" is the one of permanent self-buggering? Sade once wrote that the ultimate sexual pleasure is for a man to penetrate himself anally (having a long and plastic enough penis that can be twisted around even when erect, so that it is possible to do it)—perhaps this closed circle of self-buggery is the "truth" of the Hegelian Circle. (There is, nonetheless, a distinction between Deleuze and Hegel-Lacan with regard to practicing philosophy as buggery: while Deleuze himself does the act of buggery, Hegel and Lacan adopt the position of a perverse observer who stages the spectacle of buggery and then watches for what the outcome will be. Lacan thus stages the scene of Sade taking

Kant from behind—this is how one has to read "Kant *with* Sade"—to see the monster of Kant-Sade being born; and Hegel also is the observer of a philosophical edifice buggering itself, thus generating the monster of another philosophy.)

At a recent public discussion that followed a talk on the ethics of betrayal (the Nietzschean "noble betrayal" as the highest sign of love and respect, of fidelity even), the author (a Derridean) was asked about his own attitude toward Derrida: where is *his own* "noble betrayal" of Derrida, whom he never criticizes? The author's reply was that Derrida has no need of it, since he is all the time already betraying himself (questioning his own previous positions, etc.). But, does the same not go much more for Lacan? Is he not permanently changing his position, so that when, in his great negative statement, he pathetically proclaims that "there is no Other of the Other," and so forth, the question to be asked is But who was the poor idiot who *claimed* that there *is* an "Other of the Other" in the first place? The answer is always *Lacan himself a couple of years ago.* And, is not the highest case of this procedure Lacan's standardized attacks on Hegel in the style of "whatever I am saying, one thing is sure: it is not the Hegelian absolute knowledge, the Hegelian perfect circle of dialectical mediation?" What if this "not" is Lacan's version of "This is not my mother"? And, what if the same goes for Deleuze? What if this exceptional role of Hegel, this refusal to take him from behind, betrays a fear of excessive proximity? What if Deleuze has to elevate Hegel into an absolute Other who cannot be appropriated by free indirect speech because taking Hegel from behind would produce a monster unbearable for Deleuze himself?

Deleuze equals Hegel: is this the ultimate infinite judgment? Or, as Catherine Malabou puts it,[53] *Deleuze : Hegel = Ahab : White Whale* (the fixed exception, the One as the unity beneath multiplicity)—no complexity, no impersonal intensities, no multitudes, just Falsity embodied. This is why Deleuze even enjoins us to forget Hegel. This absolute rejection, this urge to "stupidize" Hegel, to present a straw man image of him (as amply demonstrated by Malabou), conceals, of course, a disavowed affinity. Fredric Jameson already drew attention to the fact that the central reference of *Anti-Oedipus,* the underlying scheme of its larger historical framework, is "The Pre-Capitalist Modes of Production," the long fragment from the *Grundrisse* manuscripts in which we encounter Marx at his most Hegelian (its entire scheme of the global historical movement relying on the Hegelian process from substance to subject). And, what about the other key Deleuzian concept literally taken over

---

[53] Catherine Malabou, "Who's Afraid of Hegelian Wolves?" in *Deleuze: A Critical Reader,* edited by Paul Patton (Oxford: Blackwell, 1996).

from Hegel, that of the "concrete universal"? (What Deleuze aims at with the "concrete universality" is the formal generative model of a process of BECOMING as opposed to the "abstract" universals [genuses and species] that serve to categorize modes of being, of established reality.) Is Deleuze's critique of the Platonic logic of ideal universal types designating the same quality (set of properties) in the elements comprised by the type not strangely close to Hegel's critique of abstract universality?

What is, effectively, the Hegelian "self-movement of the Notion" about? Recall a boring academic textbook that, apropos of a philosophical problem or discipline, enumerates the series of predominant opinions or claims: "The philosopher A claimed that soul is immortal, while the philosopher B claimed that there is no soul, and the philosopher C that soul is only the form of the body. . . ." There is something blatantly ridiculous and inadequate in presenting such a panoply of "opinions of philosophers"—why? We, the readers, somehow "feel" that this is not philosophy, that a "true" philosophy must systematically account for this very multitude of "opinions" (positions), not just enumerate them. In short, what we expect is to get a report on how one "opinion" arises out of the inconsistencies or insufficiencies of another "opinion" so that the chain of these "opinions" forms an organic Whole—or, as Hegel would have put it, the history of philosophy itself is part of philosophy, not just a comparative report on whether and how different "opinions" are right or wrong. This organic interweaving of "opinions" (positions) is what Hegel calls the "self-movement of the Notion." This is why, when someone—even if, like Francis Fukuyama, he claims to be a Hegelian—begins a sentence with "Hegel believes that . . . ," he thereby automatically disqualifies himself not only as a Hegelian but also as a serious philosopher. Philosophy is emphatically *not* about the "beliefs" of different individual persons.

And, what is the Hegelian *Begriff* as opposed to the nominalist "notion," the result of abstracting shared features from a series of particular objects? Often, we stumble on a particular case that does not fully "fit" its universal species, that is "atypical"; the next step is to acknowledge that *every* particular is "atypical," that *the universal species exists only in exceptions,* that there is a structural tension between the Universal and the Particular. At this point, we become aware that the Universal is no longer just an empty neutral container of its subspecies but an entity in tension with each and every one of its species. The universal Notion thus acquires a dynamics of its own. More precisely, the true Universal *is* this very antagonistic dynamics between the Universal and the Particular. It is at this point that we pass from "abstract" to "concrete" Universal—at the point when we acknowledge that every Particular is an "exception," and, consequently, that the Universal, far from "containing" its particular content, *excludes* it (or is excluded *by* it). This exclusion renders the Universal itself particular (it is not truly universal, since it cannot grasp or contain the particular content), yet this very failure is its strength: the Universal is thus simultaneously posited as the Particular. The supreme political case of such a gesture is the moment of revolutionary "councils" taking over—the moment of "ahistorical" collective freedom, of "eternity in time," of what Benjamin called "dialectic in suspense." Or, as Alain Badiou would have put it in his Platonic terms, in such historical moments, the eternal Idea of Freedom appears/transpires. Even if its realization is always "impure," one should stick to the eternal Idea, which is not just a "generalization" of particular experiences of freedom but their inherent Measure. (To which, of course, Hegel would have retorted that the Thermidor occurs because such a direct actualization of freedom has to appear as Terror.) One should insert this appearance of Freedom into the series of exceptional temporalities, together with the Messianic time first formulated by Paul—the time when "the end is near," the time of the end of time (as Giorgio Agamben puts it) when, in an ontological "state of emergency," one should suspend one's full identification with one's sociosymbolic identity and act *as if* this identity is unimportant, a matter of indifference. (This exceptional temporality is to be strictly distinguished from the ecstatic-carnivalesque suspension of Order in which things are turned upside-down in a generalized orgy.)

This story of the Hegelian Deleuze goes on ad infinitum. When, with reference to Darwin, Deleuze emphasizes how variations within a universal kind are not the inessential, contingent particularities of a species (the "irrational," conceptually irrelevant differences between individuals) but the crucial moments of evolution, of the emergence of the New, is he not more Hegelian than he is ready to admit? What's more, is the Deleuzian "phase transition" not strangely close to the old Hegelian (and, later, dialectical-materialist) notion of the passage of quantity into new quality, namely, to the Hegelian critique of considering quantity independently of quality? (No wonder one of Deleuze's references here is Ilya Prigogine, who, unique among today's theoreticians, had the courage to point out that, taken in itself, outside its ideological role, the philosophy of dialectical materialism is not without its merits).[54] So, what if, like Ahab's "becoming-whale," Deleuze himself is caught in a strange "becoming-Hegel"? The difference between Hegel and Deleuze is here much more difficult to determine than it may appear: grosso modo,

---

[54] See Ilya Prigogine, *From Being to Becoming: Time and Complexity in the Physical Sciences* (New York: W. H. Freeman, 1981).

Deleuze wants to assert the primacy of the genetic process of differentiation against any mode of universal Being, whereas Hegel's aim is to introduce (self)movement into the very heart of conceptual universality. However, in this sense, is Hegel not also a "conceptual nominalist" like Deleuze? When Deleuze conceives of universality as individual, is he not again close to Hegel's notion of individuality as universal (in its self-relating negation of its particular properties)?

Deleuze's great anti-Hegelian motif is that of absolute positivity, his thorough rejection of negativity. For Deleuze, Hegelian negativity is precisely the way to subordinate difference to Identity, to reduce it to a sublated moment of identity's self-mediation ("identity of identity and difference"). The accusation against Hegel is thus double. Hegel introduces negativity into the pure positivity of Being, *and* Hegel introduces negativity in order to reduce differentiation to a subordinated/sublatable moment of the positive One. What remains unthinkable for Deleuze is simply a negativity that is *not* just a detour on the path of the One's self-mediation. One is tempted to defend Hegel here: is what Hegel ultimately does to negativity not the unheard-of *"positivization" of negativity itself*? Recall the most famous lines of all from the Sherlock Holmes stories, found in "The Silver Blaze": " 'Is there any point to which you wish to draw my attention?' 'To the curious incident of the dog in the night time.' 'The dog did nothing in the night time.' 'That was the curious incident,' remarked Sherlock Holmes."

The absence itself is here perceived as a positive fact; we thus obtain a curious field in which absences accompany presences as just another set of positive facts. Perhaps this is how one should read Pascal: "A picture includes absence and presence, pleasant and unpleasant. Reality excludes absence and unpleasantness."[55] A picture (here synonymous with what Deleuze calls the flow of the Sense-Event) is an immaterial texture in which absences themselves have positive existence, in contrast to the bodily Real in which, as Lacan put it, nothing lacks, there are no absences. When, in February 2003, Colin Powell addressed the UN Security Council to advocate the attack on Iraq, the U.S. delegation asked the large reproduction of Picasso's "Guernica" on the wall behind the speaker's podium to be covered with a different visual ornament. Although the official explanation was that "Guernica" does not provide the adequate optical background for the televised transmission of Powell's speech, it was clear to everyone what the U.S. delegation was afraid of: that "Guernica," the painting supposed to be "about" the catastrophic results of the German aerial bombing of the Spanish city in the civil war,

---

would give rise to the "wrong kind of associations" if it were to serve as the background to Powell advocating precisely the bombing of Iraq by the far superior U.S. Air Force. This is the power of negativity at its most elementary. If the U.S. delegation were to abstain from demanding that "Guernica" be covered up, probably no one would associate Powell's speech with the painting displayed behind him—the very change, the very gesture of concealing the painting, drew attention to it and imposed the "wrong association," confirming its truth.

Another subterranean link between Deleuze and Hegel is that of *immanence*. If there ever was a philosopher of unconditional immanence, it is Hegel. Is Hegel's elementary procedure not best encapsulated by his motto, from the introduction to *Phenomenology,* according to which the difference between For-us and In-itself is itself "for us": it is ourselves, in the immanence of our thought, who experience the distinction between the way things appear to us and the way they are in themselves. The distinction between appearance and transcendent reality is itself a fact of our experiential appearance; when we say that a thing is, in itelf, in a certain way, this means it *appears* to us in this mode of being. More generally, absolute immanence also determines the status of Hegel's critique of Kant and the Kantian handling of antinomies/contradictions. Far from denying us access to the Thing-in-itself, the antinomic or contradictory character of our experience of a Thing is what brings us into direct contact with it. This is also how Hegel would have approached Kafka. The Castle or Court "in themselves" are just a reified projection of the immanent movement of our thought-experience—it is not the inaccessible Thing-Castle that is refracted inadequately in our inconsistent experience. On the contrary, the spectre of the Thing-Castle is the *result* of the inherent-immanent refraction of our experience. And, finally, does the passage from one to another "shape of consciousness" in the *Phenomenology* also not rely on the turn toward absolute immanence? When Hegel refutes ascetism, he does not proclaim it inadequate to the objective state of things; he simply compares it with the immanent LIFE-PRACTICE of the ascetic subject—it is this practice (in Deleuzian terms: what an ascetic subject "does" with ascetism, on behalf of it) that refutes what ascetism "is."

The wager of Deleuze's concept of the "plane of consistency," which points in the direction of absolute immanence, is that of his insistence on the univocity of being. In his "flat ontology," all heterogeneous entities of an assemblage can be conceived at the same level, without any ontological exceptions or priorities. To refer to the well-known paradoxes of inconsistent classification, the plane of consistency would be something like a mixture of elements thrown together through a multitude of divergent criteria (recall Borges's famous taxonomy: brown dogs, dogs who belong to the emperor, dogs who don't bark, and so forth—up to dogs who do not belong to this list). It would be all too easy to counter here that the Lacanian Real is precisely that which resists inclusion within the plane of consistency, the absent Cause of the heterogeneity of the assemblage. Is it, rather, not that this "plane of consistency" is what Lacan called the "feminine" non-All set, with no exceptions and, for that very reason, no totalizing agency?[56] When, at the very end of *Seminar XI*, Lacan refers to Spinoza as the philosopher of the universal signifier and, as such, the true antipode of Kant,[57] he makes the same point: Spinoza is the philosopher of feminine *assemblage,* against Kant as the philosopher of the masculine Exception (the moral Law that suspends the imbrication of phenomenal causes and effects). The Spinozan One-Whole is thus a nontotalized Real, bringing us back to Lacan's fundamental thesis: the Real is not simply external to the Symbolic but, rather, the Symbolic itself deprived of its externality, of its founding exception.

What about Hegel? What if Hegel "feminized" Kant again by way of reducing the Kantian ontological opposition between phenomena and the Thing-in-itself to the absolutely immanent tension inhering within phenomena themselves? It is thus already with Hegel that the logic of Transgression, the idea that, to attain Truth or ultimate Reality, one has to violate the superficial order (with its rules) and force the passage to another dimension hidden beneath, is suspended. Hegel would un-doubtedly fully endorse Deleuze's scathing remark about Bataille, the ultimate thinker of Transgression:

> "Transgression," a concept good for seminarists under the law of a Pope or a priest, the tricksters. Georges Bataille is a very French author. He made the little secret the essence of literature, with a mother within, a priest beneath, an eye above.[58]

In a late story by Somerset Maugham, an older Frenchmen has a paid young concubine. When he finds her in bed with a young man and she confesses that they really love each other, he proposes a unique solution. The two of them should marry; he will provide them with an apartment and a job for the young man—the price is that, twice a week, while the young man is at work, the old man will visit the young wife and make love to her. The solution is thus the reversal of the usual situation: instead of the young woman living with an old man and cheating

[56] See chapter VI of Jacques Lacan, *Le séminaire, livre XX: Encore* (Paris: Editions du Seuil, 1975).
[57] Jacques Lacan, *The Four Fundamental Concepts of Psycho-Analysis* (New York: Norton, 1977), p. 253.
[58] Gilles Deleuze and Claire Parnet, *Dialogues II* (New York: Columbia University Press, 2002), p. 47.

on him with a young lover, she will live with the man whom she really loves and cheat on him with the old, unattractive man. Does this story not provide the clearest staging of the Bataillean transgression? Bataille's ultimate horizon is the tension between homogeneity and its heterogeneous excess—between the profane and the sacred, the domain of exchange, and the excess of pure expenditure. (And, insofar as Bataille's opposition of homogeneity and heterogeneity echoes Lacan's couple of S_2 and S_1, the chain of "ordinary" signifiers and the Master-Signifier, this is how one should also read the series of S_1 in Lacan's seminar *Encore:* not as an ordinal series but as the series of excesses themselves).[59] Or, to put it in Chesterton's terms: a miracle is no longer the irrational exception that disturbs the rational order, since *everything* becomes a miracle; there is no longer the need to assert excess against normality, since *everything* becomes an excess—excess is everywhere, in an unbearable intensity. Therein resides the true transgression. It occurs when the tension between the ordinary phenomenal reality and the transgressive Excess of the Real Thing is abolished. In other words, the truly subversive agent asserts the univocity of Being, assembling all the heterogeneous elements within the same "plane of consistency." Instead of the ridiculously pathetic fake heroism of forcing the established order toward its transcendent traumatic core, we get a profoundly indifferent enumeration that, without the blink of an eye, puts in the same series ethics and buggery.

Hegel 2: From Epistemology to Ontology... and Back

This brings us to the basic Hegelian motif of Deleuze, his reversal of the standard relationship between a problem and its solution(s), his affirmation of an irreducible *excess* of the problem over its solution(s), which is the same as the excess of the virtual over its actualizations:

> In Deleuze's approach the relation between well-posed explanatory problems and their true or false solutions is the epistemological counterpart of the ontological relation between the virtual and the actual. Explanatory problems would be the counterpart of virtual multiplicities since, as he says, "the virtual possesses the reality of a task to be performed or a problem to be solved." Individual solutions, on the other hand, would be the counterpart of actual individual beings: "An organism is nothing if not the solution to a problem, as are each of its differenciated organs, such as the eye which solves a light problem."[60]

---

[59] See chapter XI of Jacques Lacan, *Le séminaire, livre XX: Encore.*
[60] Manuel DeLanda, *Intensive Science and Virtual Philosophy* (New York: Continuum, 2002), p. 135.

The philosophical consequences of this "intimate relation between epistemology and ontology" are crucial: the traditional opposition between epistemology and ontology should be left behind. It is no longer that we, subjects of a scientific investigation engaged in the difficult path of getting to know objective reality by gradually approaching it, formulate and solve problems, while reality just *is* out there, fully constituted and given, unconcerned by our slow progress. In a properly Hegelian way, our painful progress of knowledge, our confusions, our search for solutions, that is to say, precisely that which seems to *separate* us from the way reality really is out there, is already the innermost constituent of reality itself. When we try to establish the function of some organ in an animal, we are thereby repeating the "objective" process itself through which the animal "invented" this organ as the solution of some problem. Our process of approaching constituted objective reality repeats the virtual process of Becoming of this reality itself. The fact that we cannot ever "fully know" reality is thus not a sign of the limitation of our knowledge but the sign that reality itself is "incomplete," open, an actualization of the underlying virtual process of Becoming.[61]

Such a reflective twist by means of which the subject assumes the inexistence of the big Other defines the subjective position of the analyst, what Lacan calls the "discourse of the analyst," and he does give a clear hint that this, effectively, is Hegel's position. In his Seminar XVII (*L'envers de la psychanalyse*), Lacan, in an apparently inconsistent way, designates Hegel as the "most sublime of hysterics," as an exemplary figure of the Master, as the model of the discourse of the University. On page 20, Lacan emphasizes how "it sticks out in Hegel (*c'est saillant chez Hegel*)" that philosophy "is at the level of the discourse of the master"; on page 38,

---

[61] This is also how Deleuze determines the difference between philosophy and science. Science aims at solutions, philosophy tries to extract problems that orient scientists in their search for solutions. There is, however, a fundamental ambiguity in how Deleuze characterizes philosophy as syntagmatic, in contrast to Kuhn's notion of a scientific paradigm (i.e., of science as paradigmatic). Science is a slow-motion, freeze-frame procedure, a reduction to a fixed system of functional coordinates, in contrast to the philosophical acceleration of motion; on the other hand, Deleuze claims that science operates in a serial time (linear development, rupture, reconnection), while philosophy operates according to a "stratigraphic" time in which what comes after is always superimposed on what comes before. But is serial time not precisely *syntagmatic* (linear succession in time), in contrast to the "stratigraphic" crystallization, namely, *paradigmatic* superimposition? The key resides in the exact implications of these two modalities of time: the "stratigraphic" paradigmatic superimposition is precisely the ultimate result of time catching up with itself in an inner fold, of a past crystal-image superimposing itself on a future image, while the time of science is that of the linear temporal movement of the constituted reality *in* time, which means, precisely, *within* a certain given paradigm of what reality is. The true opposition is thus not simply between movement and static structure but between movement *in* time, correlative to a paradigmatic order, and the movement *of* time itself in a short circuit of past and present. The ultimate movement, the ultimate subversion of static order, is the very "stratigraphic" stasis in which past and future coincide in a superimposed crystallized image.

Hegel is designated as "the most sublime of all hysterics (*le plus sublime des hysteriques*)," and, on page 200, one reads "Hegel, the sublime representative of the discourse of knowledge (*le discours du savoir*), and of the university knowledge (*savoir universitaire*)."[62] It is easy to see how each of these designations is justified in its own terms. Hegel's system is the extreme case of the all-encompassing university Knowledge, allocating each particular topic to its own proper place; if there ever was a figure of the towering Master in the history of philosophy, it is Hegel; and, Hegel's dialectical procedure can best be determined as the permanent hystericization—hysterical questioning—of the hegemonic figure of the Master. So, which of these three positions is the "real" Hegel? The answer is obvious: *the fourth one*, the discourse of the analyst—as if to point in this direction, Lacan, in this seminar dedicated to the four discourses, applies to Hegel the first three positions (Master, Hysteric, University), leaving out the fourth position. Do we not get here a clear case of the logic of the borrowed kettle, mentioned by Freud to render transparent the strange procedure of dreams, namely, the enumeration of mutually exclusive answers to a reproach (that I returned to a friend a broken kettle): (1) I never borrowed a kettle from you, (2) I returned it to you unbroken, (3) the kettle was already broken when I got it from you? For Freud, such an enumeration of inconsistent arguments confirms, of course, *per negationem* what it endeavors to deny: that I returned to you a broken kettle—or, in Hegel's case, that he occupies the position of the analyst. A further proof of this fact is Lacan's claim that the discourse of the analyst is not simply one among the four—it is simultaneously a discourse that emerges when we pass from one discourse to another (say, from that of the Master to that of the University). If, then, the discourse of the analyst is located in the very passage or shift from one to another discourse, is the true position of Hegel, who is a Master, a Hysteric, and the agent of the discourse of the University, not that of an incessant passage between these three, that is to say, that of the analyst?

It is here that we can clearly pinpoint what is arguably Deleuze's crucial misunderstanding of Hegel's move against/beyond Kant: Deleuze continues to read Hegel in a traditional way, as the one who returned from Kant to an absolute metaphysics that articulates the totally self-transparent and fully actualized logical structure of Being. Already in

---

[62] I owe these indications to Mladen Dolar. And, incidentally, the last determination (of Hegel as the representative of the discourse of university) has to be read against the background of Lacan's reference to the reading of Hegel developed by Alexandre Kojeve who interpreted the Stalinist bureaucratic state as the historical actualization of the Hegelian "end of history"—no wonder that, for Lacan, "what reigns in what one calls the Union of the Soviet Socialist Republics is University" (Jacques Lacan, *Le séminaire, livre XVII: L'envers de la psychanalyse*, p. 237), that is, in the USSR, "knowledge is the king" (op. cit., p. 238).

Difference and Repetition, Deleuze interprets Kant's transcendental Ideas from the perspective of his notion of "problematicity," as the excess of the question over answers to it: a transcendental Idea designates not an ideal but a problem, a question, a task, which no answer, no actualization, can fully meet. So, Deleuze can only read the excess of the problem over its solutions as an anti-Hegelian motif, insofar as he perceives Hegel as the one who, as it were, filled in the gaps of the Kantian system and passed from Kant's openness and indeterminacy to the notion's complete actualization/determination.[63] What, however, if Hegel does not *add* any positive content to Kant, does not fill in the gaps—what if he just accomplishes a shift of perspective in and through which the problem already appears as its own solution? What if, for Hegel, "absolute Knowing" is not the absurd position of "knowing everything" but the insight into how the path toward Truth is already Truth itself, into how the Absolute is precisely—to put it in Deleuzean terms—the virtuality of the eternal process of its own actualization?

We are thereby within the very heart of the problem of *freedom:* the only way to save freedom is through this short circuit between epistemology and ontology—the moment we reduce our process of knowledge to a process external to the thing itself, to an endless approximation to the thing, freedom is lost, because "reality" is conceived of as a completed, positive order of Being, as a full and exhaustive ontological domain. The inconsistency of Kant apropos of freedom is here crucial in its structural necessity. On one hand, the subject is free in the noumenal sense—its freedom attests to the fact that it does not belong to the realm of the phenomenal enchainment of causes and effects, that it is capable of absolute spontaneity. On the other hand, spontaneity is transcendental, not transcendent: it is the way the subject appears to itself—as we learn in the final paragraphs of Part I of the *Critique of Practical Reason,* it may well be that, in ourselves at the noumenal level, we are just marionettes in the hands of the all-powerful God. The only solution is here the Hegelo-Deleuzian [*sic*] one: to transpose the incompleteness and openness (the surplus of the virtual over the actual, of the problem over its solutions) *into the thing itself.*

This unexpected transposition is not without its comic aspect. Bertolt Brecht once wrote that there is no dialectics without humor: the dialectical reversals are deeply connected to comical twists and unexpected shifts of perspective. In his book on jokes, Freud refers to the well-known story of a middleman who tries to convince a young man to marry a woman

---

[63] For a succinct account of the complex, shifting, and often inconsistent way Deleuze relates to the triad of Spinoza, Kant, and Hegel, see Christian Kerslake, "The Vertigo of Philosophy: Deleuze and the Problem of Immanence," in *Radical Philosophy,* 38.

he represents; his strategy is to reinterpret every objection into a praise. When the man says "But the woman is ugly!" he answers, "So you will not have to worry that she will deceive you with others!" "She is poor!" "So she will be used not to spend too much of your money!" and so on, until, finally, when the man formulates a reproach impossible to reinterpret in this way, the middleman explodes, "But what do you want? Perfection? Nobody is totally without a fault!"[64] Would it not also be possible to discern in this joke the underlying structure of the legitmization of a Real Socialist regime? "There are not enough meat and rich food in the stores!" "So you don't have to worry about getting fat and suffering a heart attack!" "There are not enough interesting theatrical and cinema performances or good books available!" "Does this not enable you to cultivate all the more the art of intense social life, visiting friends and neighbors?" "The secret police exerts total control over my life!" "So you can just relax and lead a life safe from worries!" and so on, until . . . "But the air is so polluted from the nearby factory that all my children have life-threatening lung diseases!" "What do you want? No system is without a fault!"

Consequently, what, precisely, is the thin line that divides tragedy from comedy, the final tragic insight from the final twist of a joke? In many a good joke, the unexpected final twist occurs when the position of enunciation itself falls into the enunciated content. Recall the familiar story about a Pole and a Jew sharing the same train compartment, with the Pole starting the conversation by asking the Jew, "Tell me, how do you Jews manage to squeeze the last bit of money from the people?" "OK," replies the Jew, "but this will cost you 10$!" Upon getting the money, the Jew goes on, "Well, at midnight, you go to the cemetery, you burn there a fire of special wood . . ." "What wood?" eagerly asks the Pole. "This will call you another 10$!" snaps back the Jew, and so on endlessly, until the Pole explodes, "But there is no final secret, no end to this story, you are just trying to squeeze all the money from me . . ." "Now you see how we Jews . . ." replies the Jew calmly. In short, what the poor Pole, eager to learn and focused upon the secret to which he expected to be initiated, forgot to take into account was the very process into which he was drawn while searching for the secret. The question is, What would make such a story (if not a tragedy proper, then at least) a nonjoke, a

---

[64] It is interesting to note that, when, in his Seminar V on *Les formations de l'inconscient* (Paris: Editions du Seuil, 1998), Lacan retells this story, he omits the final inversion—the very feature that appears to us today as its properly "Lacanian" point, and he just says that the game of critical remarks and answers goes on indefinitely. Is this slip not the best proof of how, in that period (mid-1950s), Lacan was still in the thrall of the signifying process of endless interpretation, unable to properly conceptualize the structural necessity of a cut that interrupts this unending signifying drift?

story with a painful final twist that brings no release in laughter? Would it be enough for the Pole himself to come to the insight, so that, at a certain moment, *he* exclaims, "My god, now I know how you Jews..."? Or would a simple, more dramatic twist be sufficient—imagine the Pole deprived of his last penny, his family ruined, he himself lying ill and announcing that he no longer has any money, when the Jew (caricatured as the evil figure) tells him with a vicious smile, "There is no secret! I just wanted to teach you a lesson and really show you how we Jews..."? Or, to ask the same question the other way around, since the Oedipus story involves a homologous twist (in his search, the hero forgets to include himself), what change would suffice to make it a comedy? One can effectively imagine a similar story along the lines of *The Marriage of Figaro,* with the hero all of a sudden discovering that the older rich widow he married because of her money is effectively his own mother. Would it not be possible to retell, in this way, the elementary story of Christianity, namely, as a joke with the final unexpected twist? A believer is complaining, "I was promised contact with God, divine grace, but now I am totally alone, abandoned by God, destitute, suffering, with only a miserable death awaiting me!" The divine voice then answers him, "You see, now you are effectively one with God, with Christ suffering on the cross!" If we take into account the radical consequences of this elementary dialectical move, then the Hegelian "absolute knowing" itself appears in a new light: no longer as a madly megalomaniac claim by the individual called "Hegel" who, in the 1820s, stated that he "knows and is able to deduce everything there is to know," but as an attempt at delineating the radical closure/finitude of a knowledge grounded in its historical constellation. In "absolute knowing," the limitations of our knowledge are correlated to the limitations of the known constellation itself, its "absolute" character thus emerging from the intersection of these two limitations.

Hegel 3: The Minimal Difference

In what, then, effectively resides the difference between Hegel and Deleuze? Perhaps the difference is not between immanence and transcendence but between flux and gap. The "ultimate fact" of Deleuze's transcendental empiricism is the absolute immanence of the continuous flux of pure becoming, while the "ultimate fact" of Hegel is the irreducible *rupture* of/in immanence. Here, one should evoke Einstein's passage from special to general theories of relativity: for Hegel, the gap between phenomena and their transcendent Ground is a secondary effect of the *absolutely immanent* gap of/in the phenomena themselves.

"Transcendence" is the illusory reflection of the fact that the immanence of phenomena is ruptured, broken, inconsistent. To put it in somewhat simplified terms, it is not that phenomena are broken, that we have multiple partial perspectives, because the transcendent Thing eludes our grasp; on the contrary, the specter of this Thing is the "reified" *effect* of the inconsistency of the phenomena. What if this gap in the immanence (which is not caused by any transcendence but is itself its own cause) is what Deleuze cannot accept? Therein resides Hegel's true lesson: immanence generates the specter of transcendence because it is already inconsistent in itself. This movement is best exemplified by the "Christian syllogism," consisting of three judgments/divisions (*Ur-Teile*):

(1) The starting point is the experience of transcendence: one begins with positing the radical split between man and transcendent God—as exemplified by the figure of Job, who finds himself perplexed by what God is doing to him.
(2) In the second judgment, this split is reflected into God himself, in the guise of the split between God-the-Father and Christ: in the figure of Christ dying on the cross, God himself turns into an atheist, experiencing himself as abandoned by God-the-Father.
(3) Finally, this split falls back into the split between man and man-Christ, the "minimal difference" separating the two. This final figure is the "truth" of the entire movement.

What this syllogism demonstrates is how immanence is not the starting point but the conclusion: *immanence is not an immediate fact but the result that occurs when transcendence is sacrificed and falls back into immanence.*[65] Recall the well-known joke that perfectly renders the logic of the (in)famous Hegelian triad: Three friends have a drink at a bar; the first one says, "A horrible thing happened to me. At my travel agency, I wanted to say 'A ticket to Pittsburgh!' and I said 'A picket to Tittsburgh!'" The second one replies, "That's nothing. At breakfast, I wanted to say to my wife 'Could you pass me the sugar, honey?' and what I said was 'You dirty bitch, you ruined my entire life!'" The third one concludes, "Wait till you hear what happened to me. After gathering the courage all night, I decided to say to my wife at breakfast exactly what you said to yours, and I ended up saying 'Could you pass me the sugar, honey?'" At the very bottom of despair, we thus get the most common family scene, that of the husband asking his wife for sugar. In short, the joke should be read as deploying the hidden genesis of normal, everyday family life: the immanence of normal family life is grounded in the silent despair

---

[65] Do we not find the same structure in psychoanalytic treatment: self-analysis is structurally impossible since one must start with the transferential illusion of the "subject supposed to know"?

when not only our dreams are betrayed by us but we are not even able to explode in rage against this failure.

Or, to put it in Nietzschean terms, truth is not one perspective, "the true one," against the other, illusory one; it only occurs in the very *passage* from one to another perspective (is this not what Lacan was aiming at when, in his *Seminar XX,* he emphasized that the discourse of the analyst emerges briefly in every passage-shift from one to another discourse?). René Girard made the same point apropos of the book of Job. What makes it so subversive (in short, so *true*) is the very shift from one (divine) to another (Job's) perspective, along with the ultimate incompatibility of the two perspectives.[66] Similarly, immanence only emerges as the shifting of transcendence, that is, at the moment when it suddenly strikes us how the gap that separates us from the transcendent Beyond is just a fetishized misperception-effect of the gap within immanence (the gap between "ordinary" phenomena and the phenomena in which the Beyond "shines through"). There is a homologous triad with regard to the Real (the inaccessible Beyond of representations, the hard core around which our representations circulate):

(1) we first posit the Real as the transcendent hard kernel, always perceived in a refracted way;

(2) we then accomplish the "postmodern" reversal: there is no need for any Beyond of the transcendent Real, since the play of refracted appearances is all there is;

(3) the "synthesis" of the two positions is the return to the Real, but a de-substantialized Real, a Real reduced to an elusive "minimal difference" between appearances: the Real is the very cause of refraction, not the inner core beyond refraction.

How are we to understand this? In the naive Marxist polemics about the knowability of the Thing-in-itself back in the 1920s, Karl Kautsky argued that it is easy to arrive at the thing-in-itself (i.e., to establish the difference, in the perceived objects, between what is only appearance-to-us and what belongs to the thing-in-itself). We simply compare our different perceptions of the same object, and that in regard to which these perceptions differ is clearly caused by our perception while that which remains the same must belong to the perceived thing itself. The Lacanian Real inverts this scheme. While reality is what remains the same out there and is perceived by us in an always partial, distorted way, the Real is the very *cause* of this distortion, that X on account of which our perception of reality is always distorted. The Real is thus not the kernel of the Same out there, inaccessible to us; rather, it is located in the very *gap*

---

[66] See René Girard, *Job: The Victim of His People* (Stanford, Calif.: Stanford University Press, 1987).

that separates our perceptions—in the "interstice" between perceptions, as Deleuze would have put it.

Recall the good old example of class struggle. There is no "neutral" view on class struggle, given that every notion of class struggle already implies that we took sides in the class struggle. The "real" of the class struggle is thus the very obstacle that prevents us from adopting a neutral perspective in relation to it. The third version of this syllogism would be that of truth itself:

(1) First, truth is posited as the inaccessible Beyond, something that can only be approached, something that the subject always misses;

(2) Then, the accent shifts to the psychoanalytic notion of truth as intervening in the moments of slips and distortions, in the interstices of "ordinary" discourse: truth erupts when the continuous line of our speech gets interrupted and perturbed;

(3) Finally, we arrive at a third position, that of *moi, la verité, je parle.*[67] The shift from subject to object is crucial here. It is not that what the subject says is true—it is truth itself which speaks, which turns from predicate (a qualification of subject's statements) to subject (of enunciation). It is here that Truth turns into an "organ without a body" that starts to speak.

The first two versions share the notion that Truth is an inaccessible beyond, they are precisely two versions of it: since its place is Beyond, the Truth never appears "as such" but always only in a refracted/distorted mode—or, as Lacan put it, *la verité ne peut que se mi-dire,* it can only be half-told. It is only in the third mode that truth as such *can* speak— how? In the guise of a fiction, precisely, or, to put it in another way, in the mode of the fool's (or, rather, buffon's) discourse—from Paul who designated himself as a buffon to Nietzsche. (In a closer analysis, one should subdivide the second mode in two: is the refraction/distortion the *effect* of the fact that the Truth persists outside, as an inaccessible noumenal In-itself, or are these refractions "all there is," with no Beyond to cause them?) However, is such a position of the one *through whom the Truth directly speaks (or acts)* not the ultimate perverse illusion? Does it not obviously rely on the existence of the big Other (as in the Stalinist "Marxism-Leninism," in which the party posits itself as the executor of historical Necessity)? This counterargument involves a crucial misunderstanding: *the "object" that starts to speak is the object that stands for the lack/inconsistency in the big Other, for the fact that the big Other doesn't exist.* "I, truth, speak" does not mean that through me, the big metaphysical Truth itself speaks but means that the inconsistencies and slips of my speech directly connect to the inconsistencies and the non-all of the

---

[67] "Men, listen, I am telling you the secret. I, truth, speak." Jacques Lacan, *Ecrits,* translated by Bruce Fink (New York: Norton, 2002), p. 114.

Truth itself. Lacan's "I, truth, speak" is thus to be read *together with "la verité ne peut que se mi-dire* (truth can only be half-spoken)," elaborated in the very opening paragraph of his later *Television:*

> I always speak the truth. Not the whole truth, because there's no way to say it all. Saying it all is literally impossible: words fail. Yet it's through this very impossibility that the truth holds onto the real.[68]

What this means is that the true task of thought is *to think together the notion of the "object which speaks" and the inexistence of the big Other.* "I, truth, speak" does not involve the magic overcoming of scepticism and uncertainty but involves the transposition of this uncertainty into truth itself. (Christ is such an object who speaks, his words are exemplary of "I, truth, speak" that emerges at the very point of the death of big Other qua god.) It is here that one should overcome the position of finite subjectivity, that of "we cannot ever get to know Truth itself, we can only get partial glimpses of it, our knowledge is constrained by our subjective position, we cannot every claim that the truth speaks through us.... ": what if truth itself is non-all, affected by the real-impossible of an irreducible antagonism? However, does Deleuze also not follow this path? Does he not say exactly the same thing in this key passage from *The Time-Image?*

> What counts is ... the *interstice* between images, between two images: a spacing which means that each image is plucked from the void and falls back into it. ... Given one image, another image has to be chosen which will induce an interstice *between* the two. ... The interstice is primary in relation to association. ... The fissure has become primary, and as such grows larger. ... Between two actions, between two affections, between two perceptions, between two visual images, between two sound images, between the sound and the visual: make the indiscernible, that is the frontier, visible. ... The whole undergoes a mutation, because it has ceased to be the One-Being, in order to become the constitutive between-two of images.[69]

Is this strategy of tracking down, not the *specific* difference but the *minimal* difference (the "pure" difference that differentiates an element not from other particular elements but from *itself,* from its own *place* of inscription, the minimal difference which, instead of securing the (specific) identity of the element in question, explodes this identity into the in(de)finite generative process of differentiation) not the very core of Hegelian dialectics (and, one may add, of the Lacanian "logic of the signifier")? More precisely, is this pure difference as the difference, that, in a way, *precedes* the two terms between which it is the difference not the

[68] Jacques Lacan, "Television," *October* 40 (spring 1987): 7.
[69] Gilles Deleuze, *The Time-Image* (London: Athlone Press, 1989), pp. 179–80.

very definition of the Real of an antagonism? In all antagonisms (from sexual difference to class struggle), "the fissure is primary"—as in the familiar example from Levi-Strauss in which the two drawings of the map of the village *come after* the fissure at their interstice, each of the drawings endeavoring to cover up this fissure.

When Ernesto Laclau elaborates his fundamental opposition between the logic of difference and the logic of equivalence, he asserts the coincidence of the opposites: the two logics are not simply opposed, but each logic, brought to its extreme, converts into its opposite. That is to say, as he repeatedly points out, a system of pure differentiality (a system totally defined by the differential structure of its elements, with no antagonism and/or impossibility traversing it) would lead to a pure equivalence of all its elements—they are all equivalent with regard to the void of their Outside. And, at the other extreme, a system of radical antagonism with no structure at all but just the pure opposition of Us and Them would coincide with a naturalized difference between Us and Them as the positively existing opposed species. However, from a Hegelian standpoint, the limitation of this logic is that it continues to rely on the two externally opposed poles—the fact that each of the opposites, in the abstraction from the other (i.e., brought to the extreme at which it no longer needs the other as its opposite) falls into this other, merely demonstrates their mutual reliance. What we need to do is to make a step further from this external opposition (or mutual reliance) into the direct internalized overlapping, which means: not only does one pole, when abstracted from the other and thus brought to extreme, coincide with its opposite, but also *there is no "primordial" duality of poles in the first place, only the inherent gap of the One.* Equivalence is primordially not the opposite of difference, equivalence only emerges because no system of differences can ever complete itself, it "is" only the structural effect of this incompleteness. (In a homologous way, with regard to sexual difference, woman is not the polar opposite of man, *there are women because man is not fully itself.*) The tension between immanence and transcendence is thus also secondary with regard to the gap within immanence itself: "transcendence" is a kind of perspective illusion, the way we (mis)perceive the gap/discord that inheres to immanence itself. In the same way, the tension between the Same and the Other is secondary with regard to the noncoincidence of the Same with itself.

How, then, are these two differences related: the minimal difference between the element and its place and the difference constitutive of an antagonism? The "minimal difference" is the difference between the universal and the "surnumerary" particular which directly stands in for this universal, the paradoxical particular that, precisely insofar as it has no place within the structure of the universal, directly gives body to universality. And, how does this "singular universal" relate to antagonism? The only solution is a radical one: the core of an antagonism is not the conflict between the two parts/poles of a Whole. Rather, it is inherent to the Whole itself. It runs between the two aspects of (or modes, perspectives on) the Whole: the organic structured Whole containing its elements, allocating to each of them its own place in the Whole, versus the Whole embodied in the "singular universal". It is the rift between Society as the hierarchical structure and Society for which the excluded (demos, the third estate, dissidents) stand.

This notion of minimal difference also provides a clue regarding the infamous Lacanian "decenterment." When Lacan defines the psychoanalytic subversion not as the replacement of one (false) center with another (true) one but as the very intermediate position of a "decentered center," of a center that does not coincide with itself, his original reference is here, of course, Kepler: the true revolution was not that of Copernicus (replacing the earth with the sun as the center around which planets circulate) but that of Kepler (who asserted that planets do not circulate but move in an elliptical orbit—and, what is an ellipse, if not a circle with a "decentered"/redoubled center?). It is against this background that Lacan interprets the Freudian revolution. It consists not in replacing the old center (the conscious ego) with a new center (the "deeper" unconscious self) but in sustaining an elliptical "decentered center." And, does the uniqueness of Christianity not reside in the fact that it involves the same paradox of the "decentered center?" Christianity is not halfway between pagan polytheism and "pure" Jewish (or Muslim, for that matter) monotheism; it does not add (an)other god(s) to the One. Rather, it decenters from within this One God, in the guise of the "minimal difference" that separates God-the-Father from Christ.

This reinscription of the externality of a field back into the field itself is the truly Hegelian gesture. For Hegel, Law is not simply an external totalizing force regulating the multitude of crimes/transgressions but crime's immanent self-sublation, a crime elevated to the absolute, so that the opposition of Law and crime is inherent to crime itself (and *not*, as an incorrect Hegelianism would have us think, to the Law, so that crime is reduced to a subordinate moment of the self-mediation of the Law). This *third* position is the truly subversive one: not Law as opposed to crime but Law itself as the supreme form of crime. In the same way, the question to be asked is not "How does the Oedipal matrix repress the free flow of the desiring machines?" but, rather, "What kind of a desiring machine is Oedipus?" In Deleuzian terms, one should isolate, within the field of impersonal, nomadic desiring machines, the "dark precursor" of the "official" (familial, normalizing, etc.) Oedipus complex. Or, to put it in Hegelese, the Oedipus complex, in its oppositional determination, is the place at which the very force of the repression of the desiring machines encounters ITSELF in its Otherness, as one among the desiring machines.

The difference between the Lacanian *doublure* (the inconsistency or crack in the surface of phenomenal immanence) and the Deleuzian interstice is thus that, for Deleuze, the in-between involves multitude, for Lacan, the "binary" tension is flattened or homogenized the moment that it is transformed into the difference of a multitude. There is something unique in the tension of an element with its uncanny double, in the minimal difference between an element and its place. The moment we pass from the single underlying antagonism to the multitude of antagonisms we endorse the logic of nonantagonistic One-ness: the proliferating multitude of antagonisms exists against the background of a neutral One as their medium, which is *not* itself marked or cut by an antagonism. Which is why, with regard to politics, it is crucial to "privilege" one antagonism over all others. The apparently innocent logic of "today, we know that class struggle is not the ultimate reference of all other struggles but just one in the multitude of antagonistic struggles that characterize social life" already *pacifies* the social edifice, neutralizing the impact of antagonism. As to the idea that privileging One antagonism leads to "binary logic," one should emphasize that the fact of sexual difference signals precisely the *failure* of "binary logic," the failure of the signifying couple that would "cover" sexual difference—there is sexual difference *because* the binary signifier is primordially repressed, as Lacan put it. In other words, the antagonism of/in the One does not mean the harmonious tension between the two (opposing principles, etc.) but means the inner tension, the impossibility of self-coincidence, of the One itself—or, as Alain Badiou articulates it in a concise way, "atheism is, in the end, nothing other than the immanence of the Two."[70]

The usual deconstructive movement is that of "regressing" from the domain of firm identities to the contingent process of their genesis. Say, apropos all social phenomena, one strives to demonstrate how politics is not simply one of the domains ("subsystems") of the global social system, since the very establishment of the demarcation line between what counts as political and what does not is a political gesture par excellence. Apolitical domains thus began to collapse like houses of cards: market economy is political, art is political, sex and marriage are political. Is, however, philosophically, the opposite direction not much more crucial? Instead of demonstrating how "there is nothing that is not political,"

---

[70] Alain Badiou, "The Scene of Two," *Lacanian Ink* 21 (spring 2003): 55.

one should rather focus on the opposed question: *how is it that Being itself is political,* how is our ontological space structured so that nothing can escape being tainted by the political? The answer, of course—or, rather, one of the answers—would be the above-described structure of the gap dividing the One from within, the inherent *doublure,* as the most elementary ontological fact.

Finally, this brings us to the topic of the *subject* that, according to Lacan, emerges in the interstice of the "minimal difference," in the minimal gap between two signifiers. In this sense, the subject is "a nothingness, a void, which exists." That is to say, already with animals, we cannot specify their unity, what makes an organism "one"—this unity is always ideal, since, if we analyze the body in question, we find only material parts, not what holds them together. The One-ness of an organism evaporates between our fingers. (These paradoxes were already explored in detail by Hegel in the second chapter of the *Phenomenology* on "Perception, or, the Thing and Deception.") In this sense, One is the name of the Void. With the emergence of subjectivity, this void is posited as such—it becomes For-Itself—and the empty signifier, the mark of this void, "represents the subject for other signifiers." Therein resides the passage from Hume to Kant: whereas Hume endeavors to demonstrate how there is no Self (when we look into ourselves, we only encounter particular ideas, impressions, etc., but no "Self" as such), Kant claims that this void *is* the Self.

This, then, is what Deleuze seems to get wrong in his reduction of the subject to (just another) substance. Far from belonging to the level of actualization, of distinct entities in the order of constituted reality, the dimension of the "subject" designates the *reemergence of the virtual within the order of actuality.* "Subject" names the unique space of the explosion of virtuality within constituted reality. According to *The Logic of Sense,* sense is the immaterial flow of pure becoming, and "subject" designates *not* the substantial entity whose "predicate" (attribute, property, capacity) is the sense-event but a kind of antisubstance, a negative/inverted substance—the immaterial, singular, purely abstract point that sustains the flow of sense. This is why the subject is not a person. To put it in Deleuzian terms, "person" belongs to the order of actualized reality, designating the wealth of positive features and properties that characterize an individual, whereas the subject is divided precisely in the Deleuzian sense of "dividual" as opposed to individual. Usually, "personalists" insist on the unique character of each individual as a *combinatoire* of features that cannot ever be repeated and that are organically woven together through an underlying, unidentifiable *je ne sais quoi* as the mystery of personality. The subject is, on the contrary, endlessly repeatable or divisible; it is *nothing but* the unending process of division/repetition.

Subject thus relates to substance exactly like Becoming versus Being: subject is the "absolute unrest of Becoming (*absolute Unruhe des Werdens*),"[71] (i.e., a state of things conceived from the perspective of its genesis). It was already Fichte (to whom Deleuze himself refers) who conceived the subject as pure self-positing activity: activity is not a predicate/attribute of the subject precisely because the subject "is" only (exists exclusively as) the activity of its own self-positing. In other words, the subject is a purely virtual entity in the strict Deleuzian sense of the term: the moment it is actualized, it changes into substance.

To put it in yet another way, subjectivity is the site of "true infinity." No wonder, then, that when Deleuze asserts the infinity of pure becoming as the virtuality that encompasses every actualization, he is again secretly Hegelian. Recall, in Hegel's logic, the difference of the quantitative ("spurious") and the qualitative ("true") infinite.[72] The first infinity resides in the act of going-beyond, of traversing the finite: while the finite in itself, as the objective result, is a sterile repetition of the same, what is infinite in it is the very ACT of going-beyond. We have here the opposition of becoming and being, of act and result. If we look at the results, there is no infinite; infinite is just the subjective urge to go beyond, the creative "in-between" of the two repetitions. Is this not a topic we encounter from art to politics? The fixed result always betrays us; what matters is the movement. Recall the famous episode from Dashiell Hammett's *The Maltese Falcon,* the most succinct formula of "permanent revolution": Sam Spade narrates the story of his being hired to locate a man who had suddenly left his settled job and family and vanished. Spade was unable to track him down. But, a few years later, he ran into the man in a bar in another city, where he lived under an assumed name, leading a life remarkably similar to the one he had fled when a beam from a construction site narrowly missed his head. After sharing a drink, the man tells him that, although he now leads the same life, his disappearance and his new beginning were not in vain. Is this repetition also not a model of "minimal difference"? In the repetition of the same, the minimum of the subjective excess emerges. Or, to make the same point in yet another way, this "minimal" difference is not a difference at the level of the enunciated content but a difference at the level of the tension between enunciated and enunciation. The very "no difference at all" at the level of the enunciated content confronts us with the "pure" difference between enunciated and enunciation. Lillian Hellman wrote, apropos of her turbulent relationship with the same Hammett, "In the early years,

---

[71] G. W. F. Hegel, *Science of Logic* (Atlantic Highlands, N.J.: Humanities Press International, 1969), p. 545.
[72] Hegel, op. cit., p. 226 ff.

I would say, 'Tell me more about the girl in San Francisco. The silly one who lived across the hall in Pine Street.' And he would laugh and say, 'She lived across the hall in Pine Street and was silly.' "[73] Here, again, we encounter the difference between enunciation and enunciated (content) at its purest: at the level of the enunciated, Hammett's repetition does not add anything while, at the level of enunciation (of his subjective position from which he speaks), his answer is telltale, since it displays a stance of resigned, ironic self-detachment. In short, through the very fact that we do not learn more about the girl who lived across the hall in Pine Street and was silly, we learn quite a lot about Hammett himself. In contrast to it, the true infinite offers the inverse paradox: the finite activity's *outcome* is an infinite result. Recall the Hegelian topic of State as the infinite social Substance: thousands of finite wills working and struggling, with the result being the self-relating Infinite of the State. We find here again the *political* tension between celebrating the infinite subversive movement and focusing on the Result. And, the same goes for Christ himself. It is not that his death (finitude) at the level of the enunciated content asserts the infinity (eternity) of his position of enunciation but, on the contrary, that his subjectively assumed finitude (the finitude of his position of enunciation) gives birth to the infinite collective of the Holy Ghost.[74]

So, why this exceptional, strangely reductionist misreading of Hegel on Deleuze's part, a misreading where the point is not (as is the rule in Deleuze's great interpretations) to write about an author in the famous "free indirect style" in order for Deleuze himself to use the interpreted author as his "interceptor" and speak (articulate his own innermost position) through him? Instead of such a violent productive reappropriation, what we get, in the case of Hegel (and the Oedipus complex), is a flat, totally homogenous image of the Enemy, with whom we are confronted in a clear face to face of "our" versus "his" position, each of us fully speaking in his own name, with no "free indirect style" voices confusing

---

[73] Lillian Hellman, "Introduction," in Dashiell Hammett, *The Big Knockover* (New York: Vintage Books, 1972), p. v.

[74] A similar point can be made apropos of the different types of reflexivity with regard to the way man and woman relate to erection. For a woman, a man's erection is clearly a reflexive determination of her own attractiveness: what she sees/reads in her partner's erection is the reflection of her sexual attraction (i.e., the fact of erection materializes her own ability to arouse the man). For a man, on the contrary, since, as we learned from Otto Weininger, a woman is his fantasy-formation, the naked woman's attractiveness itself is the projection of his sexual longing. It is not only that an attractive woman arouses a man but, moreover, the woman's very attractiveness is the reflection-into-her of the man's desire for her. Men not only desire beautiful women but also being an object of desire is what *makes* a woman beautiful. It is here that one should repeat Marx's words regarding the King: it is not that men desire a woman who is, in herself, beautiful; her beauty merely objectivizes man's desire. From this standpoint, erection is doubly reflective and, as such, masturbatory: it reinscibes back into the male body the fascination of the man's own product.

the unambiguous picture. Perhaps the answer is designated by Jameson's perspicuous observation on how Deleuze's drive toward unconditional monism

> is paradoxically the source of the later dualisms. For the principle of desire it-self would be a monism: everything is libidinal investment, everything is de-sire; there is nothing which is not desire, nothing outside desire. This means, of course, that fascism is a desire . . . , that bureaucracy is desire, the State is desire, capitalism preeminently desire, even the much maligned Oedipus complex has to correspond to a certain desire in order to take on its inveterate authority. . . . If the mission of the One lies in subordinating illusory pairs, doubles, oppositions of all kinds, then it turns out that we are still in dual-ism, for the task is conceived as the working through of the opposition—the dualism—between dualism and monism.[75]

Where, then, do we encounter dualism here? The answer is provided by the strange complementarity of the relationship between Deleuze and Foucault. The tension between Deleuze and Foucault sometimes appears to have the structure of a mutual implication. At the extreme point of his development marked by *Discipline and Punish* (as well as the first volume of *History of Sexuality*), Foucault conceived of the eman-cipation/liberation from power as totally inherent to power itself. Since power generates the very resistance to itself, the subject that strives to liberate itself from the clutches of power is already a product of power, of its disciplinary and controlling mechanisms. For instance, the very "repressive" mechanism that regulates our sexual lives generates Sex as the excess, the "dark continent," that needs to be regulated. In a strictly symmetrical way, Deleuze, in *Anti-Oedipus*, at least, conceives of the force of "repression" as inherent to desire. In a kind of Nietzschean geneal-ogy, Deleuze and Guattari endeavor to explain, from the very immanent deployment of desire, the reactive, life-negating attitude of lack and re-nunciation. In both cases, the structure is that of the absolute immanence of the two opposed poles. The circle is thus closed, except only from the opposite direction, as it were. To put it in Hegelian terms, in Foucault, power is the encompassing unity of itself and its opposite (i.e., the resis-tance to itself), whereas, in Deleuze, desire is the encompassing unity of itself and its "repression" (i.e., its negating force). Of course, the crucial question here is, Are these two operations fully symmetrical or is there a hidden dissymmetry between the two? It is *here* that one should follow the Hegelian path: the question is that of the encompassing Subject of the process. For Deleuze, the (acephalous, anonymous, impersonal . . .)

---

[75] Fredric Jameson, "Marxism and Dualism," in *A Deleuzian Century?* edited by Ian Buchanan (Durham, N.C.: Duke University Press, 1999), p. 30.

Subject is Desire itself, which encompasses/generates its opposite ("repression"), whereas, for Foucault, the (again: acephalous, anonymous, impersonal . . .) Subject is Power, which encompasses/generates its opposite (resistance). And the Hegelian gesture here is precisely to explode from within the unity of this presupposed, encompassing subject: the subject passes into its predicate. In other words, at the beginning of the process, Desire generates the structure of Power, which then, retroactively, poses itself as the process' subject—this is what Hegel calls "the speculative passage of subject into predicate."

In other words, Hegel is here a kind of dialectical synthesis of the opposite positions of Deleuze and Foucault, that is, their speculative identity. It is only *such* a "monism" of the process itself with a constant displacement of its subject that effectively allows us to overcome dualism. As long as we stick to *one* Subject, a dualism *has* to return as the very inherent result of our monism. The paradox here is, of course, that what we are reproaching Deleuze with is that, in missing this Hegelian point, he is not Deleuzian enough: the drift of his monism into dualism bears witness to the fact that his process of Becoming is itself secretly anchored in a unified Subject. When Deleuze opposes being and becoming, when he insists on how becoming is not a becoming *of* a being as an established entity but a process that itself establishes being(s) and transforms them, does he not thereby point toward the Hegelian "speculative judgment" as a process in the course of which subject and predicate exchange places, so that the process is not the process *of* a subject, but generates new subjects of itself, involving shifts from one to another subjectivity?[76] Is, then, from this Hegelian perspective, what Deleuze attacks as Hegelianism not precisely subject *as* (still) *substance,* the self-identical foundation/ground of a process, and not yet $, the empty, nonsubstantial subject? What this means is that the topic of subject insists: it eludes the opposition of impersonal intensities and positive self-identical entities. (The late Foucault sensed this when he reasserted the topic of subjectivity.)

However, even if there is a grain of truth in the reproach of Deleuze's "dualism," and in the remark that the opposition(s) between nomadic and State, molecular and molar, and so forth is not simply the opposition between the Good (nomadic . . .) and the Evil (state . . .), Deleuze is as far as possible from asserting any kind of complementarity between the two poles (in the sense that, while the molar State alone is oppressive, suffocating the flow of desire, the opposite extreme, as the total abolition

---

[76] No wonder that Cutrofello, in his wonderful sequel to Hegel's *Phenomenology* (covering the period from Hegel's death until today) reads Deleuze—*the* anti-Hegelian—as the concluding moment of the entire process. See Andrew Cutrofello, *The Owl at Dawn: A Sequel to Hegel's Phenomenology of Spirit* (Albany: State University of New York Press, 1995).

of the State, would mean "regression" into the psychotic, self-destructive rage of the pure, pre-Oedipal flow of desire). So, what we ostensibly need is the right balance between the two. This is how, among others, Julia Kristeva reads and appropriates Deleuze: while praising his liberation of the creativity of desire from the constraints of State Power, she nonetheless warns of the destructive consequences of seeing in the State only a negative barrier to be abolished: to avoid direct self-destruction, the total revolutionary abolition of the (existing) State always reverts into a new Order, even more oppressive than the previous one. In this sense, Kristeva praises revolt—the liberation of the "wild" pre-Oedipal creative forces, the liberation that is not primarily political but more intimate, psychic, religious, artistic . . . —and condemns revolution as the installation of a new Order, the coagulation of the creative energies of the revolt.[77] From a truly Hegelian, Deleuzian, and/or Lacanian approach (a strange series of equivalences indeed), this line of argumentation should be rejected in toto: true radicality does not consist in going to the extreme and destroying the system (i.e., in disturbing too much the balance that sustains it) but consists in *changing the very coordinates that define this balance.* Say, once we accept the social-democratic idea of the modern capitalist market economy cum welfare state, it is easy to claim that one should avoid both extremes (i.e., the total freedom of the market, on one hand, and excessive state intervention, on the other hand) and find the right balance between the two. However, the true revolution would consist in transforming the very overall balance of the social edifice, in enforcing a new structural principle of social life that would render the very field of the opposition between market and state obsolete. Or, let us take the platitude about the right balance between the permissive indulgence of spontaneity and the rigors of discipline. Revolution is not the assertion of spontaneity and rejection of every discipline but the radical redefinition of what counts as true spontaneity or discipline. For instance, in the Kantian philosophical revolution, true (transcendental) spontaneity occurs not when I follow my natural instincts and needs but when I exercise my freedom, which means when I act *against* my "spontaneous" natural impulses.

There is a wonderful detail in *Superman III* (the movie): angry at the world, Superman, momentarily turned evil, flies to Pisa and straightens up the leaning tower. And, effectively, what makes Pisa interesting? It is the stupid fact that the tower is somehow "out of joint," that it does not stand straight. The worst thing one can do to it is to set it straight—this act throws the town of Pisa back into indifference, depriving it of its

---

[77] See Julia Kristeva, *The Sense and Non-Sense of Revolt* (New York: Columbia University Press, 2000).

sign of recognition. The lesson of this story is universal and contains fundamental ontological consequences: for something to exist, it has to rely on something that stands out, that disturbs the balance. As quantum cosmology has taught us, the universe emerged out of the void, ex nihilo, through a disturbance/disruption of balance.

The Torsion of Meaning

The standard topos of the critique of idealism is that at the point at which the conceptual deployment/presentation (*logos*) fails, touches its limit, a narrative (*mythos*) has to intervene—this holds from Plato through Schelling (who, in his *Weltalter*, aims at supplementing the Hegelian conceptual self-development with the narrative of the Absolute prior to *logos*) and up to Marx (the narrative of the primordial accumulation of capital) and Freud (the narrative of the primordial horde). In the face of the constant theological motive of the ineffable obscure mystery in the very heart of the divine, of what Chesterton calls "a matter more dark and awful than it is easy to discuss . . . a matter which the greatest saints and thinkers have justly feared to approach,"[78] one is tempted to propose the opposite path: far from pointing toward the dimension of the "irrational," *this mystery irrepresentable in the form of a narrative* (except in the terms of a "heretic" notion of God himself as the source of Evil, etc.) *is simply the negative of the clarity of the Concept itself,* namely, the only way the self-division that characterizes the immanent self-movement of the Concept can be represented in the medium of a narrative. In other words, when (what Hegel called) the thought constrained to the domain of Representation or Understanding mentions the Ineffable as a Beyond that eludes its grasp, one can be sure that this Beyond is nothing but the concept itself—it is the highest irony of the "mere Understanding" that it perceives as "irrational" Reason itself.

Hegel here rejoins Spinoza: Spinoza's opposition of imagination and true knowledge becomes the opposition of mere *Vorstellung* (representation), with its "stories," and the self-development of a Notion. It is the irony of the history of philosophy that it is Schelling, the one who is considered a "Spinozan" among the German Idealists, who accomplishes the return to (philosophy as) *narrative*. In what does Schelling's true philosophical revolution consist? According to the standard academic *doxa,* Schelling broke out of the idealist closure of the Notion's self-mediation by way of asserting a more balanced bipolarity of the Ideal and the Real: the "negative philosophy" (the analysis of the notional essence) must be supplemented by the "positive philosophy," which deals with the positive order of existence. In nature as well as in human history, the ideal

[78] Chesterton, *Orthodoxy,* p. 145.

rational order can thrive only against the background of the impenetrable Ground of "irrational" drives and passions. The climax of philosophical development, the standpoint of the Absolute, is thus not the "sublation" (*Aufhebung*) of all reality in its ideal Notion but the neutral medium of the two dimensions—the Absolute is ideal-real. Such a reading, however, obfuscates Schelling's true breakthrough: his distinction, first introduced in the essay on human freedom from 1809,[79] between (logical) Existence and the impenetrable Ground of Existence (as the Real of pre-logical drives): this proto-ontological domain of drives is not simply "nature" but the spectral domain of not-yet-fully constituted reality. Schelling's opposition of the proto-ontological Real of drives (the Ground of Being) and the ontologically fully constituted Being itself (which, of course, is "sexed" as the opposition of the Feminine and the Masculine) thus radically displaces the standard philosophical couples of Nature and Spirit, the Real and the Ideal, Existence and Essence, and so forth. The real Ground of Existence is impenetrable, dense, inert, and yet, at the same time, spectral, "irreal," ontologically not fully constituted—while Existence is ideal, and yet, at the same time (in contrast to the Ground), fully "real," fully existing.[80] This opposition—between the fully existing reality and its proto-ontological spectral shadow—is thus irreducible to the standard metaphysical oppositions between the Real and the Ideal, Nature and Spirit, Existence and Essence, and so on. (Furthermore, one should recall here how the space for this spectral domain of the pre-ontological "undead" was opened up by the Kantian transcendental revolution.) In his late "philosophy of revelation," Schelling withdraws from the difficulty of thinking to the end this opposition, and "regresses" (retranslates it) into the traditional ontological couples of essence and existence, the ideal and the real, and so forth.[81] The triangle of

79 See F. W. J. Schelling, "Philosophical Investigations into the Essence of Human Freedom and Related Matters," in *Philosophy of German Idealism,* edited by Ernst Behler (New York: Continuum, 1987).
80 The notion of the pre-ontological Real is crucial not only with regard to the history of ideas but even with regard to art and our daily experience of reality. Is the entire contemporary popular (but not only popular) culture not populated by entities located in this pre-ontological domain? Recall, from the Stephen King horror tradition, the spectral figure of a young boy, not yet sexualized, who is "undead," a living dead, utterly corrupted *and* innocent, infinitely fragile *and* all-powerful, the embodiment of Evil in his very purity. Do we not encounter the same figure in modern art a century ago, from the poems of Georg Trakl to the paintings of Edvard Munch, in the guise of the asexual spectral young boy, this "unborn" who stands simultaneously for vulnerable innocence and utter corruption?
81 And does, as we have already seen, the same not also apply to Deleuze? In *The Logic of Sense,* he problematizes the opposition of corporeal Being (the complex network of causes and effects) and the ostensibly separate level of Becoming (its pure effect, the sterile impassive flow of immaterial Sense), thus undermining the stability of the old ontological couples; later, however, with *Anti-Oedipus,* to avoid the difficulty of sustaining this position, he revives the traditional couple of Becoming versus Being, of the dynamic productive movement versus the "reified" order of its effects.

Spinoza-Hegel-Schelling is thus not as unambiguous as it may appear. Although Spinoza and Hegel are solidary in their effort to formulate the truth of religion in conceptual form, there is nonetheless a level at which Spinoza is closer to Schelling—more precisely, instead of Schelling, let us mention Richard Wagner, who, with regard to our topic, shares Schelling's fundamental attitude. Recall the famous beginning of Wagner's *Religion and Art:*

> One could say that when religion becomes artificial it is for art to salvage the essence of religion by construing the mythical symbols which religion wants us to believe to be literal truth in terms of their figurative value, so as to let us see their profound hidden truth through idealized representation. Whereas the priest is concerned only that the religious allegories should be regarded as factual truths, this is of no concern to the artist, since he presents his work frankly and openly as his invention.[82]

Everything is false here, in this passage which is anti-Kierkegaardian par excellence: its disgusting aestheticization of religion, its misleading anti-fetishism, that is, its rejection of the belief in the factual/literal truth on behalf of the "inner" spiritual truth. What if the true fetishism is this very belief in the "profound hidden truth" beneath the literal truth? Wagner is here the opposite of Spinoza, who, in his *Theologico-Political Tractatus,* was the first to propose a historicocritical reading of the Bible grounded in the Enlightenment notion of universal Reason. One should distinguish between the inner true meaning of the Bible (accessible to us today through philosophical analysis) and the mythical, imaginary, narrative mode of its presentation as conditioned by the immature state of humanity in the period when the Bible was written. As Spinoza puts it pointedly, if someone holds to the rational inner truth of the Bible while ignoring its explicit narrative content, he should be counted as a perfect believer; and, vice versa, if someone slavishly follows all ritualistic prescripts of the Bible while ignoring the rational inner truth, he should be counted as a nonbeliever. It is against such a stance that one should reassert the Jewish obedience of rules. Even more pointedly, it is against such a stance that one should, with as much force as possible, assert the Kierkegaardian point of pure dogma: even if one follows all the ethical rules of Christianity, if one does not do it on account of one's belief that they were revealed by the divine authority of Christ, one is lost.

Although opposed, these two readings are complementary in that they search for a "deeper" truth beneath the figurative surface. In one case, this truth is the inner ineffable spiritual message; in the other case, it is the rational conceptual insight. What they both miss is, to put it as

---

[82] Quoted from Bryan Magee, *The Tristan Chord* (New York: Henry Holt, 2000), p. 281.

Marx would, the level of form as such: the inner necessity of the content to assume such a form. The relationship between form and content is here dialectical in the strict Hegelian sense: the form articulates what is repressed in the content, its disavowed kernel—which is why, when we replace the religious form with the direct formulation of its "inner" content, we feel somehow cheated, deprived of the essential.[83] What is missing in Spinoza and Wagner is thus the inner torsion by means of which the form itself is included (or, rather, inscribes itself) within content—and this, perhaps, is the minimal definition of an EVENT.

A Comic Hegelian Interlude: Dumb and Dumber

How many people noticed that the Hegelian dialectics is unconsciously practiced by Dan Quayle and George W. Bush? We thought we had seen it all with Quayle a decade ago. However, in comparison with Bush, Quayle emerges as a rather intelligent person. With regard to his famous mistake of correcting the spelling of "potato" to "potatoe," I myself must admit it always seemed to me that Quayle was somehow right: "potatoe" comes closer to what Humboldt would have called the true "inner form" of potato. (Nonetheless, I must admit that I feel something similar apropos Bush's recent "Grecians" instead of "Greeks": "Keep good relations with the Grecians." "Grecian" does seem somehow more dignified, like "thou art" instead of "you are," while "Greek" sounds all too close to "geek"—were the founders of our noble Western civilization really just a bunch of geeks?)

How, then, does Bush compare with Quayle? Are Bush's slips, like those of Quayle at his best, at the level of the Marx brothers' supreme slips ("No wonder you remind me of Emmanuel Ravelli, since you *are* Ravelli!"), or of no less ingenious "goldwynisms," the sayings attributed to the larger-than-life Hollywood producer Sam Goldwyn (from "An oral agreement isn't worth the paper it's written on!" to the notorious "Include me out!")? Most of Quayle's and Bush's slips follow the basic formula of

---

[83] This is why neither Wagner's nor Spinoza's reading of the Bible has anything whatsoever to do with psychoanalysis, with psychoanalytic interpretation. If one wants to learn what a truly psychoanalytic reading is, one should look for it in, say, the dialogue between Joseph K. and the Priest, which, in Kafka's *The Trial,* follows the "parable" on the door of the law.

How does interpretation proper procede? Recall the charming cryptic remarks in classic detective fiction: "Did Madame's maiden wear new green socks? This means there will soon be a wide European war!" A reader would have felt cheated if, in the ensuing interpretation, he were to learn that the maiden was a spy and that her wearing green socks was a key signal to a fellow spy. A true interpretation has to be deprived of such direct references to an arbitrary code; it should rather run along the lines of: "The maiden adores green socks, and her lover brings them to her every time he visits her. Her lover is a servant of the German ambassador; if the German ambassador yesterday paid a call to Madame accompanied by his servant, it has to be in order to get from her—a covert German spy—the secret data enabling the German attack . . ."

what the French call *lapalissades,* the tautological statings of the obvious attributed to the mythical figure of Monsieur la Palice, like "One hour before his death, Monsieur la Palice was still fully alive." Indeed, la Palice's ingenious "Why don't we build cities in the countryside where the air is much cleaner?" comes pretty close to a concise formulation of the Republican Party's ecological policy, rendered perfectly by Bush's truism: "I know the human being and fish can coexist peacefully."

Here, then, are some samples of this elementary type of slips from Bush and Quayle: "If we don't succeed, we run the risk of failure." / "A low voter turnout is an indication of fewer people going to the polls." / "For NASA, space is still a high priority." These *lapalissades* get a little bit more interesting when pure tautology is emphatically offered as a causal explanation—see the following slip of Quayle: "When I have been asked who caused the riots and the killing in Los Angeles, my answer has been direct and simple: Who is to blame for the riots? The rioters are to blame. Who is to blame for the killings? The killers are to blame." (There is, of course, an implicit conservative political logic in this tautology, that is, this quote relies on an implicit negation: don't look for the "deeper" causes in social circumstances, it is the immediate perpetrators who bear the full responsibility.) Things get even more interesting when, in a strangely Hegelian way, Quayle explodes the identity by opposing the notion and its empirical exemplifications: "It isn't pollution that's harming the environment. It's the impurities in our air and water that are doing it."

While Bush is not able to follow Quayle along this road, he often does catch up with him in producing slips in which a conceptual opposition is raised to the level of dialectical self-relating (*Selbstbeziehung*). Recall how he posited the very opposition between irreversibility and reversibility as reversible: "I believe we are on an irreversible trend towards more freedom and democracy—but that could change." So it's not simply that things are either reversible or irreversible: a situation that appears irreversible could change into a reversible one. Here is an even nicer example of this reflexivity: "The future will be better tomorrow." The point is not simply that Quayle made a mistake, intending to claim that tomorrow things will be better: in the near future (tomorrow), *future itself* will look brighter to us. Did Bush not reproduce exactly the same structure in his statement: "One of the common denominators I have found is that expectations rise above that which is expected"?

With Quayle, this reflexivity culminates in the following quote in which the series of three evasions/disavowals is consummated in the speaker's self-erasure from the picture: "The Holocaust was an obscene period in our nation's history. I mean in this century's history. But we all lived in this century. I didn't live in this century." The logic of progress in this series is inexorable: first, in his eagerness to square the accounts with the dark past of his own nation, Quayle attributes to it the crime of the century, which it did *not* commit; then he retracts, specifying that the act was not committed by his nation; in a desperate attempt to return to the logic of settling the accounts with one's past, he then constitutes a new community—no longer "our nation" but all of us who lived in the last century and are thus coresponsible for the Holocaust; finally, becoming aware of the mess he talked himself into, he automatically opts for a quick escape, excluding himself from his own century. In short, in a gesture that forms the perfect reversal of Goldwyn's "include me out," Quayle "excludes himself in" his century! No wonder, then, that, after this imbroglio, he makes a statement that provides the most succinct characterization of Bush: "People that are really weird can get into sensitive positions and have a tremendous impact on history."

There are, however, two domains in which Bush goes further than Quayle; the first is that of the postmodern dialectics of certainty and uncertainty. In Bush's thought, uncertainty (about the empirical figure of the enemy), far from diminishing the danger, dialectically inverts itself into the higher certainty that there *must be* an enemy, all the more dangerous for the fact that we don't know who, exactly, he is. So the more uncertainty about the enemy, the more we can be certain of him lurking out there: "This is a world that is much more uncertain than the past. In the past we were certain, we were certain it was us versus the Russians in the past. We were certain, and therefore we had huge nuclear arsenals aimed at each other to keep peace. . . . [E]ven though it's an uncertain world, we're certain of some things. . . . We're certain there are madmen in this world, and there's terror, and there's missiles and I'm certain of this too." Bush also surpasses Quayle with regard to the refined reflexive twist of the simple Christian precept "Love your neighbor like yourself!" Bush took the lesson of the dialectics of the desire for recognition from Hegel's *Phenomenology of Spirit:* we do not directly love ourselves—what we effectively love is to be loved by others, that is, we love others to love us: "We must all hear the universal call to like your neighbor just like you like to be liked yourself."

So what should the unfortunate Bush do to avoid Quayle's sad fate and to dispel the blindness of the stupid liberal public, which is unable to appreciate the hidden dialectical finesse of his statements? As we all know, not only is it true that *du sublime au ridicule, il n'y a qu'un pas,* the same goes also the other way round. So, perhaps, Bush should just learn the Heideggerian art of generating deep insights from tautological reversals. That is to say, when we recall Heidegger's famous reversal "*das*

Wesen der Wahrheit ist die Wahrheit des Wesens (the essence of truth is the truth of the essence)" or his rhetorical strategy of excluding *das Wesen* of some domain from this domain itself ("the essence of technology is nothing technological"), it cannot but strike us how easy it would have been to change some bushism into a deep thought. Bush has said: "This is Preservation Month. I appreciate preservation. It's what you do when you run for president. You gotta preserve." This could be translated into: "The essence of preservation has nothing to do with the ontic preservation of our physical resources. The essence of preservation is the preservation of the essence of our society itself—and this is what the president of the USA has to do, even if, at the vulgar ontic level, he allows the destruction of more natural resources than in the entire previous history of the USA."[84]

The Becoming-Oedipal of Deleuze

And back to Deleuze, is the same violent sort of misreading as in the case of Hegel not also clearly discernible in Deleuze's treatment of psychoanalysis, with special regard to Lacan? What Deleuze presents as "Oedipus" is a rather ridiculous simplification, if not an outright falsification, of Lacan's position. In the last decades of Lacan's teaching, topics and subtitles like "au-delà de l'Oedipe," "l'Oedipe, un rêve de Freud," and so forth abound; not only this, but Lacan even presents the very figure of Oedipus at Colonus as a post-Oedipal figure, as a figure "beyond the Oedipus complex." What, then, if one conceives of the Lacanian "obverse of the Oedipus" as a kind of Deleuzian "dark precursor" mediating between the two series, the "official" Oedipal narrative of normalization, on the one side, and the presubjective field of intensities and desiring machines, on the other side? What if it is *this* that Deleuze desperately tries to avoid, this "vanishing mediator" between the two series? What one should do is thus to repeat, apropos of Deleuze's reductionist reading of (the Freudian) Oedipus (his other uncanny exception, in terms of a botched, simplistic interpretation), the same gesture as the one that imposes itself in relation to Hegel.

In today's theory, especially in cultural studies, reference to Oedipus is often reduced to the extreme of a ridiculous straw man: the flat scenario of the drama of the child's entry into normative heterosexuality. To fulfill this rhetorical function, the Oedipus complex has to be ascribed a multitude of inconsistent functions. Let me quote the following typical

---

[84] In learning this art, Bush will regain a chance of proving himself a worthy successor of Bill Clinton, since this Heideggerian trend in the American presidency was discernible already in the Clinton era. When Clinton answered the prosecutor's question about his relationship with Monica Levinsky ("Is it true that...?") with the infamous "It depends on what you mean by 'is,'" was he not pointing toward the Heideggerian *Seinsfrage*?

passage (which will tactfully be allowed to remain anonymous): "In the Oedipal scenario, the young boy desires to conquer his mother sexually in order to separate himself from her and begin to grow as an adult. For him to succeed, he must destroy his father, his sexual competitor." So, it is not the father whose "castrating" function is to separate the boy from his mother. In fact, the boy has to do three inconsistent things simultaneously: conquer his mother, separate himself from her, and destroy his father. What Jerry Aline Flieger did[85] is something subversive in its properly Hegelian simplicity: she reinscribed-retranslated Oedipus back into Deleuzian territory, (re)discovering in it an "abstract machine," a nomadic agent of deterritorialization, the supreme case of what Deleuze and Guattari call the "lone wolf" who stands for the limit of the pack of wolves, opening a "line of flight" toward its outside. And effectively, does Oedipus—this stranger who *blindly* (in both senses of the term) followed his trajectory—not stand for the extreme limit of the pack of human wolves, by way of realizing, acting out, the utter limit of human experience, finishing alone (or, rather, with a pack of exiles of his own) as, literally, a homeless nomad, a living dead among humans? One should thus repeat here the same operation as the one that, apropos of Hegel, enabled us to (re)discover in him the philosopher who shows how necessity emerges out of contingency, the philosopher of the vertiginous fluidity of concepts in which the subject is constantly displaced. The concept that this "Freudo-Lacanian buggery of Deleuze" should focus on is, predictably, that of the phallus, the Deleuzian term for which is "dark precursor." Deleuze introduces it in *Difference and Repetition*: "Thunderbolts explode between different intensities, but they are preceded by an invisible, imperceptible dark precursor [*precurseur sombre*], which determines their path in advance, but in reverse, as though intagliated."[86] As such, the dark precursor is the signifier of a metadifference:

> Given two heterogeneous series, two series of differences, the precursor plays the part of the differenciator of these differences. In this manner, by virtue of its own power, it puts them into immediate relation to one another: it is the in-itself of difference or the "differently different"—in other words, difference in the second degree, the self-different which relates different to different by itself. Because the path it traces is invisible and becomes visible only in reverse, to the extent that it is traveled over and covered by the phenomenon it induces within the system, it has no place other than that from which it is "missing," no identity other than that which it lacks: it is precisely the object=x, the one which is "lacking in its place" as it lacks its own identity.[87]

---

85 See Jerry Aline Flieger, "Overdetermined Oedipus," in *A Deleuzian Century?* edited by Ian Buchanan (Durham, N.C.: Duke University Press, 1999).

86 Gilles Deleuze, *Difference and Repetition* (New York: Columbia University Press, 1994), p. 119.

87 Deleuze, op. cit., pp. 119–20.

Or as Buchanan puts it in a concise way: "Dark precursors are those moments in a text which must be read in reverse if we are not to mistake effects for causes."[88] In *The Logic of Sense,* Deleuze develops this concept through a direct reference to the Lacanian notion of "pure signifier": there has to be a short circuit between the two series, that of the signifier and that of the signified, for the effect-of-sense to take place. This short circuit is what Lacan calls the "quilting point," the direct inscription of the signifier into the order of the signified in the guise of an "empty" signifier without signified. This signifier represents the (signifying) cause within the order of its effects, thus subverting the (mis)perceived "natural" order within which the signifier appears as the effect/expression of the signified.

And effectively, the relationship of Deleuze to the field generally designated as that of "structuralism" is much more ambiguous than it may appear. Not only is the key notion of "dark precursor" in *The Logic of Sense* directly developed in Lacanian structuralist terms; at the same time, Deleuze wrote "A quoi reconnait-on le structuralisme?" a brief, concise, and sympathetic account that, precisely, presents structuralism not as the thought of fixed transcendent Structures regulating the flux of experiences, but as deploying a consistent theory of the role of nonsense as the generator of the flux of sense.[89] Furthermore, Deleuze here explicitly refers to (and develops in detail) the Lacanian identification of this signifier as phallus.[90] How, then, are we to read his later obvious "hardening" of the stance toward "structuralism?" Why is the very Lacanian reference of the "dark precursor" reduced to the status of a "dark precursor" in the later Deleuze's thought, turned into a kind of "vanishing mediator" whose traces are to be erased in the finished result?

Perhaps it is all too hasty to dismiss Deleuze's endorsement of "structuralism" as a feature belonging to an epoch when he was not yet fully aware of all the consequences of his basic position (thus, the "hardening" would be conceived of as a necessary radicalization). What if this hardening is, on the contrary, a sign of "regression," of a *false* "line of flight," a false way out of a certain deadlock that resolves it by sacrificing

---

[88] Ian Buchanan, *Deleuzism* (Durham, N.C.: Duke University Press, 2000), p. 5.
[89] Gilles Deleuze, "A quoi reconnait-on le structuralisme?" in *Histoire de la philosophie,* vol. 8: *Le XXéme siécle,* edited by François Chatelet (Paris: Hachette, 1972), pp. 299–335 (written in 1967); English translation, "How Do We Recognize Structuralism?" published as an appendix in Charles J. Stivale, *The Two-Fold Thought of Deleuze and Guattari* (New York: Guilford Press, 1998), pp. 258–82. And one is tempted to claim that Deleuze's turn against Hegel is, in a homologous way, a turn against his own origins—recall one of Deleuze's early texts, his deeply sympathetic review of Hyppolite's reading of Hegel's *Logic,* reprinted in Jean Hyppolite, *Logic and Existence* (Albany: State University of New York Press, 1997), pp. 191–95.
[90] See Stivale, op. cit., pp. 277–78. For a more detailed account of the link between "dark precursor" and phallus, see *The Logic of Sense,* pp. 227–30.

its complexity? This, perhaps, is why Deleuze experienced his collaboration with Guattari as such a "relief": the fluidity of his texts cowritten with Guattari, the sense that now, finally, things run smoothly, is effectively a fake relief—it signals that the burden of thinking was successfully avoided. The true enigma is hence: why does Deleuze succumb to this strange urge to "demonize" structuralism, disavowing his own roots in it (on account of which one can effectively claim that Deleuze's attack on "structuralism" is enacted on behalf of what he got from structuralism, that it is strictly inherent to structuralism)? Again, why must he deny this link?

Is the Freudian Oedipus complex (especially in terms of its Lacanian interpretive appropriation) not the exact *opposite* of the reduction of the multitude of social intensities onto the mother-father-and-me matrix: the matrix of the explosive *opening up* of the subject onto the social space? Undergoing "symbolic castration" is a way for the subject to be thrown out of the family network, propelled into a wider social network—*Oedipus, the operator of deterritorialization.* However, what about the fact that, nonetheless, Oedipus "focuses" the initial "polymorphous perversity" of drives onto the mother-father-and-me coordinates? More precisely, is "symbolic castration" not also the name for a process by means of which the child-subject enters the order of sense proper, of the ABSTRACTION of sense, gaining the capacity to abstract a quality from its embeddedness in a bodily Whole, to conceive of it as a becoming no longer attributed to a certain substance—as Deleuze would have put it, "red" no longer stands for the predicate of the red thing but for the pure flow of becoming-red? So, far from tying us down to our bodily reality, "symbolic castration" sustains our very ability to "transcend" this reality and enter the space of immaterial Becoming. Does the autonomous smile that survives on its own when the cat's body disappears in *Alice in Wonderland* also not stand for an organ "castrated," cut off from the body? What if, then, phallus itself, as the signifier of castration, stands for such an organ without a body?

Is this not a further argument for the claim that Deleuze's quasi cause is his name for the Lacanian "phallic signifier"? Recall how, according to Deleuze, the quasi cause "*extracts singularities from the present,* and from individuals and persons which occupy this present,"[91] and, in the same movement, provides them with their relative autonomy with regard to the intensive processes as their real causes, endowing these impassive and sterile effects with their morphogenetic power—is this double movement not *exactly* that of "symbolic castration" (whose signifier is phallus)?

---

[91] Deleuze, *The Logic of Sense*, p. 166.

First, the impassive-sterile Event is cut off, extracted, from its virile, corporeal, causal base (if "castrations" means anything at all, it means *this*). Then, this flow of Sense-Event is constituted as an autonomous field of its own, the autonomy of the incorporeal symbolic order with regard to its corporeal embodiments. "Symbolic castration," as the elementary operation of the quasi cause, is thus a profoundly *materialist* concept, since it answers the basic need of any materialist analysis: "If we are to get rid of essentialist and typological thought we need some process through which virtual multiplicities are derived from the actual world and some process through which the results of this derivation may be given enough coherence and autonomy."[92]

The problem, of course, is the following one: the minimal actualization is here conceived as the actualization of the virtual, after its extraction from the preceding actual. Is, then, *every* actual the result of the actualization of the preceding virtual (so that the same goes for the actual out of which the actualized virtual was extracted), *or* is there an actual that precedes the virtual, since every virtual has to be extracted from some actual? Perhaps the way out of this predicament—is the virtual extracted from the actual as its impassive-sterile effect or is it the productive process that generates the actual?—is the ultimate, absolute identity of the two operations, an identity hinted at by Deleuze himself when he described the operation of the "pseudo cause" as that of virtualization (extraction of the virtual) and, simultaneously, minimal actualization (the pseudo cause confers on the virtual a minimum of ontological consistency). What if, as we know from Schelling, what makes from the field of potentialities an actual reality is not the addition of some raw reality (of matter) but, rather, the addition of pure ideality (of *logos*)? Kant himself was already aware of this paradox: the confused field of impressions turns into reality when supplemented by the transcendental Idea. What this fundamental lesson of transcendental idealism means is that virtualization and actualization are two sides of the same coin: *actuality constitutes itself when a VIRTUAL (symbolic) supplement is added to the pre-ontological real.* In other words, the very extraction of the virtual from the real ("symbolic castration") constitutes reality—*actual reality is the real filtered through the virtual.*

The function of the quasi cause is therefore inherently contradictory. Its task is, at one and the same time, to perform a push toward actualization (endowing multiplicities with a minimum of actuality) and to counter actualization by way of extracting virtual events from the corporeal processes that are their causes. One should conceive of these two

[92] DeLanda, op. cit., p. 115.

aspects as identical. The properly Hegelian paradox at work here is that the only way for a virtual state to actualize itself is to be supplemented by another virtual feature. (Again, recall Kant: how is a confused multiplicity of subjective sensations transformed into "objective" reality? It happens when the *subjective* function of transcendental synthesis is added to this multiplicity.) This is the "phallic" dimension at its most elementary: *the excess of the virtual that sustains actualization.* And, this reference to the phallic signifier also enables us to answer one of the standard reproaches to the Lacanian notions of phallus and castration: the idea that they involve a kind of ahistorical short circuit, that is to say, the complaint that they directly link the limitation serving as a condition of human existence as such to a particular threat (that of castration) that relies on a specific patriarchal gender constellation. The next move is, then, usually the one of trying to get rid of the notion of castration—this "ridiculous" Freudian claim—by way of claiming that the threat of castration is, at its best, just a local expression of the global limitation of the human condition, which is that of human finitude, experienced in a whole series of constraints (the existence of other people who limit our freedom, our mortality, and, also, the necessity to "choose one's sex"). Such a move from castration to an anxiety grounded in the very finitude of the human condition is, of course, the standard existential-philosophical move of "saving" Freud by way of getting rid of the embarrassing topic of castration and penis envy ("Who can take this seriously today?"). Psychoanalysis is thus redeemed, magically transformed into a respectable academic discipline that deals with how suffering human subjects cope with the anxieties of finitude. The (in)famous advice given to Freud by Jung when their boat approached the coast of the United States in 1912 (that Freud should leave out or at least limit the accent on sexuality to render psychoanalysis more acceptable to the American medical establishment) is resuscitated here.

Why is it not sufficient to emphasize how "castration" is just a particular instance of the general limitation of the human condition? Or, to put it in a slightly different way, how should one insist on the link between the universal symbolic structure and the particular corporeal economy? The old reproach against Lacan is that he conflates two levels, the allegedly neutral-universal-formal symbolic structure and the particular-gendered-bodily references; say, he emphasizes that the phallus is not the penis as an organ but as a signifier, even a "pure" signifier—so, why then call this "pure" signifier "phallus"? As it was clear to Deleuze (and not only to Lacan), the notion of castration answers a very specific question: how does the universal symbolic process detach itself from its corporeal roots? How does it *emerge* in its relative autonomy? "Castration" designates the violent bodily cut that enables us to enter the domain of the incorporeal.

And, the same goes for the topic of finitude: "castration" is not simply one of the local cases of the experience of finitude—this concept tries to answer a more fundamental "arche-transcendental" question, namely, *how do we, humans, experience ourselves as marked by finitude in the first place*? This fact is not self-evident: Heidegger was right to emphasize that only humans exist in the mode of "being-towards-death." Of course, animals are also somehow "aware" of their limitation, of their limited power, and so forth—the hare *does* try to escape the fox. And yet, this is not the same as human finitude, which emerges against the background of the small child's narcissistic attitude of illusory omnipotence (of course, we do indeed say that, in order to become mature, we have to accept our limitations). What lurks behind this narcissistic attitude is, however, the Freudian death drive, a kind of "undead" stubbornness denounced already by Kant as a violent excess absent in animals, which is why, for Kant, only humans need education through discipline. The symbolic Law does not tame and regulate nature but, precisely, applies itself to an unnatural excess. Or, to approach the same complex from another direction: at its most radical, the helplessness of the small child about which Freud speaks is not physical helplessness, the inability to provide for one's needs, but a helplessness in the face of the enigma of the Other's desire, the helpless fascination with the excess of the Other's enjoyment, and the ensuing inability to account for it in the available terms of meaning.

When Roman Jakobson wrote on phonemes and the bodily grounding of language, he focused on the crucial gap between embodied gestures and the free-floating symbolic network of phonemes—this gap is what Lacan calls "castration." Jakobson's crucial point is that it is only the SIGNIFIER, not meaning, that can do this job of deterritorialization: meaning tends to revert to our concrete life-world embeddedness (the premodern antropomorphic mirroring of interior and exterior is the attitude of meaning par excellence.) So, the phallus, far from signalling the rootedness of the symbolic in our bodily experience (its territorialization), is the "pure signifier" and, as such, the very agent of deterritorialization. Here, Jakobson introduces the key dialectical notion of secondary grounding in bodily experience: yes, our language shows overall traces of this embodiment (the word "locomotive" resembles the profile of an old steam locomotive; the word "front" is formed in the front of our oral cavity, and the word "back" in the back of it—and so on and so forth). However, all of these are reterritorializations against the background of the fundamental cut that is the condition of meaning.[93] This is why the anthropomorphic model of mirroring between language and the human

---

[93] See Roman Jakobson, *On Language* (Cambridge: Belknap, 1995).

body, the reference to the body as a fundamental frame of reference for our understanding, is to be abandoned—language is "inhuman." (The process thus has three phases: (1) primordial territorialization as the "assemblage of bodies"—an organism marks its suroundings, its exchanges with it, in a texture of affective inscriptions, tatoos, and so forth; (2) deterritorialization—passage to the immaterial, virtual production of sense—marks are freed from their origins (enunciator, reference); (3) reterritorialization—when language turns into a medium of communication, pinned down to its subject of enunciation whose thoughts it expresses, to the reality it designates.)

Phallus

So, what is symbolic castration, with the phallus as its signifier? One should begin by conceiving of the phallus as a signifier—which means what? From the traditional rituals of investiture, we know the objects that not only "symbolize" power but put the subject who acquires them into the position of effectively *exercising* power. If a king holds in his hands the scepter and wears the crown, his words will be taken as the words of a king. Such insignia are external, not part of my nature: I don them; I wear them to exert power. As such, they "castrate" me: they introduce a gap between what I immediately am and the function that I exercise (i.e., I am never fully at the level of my function). This is what the infamous "symbolic castration" means. Not "castration as symbolic, as just symbolically enacted" (in the sense in which we say that, when I am deprived of something, I am "symbolically castrated"), but the castration that occurs by the very fact of me being caught in the symbolic order, assuming a symbolic mandate. Castration is the very gap between what I immediately am and the symbolic mandate that confers on me this "authority." In this precise sense, far from being the opposite of power, it is synonymous with power; it is that which confers power on me. And one has to think of the phallus not as the organ that immediately expresses the vital force of my being, my virility, and so forth but, precisely, as such an insignia, as a mask that I put on in the same way a king or judge puts on his insignia—phallus is an "organ without a body" that I put on, which gets attached to my body, without ever becoming its "organic part," namely, forever sticking out as its incoherent, excessive supplement.[94]

---

[94] And incidentally, insofar as one provisionally accepts the vulgar "Freudian" reading of the Juan Batista mission tower in *Vertigo* as "phallic," one should stress the fact, known to every Hitchcock lover, that the tower is not really there (at the site of the real mission building)—it is just a painting incorporated at the studio into the shot of the "real" mission. Perhaps *this* is what really makes it "phallic": the fact that it does not really exist, that it is a fictional "organ" artificially attached to the "real" building.

Although the latest "radical" sexual practice in the United States appears to concern cutting, its underlying logic is entirely different. In the so-called subincision (the chirurgic vertical cutting of the penis into two, so that each half then functions as its own, also with its own erection), the aim is not any kind of self-punishment or inflicting of pain but—this is precisely what's at stake in this practice—the redoubling of penis. The question, of course, is, How does this redoubling of the *penis* effect the symbolic functioning of the *phallus* as signifier? Here, one can again observe "in practice" the gap that separates penis-as-organ from phallus-as-signifier. One is tempted to argue that this redoubling of the penis, this staging of a "divided penis," far from symmetrically redoubling the phallus, is an attempt to change the phallus into an(other) *objet petit a.* One of the definitions of *objet a* is that it is the spectral indivisible remainder of the operation of division, and, in this case, this indivisible remainder is the phallus itself. And is not the feminine counterpoint to this practice that of "butch lesbians" who adopt a masculine stance and dress and, in their sexual practice, renounce their own pleasure, focusing only on giving pleasure to their partner (with the help of dildos, etc.). The paradox here is that, precisely by adopting the masculine mask, "butch lesbians" stand for the feminine subjective position at its purest, for the *jouissance* of the Other as opposed to phallic *jouissance.*

"Symbolic castration" is an answer to the question: how we are to conceive the passage from bodily depth to the surface event, the rupture that has to occur at the level of bodily depth if the effect-of-sense is to emerge? In short, how are we to articulate the "materialist" genesis of Sense? This problem of the emergence of mind out of matter, as its "emerging property," is the problem Deleuze is struggling with in *The Logic of Sense,* tracing it back to the ancient Stoic opposition of bodies and immaterial events. To ask this question is to enter the problematic of dialectical materialism. Thus conceived, dialectical materialism is strictly opposed to mechanical materialism, which is reductionist by definition. The latter sort of materialism does not acknowledge the radical heteronomy of the effect with regard to the cause (i.e., it conceives of the surface of sense-effect as a simple appearance, the appearance of an underlying, deeper material Essence). Idealism, on the contrary, denies that sense-effect is an effect of bodily depth; it fetishizes sense-effect into a self-generated entity. The price it pays for this denial is the substantialization of sense-effect: idealism covertly qualifies sense-effect as a new Body (the immaterial body of Platonic Forms, for example). Paradoxical as it may sound, only dialectical materialism can think the effect of Sense, sense qua event, in its specific autonomy, without a substantialist reduction (which is why vulgar mechanical materialism forms the necessary complement to idealism). Only (dialectical) materialism can effectively *think* the "immaterial" void, the gap of negativity, in which mental Events emerge. Idealism, by contrast, substantializes this void.

The universe of Sense qua "autonomous" forms a vicious circle. We are always-already part of it, since the moment we assume toward it the attitude of external distance and turn our gaze from the effect to its cause, we lose the effect. The fundamental problem of dialectical materialism is therefore: how does this circle of Sense, allowing for no externality, emerge? How can the immixture of bodies give rise to "neutral" thought, that is, to the symbolic field that is "free" in the precise sense of not being bound by the economy of bodily drives, of not functioning as a prolongation of the drive's striving for satisfaction? The Freudian hypothesis is: through the inherent impasse of sexuality. It is not possible to derive the emergence of "disinterested" thought from other bodily drives (hunger, self-preservation . . .)—why not? Sexuality is the only drive that is, in itself, hindered and perverted, being simultaneously insufficient and excessive (with excess as the form of appearance of lack). On one hand, sexuality is characterized by the universal capacity to provide the metaphorical meaning or innuendo of any activity or object—any element, including the most abstract reflection, can be experienced as "alluding to that" (suffice it to recall the proverbial example of the adolescent who, in order to forget his sexual obsessions, takes refuge in pure mathematics and physics—whatever he does here again reminds him of "that": how much volume is needed to fill out an empty cylinder? how much energy is discharged when two bodies collide? . . .). This universal surplus—this capacity of sexuality to overflow the entire field of human experience so that everything, from eating to excretion, from beating up our fellow man (or getting beaten up by him) to the exercise of power, can acquire a sexual connotation—is not the sign of its preponderance. Rather, it is the sign of a certain structural faultiness: sexuality strives outward and overflows the adjoining domains precisely because it cannot find satisfaction in itself, because it never attains its goal. How, precisely, does an activity that is, in itself, definitely asexual acquire sexual connotations? It is "sexualized" when it fails to achieve its asexual goal and gets caught in the vicious circle of futile repetition. We enter sexuality when a gesture that "officially" serves some instrumental goal becomes an end-in-itself, when we start to enjoy the very "dysfunctional" repetition of this gesture and thereby suspend its purposefulness.

Sexuality can function as a co-sense that supplements the "desexualized" neutral-literal meaning precisely insofar as this neutral meaning is already here. As was demonstrated by Deleuze, perversion enters the stage as an inherent reversal of this "normal" relationship between the asexual, literal sense and the sexual co-sense. In perversion, sexuality is made into a direct object of our speech, but the price we pay for it is the desexualization of our attitude toward sexuality—sexuality becomes one desexualized object among others. The exemplary case of such an attitude is the "scientific" disinterested approach to sexuality or the Sadean approach that treats sexuality as the object of an instrumental activity. Suffice it to recall the role of Jennifer Jason Leigh in Altman's *Short Cuts*: a housewife who earns supplementary money by paid phone sex, entertaining customers with pep talk. She is so well accustomed to her job that she can improvise into the receiver, describing, for instance, how she is all wet between her thighs, while changing her baby or preparing lunch—she maintains a wholly external, instrumental attitude toward sexual fantasies. They simply do not concern her. What Lacan aims at with the notion of "symbolic castration" is precisely this *vel*, this choice: either we accept the desexualization of the literal sense, entailing the displacement of sexuality to a "co-sense," to the supplementary dimension of sexual connotation-innuendo; or, we approach sexuality "directly," we make sexuality the subject of literal speech, which we pay for with the "desexualization" of our subjective attitude to it. What we lose in every case is a direct approach, a literal talk about sexuality that would remain "sexualized."

In this precise sense, the phallus is the signifier of castration. Far from acting as the potent organ-symbol of sexuality qua universal creative power, it is the signifier, organ, or both of desexualization itself, of the "impossible" passage of "body" into symbolic "thought," the signifier that sustains the neutral surface of "asexual" sense. Deleuze conceptualizes this passage as the inversion of the "phallus of coordination" into the "phallus of castration": the "phallus of coordination" is an imago, a figure the subject refers to in order to coordinate the dispersed erogenous zones into the totality of a unified body, whereas the "phallus of castration" is a signifier. Those who conceive of the phallic signifier after the model of the mirror stage, as a privileged image or bodily part that provides the central point of reference enabling the subject to totalize the dispersed multitude of erogenous zones into a unique, hierarchically ordered totality, remain at the level of the "phallus of coordination." They thereby reproach Lacan with what is actually his fundamental insight: this coordination through the central phallic image necessarily fails. The outcome of this failure, however, is not a return to the uncoordinated plurality of erogenous zones but, precisely, a "symbolic castration": sexuality retains its universal dimension and continues to function as the (potential) connotation of every act, object, and so forth only if it "sacrifices" literal meaning (i.e., only if literal meaning is "desexualized"). The step from the "phallus of coordination" to the "phallus of castration" is the step from the impossible-failed total sexualization, from the state in which "everything has sexual meaning," to the state in which this sexual meaning becomes secondary, changes into the "universal innuendo," into the co-sense that potentially supplements every literal, neutral-asexual sense.

How, then, do we pass from the state in which "the meaning of everything is sexual," in which sexuality functions as the universal signified, to the surface of the neutral-desexualized literal sense? The desexualization of the signified occurs when the very element that coordinated (or failed to coordinate) the universal sexual meaning (i.e., the phallus) is reduced to a signifier. The phallus is the "organ of desexualization" precisely in its capacity as a signifier without signified. It is the operator of the evacuation of sexual meaning (i.e., of the reduction of sexuality qua signified content to an empty signifier). In short, the phallus designates the following paradox: sexuality can universalize itself only by way of desexualization, only by undergoing a kind of transubstantiation in which it changes into a supplement-connotation of the neutral, asexual literal sense.

Therein resides the materialist "wager" of Deleuze and Lacan: the "desexualization," the miracle of the advent of the neutral-desexualized surface of Sense-Event, does not rely on the intervention of some transcendent, extrabodily force. It can be derived from the inherent impasse of the sexualized body itself. In this precise sense—shocking as it may sound to vulgar materialists and obscurantists in their unacknowledged solidarity—the phallus, the phallic element as the signifier of "castration," is the fundamental category of dialectical materialism. Phallus qua signifier of "castration" mediates the emergence of the pure surface of Sense-Event. As such, it is the "transcendental signifier"—nonsense within the field of sense—that distributes and regulates the series of Sense. Its "transcendental" status means that there is nothing "substantial" about it: phallus is the semblance par excellence. What the phallus "causes" is the gap that separates the surface-event from bodily density: it is the "pseudo cause" that sustains the autonomy of the field of Sense with regard to its true, effective, bodily cause. One should recall here Adorno's observation on how the notion of transcendental constitution results from a kind of perspectival inversion: what the subject (mis)perceives as his constitutive power is actually his impotence, his incapacity to reach beyond the imposed limitations of his horizon. The transcendental constitutive power is a pseudo power representing the flip side of the subject's blindness concerning true bodily causes. Phallus qua cause is the pure semblance of a cause. There is no place for Deleuze's key concept of "quasi-cause" in the *Anti-Oedipus* dispositive of productive becoming versus reified being: "quasi-cause" enters to sustain the autonomy of the sterile and impassive flow of events with regard to their corporeal causes.

There is no structure without the "phallic" moment as the crossing point of the two series (of signifier and signified), as the point of the short circuit at which—as Lacan puts it in a very precise way—"the signifier falls into the signified." The point of nonsense within the field of Sense is the point at which the signifier's cause is inscribed into the field of Sense. Without this short circuit, the signifier's structure would act as an external bodily cause and would thus be unable to produce the effect of Sense. On that account, the two series (of the signifier and the signified) always contain a paradoxical entity that is "doubly inscribed" (i.e., that is simultaneously surplus and lack): a surplus of the signifier over the signified (the empty signifier without a signified) and the lack of the signified (the point of nonsense within the field of Sense). That is to say, as soon as the symbolic order emerges, we are dealing with the minimal difference between a structural place and the element that occupies, fills out, this place: an element is always logically preceded by the place in the structure it fills out. The two series can, therefore, also be described as the "empty" formal structure (signifier) and the series of elements filling out the empty places in the structure (signified). From this perspective, the paradox consists in the fact that the two series never overlap: we always encounter an entity that is simultaneously—with regard to the structure—an empty, unoccupied place and—with regard to the elements—a rapidly moving, elusive object, an occupant without a place. We have thereby produced Lacan's formula of fantasy ($—a), since the matheme for the subject is $, an empty place in the structure, an elided signifier, while *objet a* is, by definition, an excessive object, an object that lacks its place in the structure. Consequently, the point is not that there is simply the surplus of an element over the places available in the structure or the surplus of a place that has no element to fill it out. An empty place in the structure would still sustain the fantasy of an element that will emerge and fill out this place; an excessive element lacking its place would still sustain the fantasy of some yet unknown place waiting for it. The point is, rather, that the empty place in the structure is strictly correlative to the errant element lacking its place. They are not two different entities but the front and the back of one and the same entity, that is, one and the same entity inscribed onto the two surfaces of a Moebius strip. In short, the subject qua $ does not belong to the depth: it emerges from a topological twist of the surface itself. It is here that psychoanalysis can supplement Heidegger who, toward the end of his life, conceded that, for him, "the body phenomenon is the most difficult problem":

> The bodily (*das Leibliche*) in the human is not something animalistic. The manner of understanding that accompanies it is something that metaphysics up till now has not touched on.[95]

One is tempted to risk the hypothesis that it is precisely psychoanalytic theory that was the first to touch on this key question. Is not the Freudian eroticized body, sustained by libido, organized around erogenous zones, precisely the nonanimalistic, nonbiological body? Is not *this* (and not the animalistic) body the proper object of psychoanalysis? What happens in hysteria is, to quote Jacques-Alain Miller, a double refusal of the body, according to the shift from subjective to objective genitive: first, the body refuses to obey the soul and starts to speak on its own, in the symptoms in which the subject's soul cannot recognize itself; second, the hysteric's unconscious rejects the body itself (the body in its biological dimension), using it as a medium through which unconscious drives and desires running against the body's biological interests (well-being, survival, reproduction) express themselves. The Unconscious is a parasite that uses the body, forcefully distorting its normal functioning. For that reason, a hysterical subject turns away from her biological body in disgust, unable to accept that she "is" her body.[96] In the strict psychoanalytic perspective, one should thus distinguish between *two* bodies: what Miller calls the "body-knowledge," the biological body regulated by the knowledge contained in its genome, and the "body-*jouissance*," the body that is the proper object of psychoanalysis, the body as the inconsistent composite of erogenous zones, the body as the surface of the inscription of the traces of traumas and excessive enjoyments, the body through which the unconscious speaks.[97]

Consequently, if we try to locate psychoanalysis within this Deleuzian opposition of bodily causes and the flow of immaterial becoming, it is crucial to emphasize that it is *not* the science of the "real" bodily causes of psychic life, but a science that moves entirely at the "surface" level of the flow of events—even (and precisely) when it deals with the body, it is not the biological "interior" of the body but the body as the multitude of erogenous zones that are all located upon the SURFACE. Even when we penetrate the subject's innermost sanctum, the very core of its Unconscious, what we find there is the pure surface of a fantasmatic screen.

---

[95] Martin Heidegger, with Eugen Fink, *Heraclitus Seminar* (Tuscaloosa: University of Alabama Press, 1979), p. 146.

[96] See Jacques-Alain Miller, "The Symptom and the Body Event," *Lacanian Ink* 19, (2001): 16.

[97] Miller, op. cit., p. 21.

Fantasy

The ontological scandal of the notion of fantasy resides in the fact that it subverts the standard opposition of "subjective" and "objective." Of course, fantasy is, by definition, not "objective" (in the naive sense of "existing independently of the subject's perceptions"). However, it is also not "subjective" (in the sense of being reducible to the subject's consciously experienced intuitions). Rather, fantasy belongs to the "bizarre category of the objectively subjective—the way things actually, objectively seem to you even if they don't seem that way to you."[98] When, for example, we claim that someone who is consciously well disposed toward Jews nonetheless harbors profound anti-Semitic prejudices he is not consciously aware of, do we not claim that (insofar as these prejudices do not render the way Jews really are but render the way they appear to him) he is not aware of how Jews really seem to him? Apropos of commodity fetishism, Marx himself uses the term "objectively-necessary appearance." So, when a critical Marxist encounters a bourgeois subject immersed in commodity fetishism, the Marxist's reproach to him is not "The commodity may seem to you to be a magical object endowed with special powers, but it really is just a reified expression of relations between people." The actual Marxist's reproach is, rather, "You may think that the commodity appears to you as a simple embodiment of social relations (that, for example, money is just a kind of voucher entitling you to a part of the social product), but this is not how things really seem to you—in your social reality, by means of your participation in social exchange, you bear witness to the uncanny fact that a commodity really appears to you as a magical object endowed with special powers." This is what Marx is aiming at in his famous fiction of commodities that start to speak to each other:

> If commodities could speak, they would say this: our use-value may interest men, but it does not belong to us as objects. What does belong to us as objects, however, is our value. Our own intercourse as commodities proves it. We relate to each other merely as exchange-values.[99]

Marx quotes here ironically Dogberry's advice to Seacoal from Shakespeare's *Much Ado about Nothing* (Act 3, Scene 3), which concludes chapter 1 of *Capital*: "To be a well-favoured man is the gift of fortune; but reading and writing comes by nature." This reversal is not simply a fiction in the sense of subjective illusion—on the contrary, its status is objective, that of "objective appearance," of how things "effectively

---

[98] Daniel C. Dennett, *Consciousness Explained* (New York: Little, Brown, 1991), p. 132. (Dennett, of course, evokes this concept in a purely negative way, as a nonsensical *contradictio in adjecto*.)

[99] Karl Marx, *Capital*, vol. 1 (Harmondsworth, England: Penguin Books, 1990), pp. 176–77.

appear to me," as opposed to how they immediately appear to me: the categories of bourgeois economics

> are forms of thought which are socially valid, and therefore objective, for the relations of production belonging to this historically determined mode of social production, i.e. commodity production.[100]

In March 2003, Donald Rumsfeld engaged in a little bit of amateur philosophizing about the relationship between the known and the unknown: "There are known knowns. These are things we know that we know. There are known unknowns. That is to say, there are things that we know we don't know. But there are also unknown unknowns. There are things we don't know we don't know." What he forgot to add was the crucial fourth term: the "unknown knowns," things we don't know that we know, which is precisely the Freudian unconscious, the "knowledge which doesn't know itself," as Lacan used to say. If Rumsfeld thinks that the main dangers in the confrontation with Iraq are the "unknown unknowns," the threats from Saddam about which we do not even suspect what they may be, what we should reply is that the main dangers are, on the contrary, the "unknown knowns," the disavowed beliefs and suppositions we are not even aware of adhering to ourselves. The risk to be taken is to *assume* these fantasmatic unknowns. In a story by Somerset Maugham from the 1920s, an Englishman in his forties, who, for decades, worked in colonial Shanghai, finally earns enough to realize the dream that sustained him through the years—to move to London and live the comfortable life of a bachelor there. However, after a couple of weeks in London, he gets terribly bored and depressed, and starts to long for the life back in Shanghai; so, he boards a boat back to China. But, on the long trip back, while the boat makes a stop in Hanoi, he leaves it and remains permanently in Hanoi. After being disappointed by the realization of a lifetime dream, he knows that he cannot afford another such experience, so he decides to stay forever close to China, forever dreaming about how nice life would have been in Shanghai. This is what Lacan means by "compromising one's desire": the refusal to "traverse one's fantasy" by way of risking its actualization.

This is also one of the ways of specifying the meaning of Lacan's assertion of the subject's constitutive "decenterment." Its point is not that my subjective experience is regulated by objective unconscious mechanisms that are "decentered" with regard to my self-experience and, as such, beyond my control (a point asserted by every materialist) but, rather, is something much more unsettling: I am deprived of even my most intimate "subjective" experience, the way things "really seem to me," that of

[100] Marx, op. cit., p. 169.

the fundamental fantasy that constitutes and guarantees the core of my being, since I can never consciously experience it and assume it. According to the standard view, the dimension that is constitutive of subjectivity is that of phenomenal (self)experience: I am a subject the moment I can say to myself, "No matter what unknown mechanism governs my acts, perceptions, and thoughts, nobody can take from me what I see and feel now." Say, when I am passionately in love, and a biochemist informs me that all my intense sentiments are just the result of biochemical processes in my body, I can answer him by clinging to the appearance: "All that you're saying may be true, but, nonetheless, nothing can take from me the intensity of the passion that I am experiencing now." Lacan's point, however, is that the psychoanalyst is the one who, precisely, *can* take this from the subject—his ultimate aim is to deprive the subject of the very fundamental fantasy that regulates the universe of his (self)experience. The Freudian "subject of the Unconscious" emerges only when a key aspect of the subject's phenomenal (self)experience (his "fundamental fantasy") becomes inaccessible to him (i.e., is "primordially repressed"). At its most radical, the Unconscious is the inaccessible phenomenon, not the objective mechanism that regulates my phenomenal experience. So, in contrast to the commonplace that we are dealing with a subject the moment an entity displays signs of "inner life" (i.e., of a fantasmatic self-experience that cannot be reduced to external behavior), one should claim that what characterizes human subjectivity proper is, rather, the gap that separates the two, namely, the fact that fantasy, at its most elementary, becomes inaccessible to the subject. It is this inaccessibility that makes the subject "empty." We thus obtain a relationship that totally subverts the standard notion of the subject who directly experiences himself via his "inner states": an "impossible" relationship between the empty, nonphenomenal subject and the phenomena that remain inaccessible to the subject. In other words, psychoanalysis (and Deleuze) allows us to formulate a paradoxical *phenomenology without a subject*—phenomena arise that are not phenomena *of* a subject, appearing *to* it. This does not mean that the subject is not involved here—it is, but, precisely, in the mode of EXCLUSION, as the negative agency that is not able to assume these phenomena.

In what, then, resides the gap between the neuroscientific image of the human mind and psychoanalysis? It is not simply that, while animals find the coordinates of their mating activity embedded in their natural instincts, humans lack them and therefore need their "second nature," the symbolic institution, to provide them with these coordinates. The coordinates of the symbolic order are here to enable us to cope with the impasse of the Other's desire, and the problem is that the symbolic order ultimately always fails. As Jean Laplanche points out, the traumatic impact of the "primordial scene," the enigma of the signifiers of the Other's desire, generates an excess that cannot ever be fully "sublated" in symbolic ordering. The notorious "lack" cosubstantial with the human animal is not simply negative, an absence of instinctual coordinates; it is a lack with regard to an excess, to the excessive presence of traumatic enjoyment.[101] The paradox is that there is signification precisely because there is an excessive, nonsignifiable, erotic fascination and attachment: the condition of possibility of signification is its condition of impossibility. What if, then, the ultimate resort of the excessive development of human intelligence is the effort to decipher the abyss of *"Che vuoi?"* the enigma of Other's desire? What if therein resides the reason why humans are fixated on solving tasks that cannot be solved, on trying to answer unanswerable questions? What if the link between metaphysics and sexuality (or, more precisely, human eroticism) is to be taken quite literally? Ultimately, this traumatic, indigestible kernel, as the nonsensical support of sense, is the fundamental fantasy itself. As is well known, Wagner's musical hatred was directed against Meyerbeer, who, for him, stood for fake commercial Jewish music. What is less known is that, at the lowest point of his despair (on May 3, 1840), Wagner wrote a letter to Meyerbeer exhibiting a strange, groveling sycophancy stripped of the last vestiges of self-respect:

> It is *Meyerbeer* and *Meyerbeer* alone, and you will readily understand me when I tell you that I weep tears of the deepest emotion whenever I think of the man who is *everything* to me, *everything*. . . . I realize that I must become your slave, body and soul, in order to find food and strength for my work, which will one day tell you of my gratitude. I shall be a loyal and honest slave,—for I openly admit that I am a slave by nature; it gives me endless pleasure to be able to devote myself unconditionally to another person, recklessly, and in blind trust. The knowledge that I am working and striving for you, and you *alone,* makes that effort and industry seem all the more agreeable and all the more worthwhile. Buy me, therefore, Sir, it is by no means a wholly worthless purchase! . . . Your property, Richard Wagner.[102]

There probably has never been a more direct and shameless display of masochist enjoyment. Does this position of thorough and shameless servitude not render Wagner's "fundamental fantasy," the disavowed core of his subjective identity that had to be denied in the guise of virulent anti-Semitism? It is precisely the status of fantasy that brings us to the ultimate point of the irreconcilable difference between psychoanalysis and feminism, that of rape (or the masochistic fantasies sustaining it).

---

101 See Jean Laplanche, *New Foundations for Psychoanalysis* (Oxford: Basil Blackwell, 1989).
102 Quoted from Bryan Magee, *The Tristan Chord* (New York: Owl Books, 2001), pp. 345–46.

For standard feminism, at least, it is an a priori axiom that rape is a violence imposed from without: even if a woman fantasizes about being raped, this only bears witness to the deplorable fact that she internalized male attitudes. The reaction is here one of pure panic. The moment one mentions that a woman may fantasize about being raped or at least brutally mishandled, one hears cries: This is like saying that Jews fantasize about being gassed in the camps or African Americans fantasize about being lynched! From this perspective, the split hysterical position (that of complaining about being sexually misused and exploited while simultaneously desiring it and provoking man to seduce her) is secondary, whereas for Freud, it is primary, constitutive of subjectivity. Consequently, the problem with rape, in Freud's view, is that it has such a traumatic impact not simply because it is a case of such brutal external violence but because it also touches on something disavowed in the victim herself. So, when Freud writes, "If what [subjects] long for most intensely in their phantasies is presented to them in reality, they none the less flee from it,"[103] his point is not merely that this occurs because of censorship but, rather, because the core of our fantasy is unbearable to us.

The original site of fantasy is that of a small child overhearing or witnessing parental coitus and unable to make sense of it: what does all of this *mean*, the intense whispers, the strange sounds in the bedroom, and so forth? So, the child fantasizes a scene that would account for these strangely intense fragments—recall the best-known scene from David Lynch's *Blue Velvet*, in which Kyle MacLachlan, hidden in the closet, witnesses the weird sexual interplay between Isabella Rossellini and Dennis Hopper. What he sees is a clear fantasmatic supplement destined to account for what he hears. When Hopper puts on a mask through which he breathes, is this not an imagined scene that is to account for the intense breathing that accompanies sexual activity? And, the fundamental paradox of the fantasy is that the subject never arrives at the moment when he can say "OK, now I fully understand it, my parents were having sex, I no longer need a fantasy!" *This* is, among other things, what Lacan meant with his "*il n'y a pas de rapport sexuel.*" Every *sense* has to rely on some nonsensical fantasmatic frame—when we say "OK, now I understand it!" what this ultimately means is "Now I can locate it within my fantasmatic framework." Or, to resort again to the old Derridean twist, fantasy as the condition of impossibility, the limit, of sense, the nonsensical kernel, is, at the same time, its irreducible condition of possibility.

---

[103] Sigmund Freud, *Dora: An Analysis of a Case of Hysteria* (New York: Macmillan, 1963), p. 101.

So, when, in *Seminar XX (Encore)*, Lacan repeatedly asserts that "*y'a de l'un* /there is something of the one/,"[104] this One is not the totalizing One of the Master-Signifier, but the "supplementary" partial object (organ without a body) that functions as the enabling obstacle of the sexual relationship, as its condition of (im)possibility. *Y'a de l'un* is thus strictly correlative to *il n'y a pas de rapport sexuel:* the two sexual partners are never alone, since their activity has to involve a fantasmatic supplement that sustains their desire (and that can ultimately be just an imagined gaze observing them while they are engaged in sexual intercourse). *Y'a de l'un* means that every erotic couple is a couple of three: $1 + 1 + a$, the "pathological" stain that disturbs the pure immersion of the couple. In short, this "one" is precisely that which *prevents* the fusion of the amorous couple into One. (And, one can well argue that, in the case of a lesbian couple, this "one" is none other than phallus itself [occasionally materialized in dildo]—so that, when Judith Butler ironically proposes the term "lesbian phallus," one should fully agree with her, just adding that this "lesbian phallus" is phallus *tout court*.)[105] Furthermore, not only is this Real of the One not opposed to freedom—it is its very condition. The shocking impact of being affected or "seduced" by the enigmatic message of the Other derails the subject's automaton, opens up a gap that the subject is free to fill in with his (ultimately failed) endeavors to symbolize it. Freedom is ultimately *nothing but* the space opened up by the traumatic encounter, the space to be filled in by its contingent/inadequate symbolizations/translations.

In short, freedom is strictly correlative to the gap in—inconsistency of—the "big Other" (the substantial symbolic order). The first move in the ideologicocritical debunking of the big Other is the denunciation of its inherent *stupidity*. Recall Paul Robeson's later rewriting of his legendary "Ol' Man River" as a model of simple and efficient criticoideological intervention. In the original version from the Hollywood musical *Showboat* (1936), the river (Mississippi) is presented as the embodiment of the enigmatic and indifferent Fate, an old wise man who "must know somethin', but don't say nothin'," and just keeps rolling, retaining its silent wisdom. In the new version—now available in the indispensable recording of his notorious Moscow concert in 1949 (*Russian Revelation*, RV 70004) with a brief spoken introduction by Robeson himself in perfect Russian—the river is no longer the bearer of an anonymous, unfathomable collective wisdom but, rather, the bearer of collective *stupidity*, of the stupid, passive tolerance for meaningless suffering. This

---

[104] See chapter 11 of Jacques Lacan, *Le séminaire, livre XX: Encore*.
[105] See Judith Butler, *Bodies That Matter* (New York: Routledge, 1993), p. 127.

repositioning of the big Other from wisdom to stupidity is crucial. Here are the final lines of the original song: " . . . You gets a little drunk, / an' you land in jail. / But I gets weary, / and sick of tryin', / I'm tired of livin', / and scared of dyin'. / But ol' man river, / he just keeps rollin' along." And here is the changed version: "You show a little grit, / an' you lands in jail. / But I keeps laughin', / instead of cryin', / I must keep fightin', / until I'm dyin'. / And ol' man river, / he'll just keeps rollin' along."

Of course, one should not underestimate the emancipatory power of the original song in its historical context. For the first time in Hollywood, African Americans were presented as hard laborers caught in meaningless permanent suffering, that is, a wide crack appeared in the standard image of them as happy children with no constraints, either smiling and dancing or getting drunk, horny, and violent (recall the racist cliché of a horny Negro from the Hollywood silent comedies: a black worker carries a large block of ice up the stairs to deliver it; when, through a crack in the half-open door, he sees a white woman taking a bath, he gets so aroused that the whole block melts on his back instantly. Is there not something almost charming in the unabashed directness of this cliché?). However, the price of this "serious" depiction of suffering is that African Americans are portrayed as passive, resigned to their sad Fate. But, again, one should not miss the point here: what the changed words accomplish is not the simple passage from the passive acceptance of fate into optimistic, active engagement and struggle—recall that the last line of the new version remains the same, "And ol' man river, / he'll just keeps rollin' along." In other words, *the blind Fate remains,* but is deprived of its aura of unfathomable Wisdom, reduced—not simply to historical contingency but—to the inherent stupidity of the ideological big Other.

"The only good God is a dead God" is effectively the founding statement of the big Other, and, as such, far from a truly atheistic statement: one is even tempted to claim that the ultimate aim of theology is to mortify god, to keep him at a proper distance, to prevent him getting too close to us and thus turning into a voracious monster. The support of the symbolic Law is by definition a dead ("castrated") god: "The point of psychoanalysis is for sure atheism, on condition that we confer on this term a meaning different from that of *God is dead,* since everything indicates that this statement, far from undermining what is at stake here, namely the law, rather consolidates it."[106] It is precisely in so-called totalitarian regimes that the "noncastrated" authority figure returns, in the guise of what one usually refers to as the "Father of the People" who, according to Lacan, is related to the "real father as the agent of castration."[107] That is to

[106] Jacques Lacan, *Le séminaire, livre XVII: L'envers de la psychanalyse* (Paris: Editions du Seuil, 1991), p. 139.
[107] Lacan, op. cit., p. 147.

say, the outside-law (*hors-loi*) aspect of the "totalitarian" leader means precisely that, instead of himself assuming castration (the price to be paid for acting as the agent of the law), he himself turns into an agent of castration, strictly homologous to the Freudian primordial father.

The second move consists in the shift of the emphasis to the "barred" (inconsistent, lacking) big Other, to the question emerging from the Other ("*Che vuoi?*"): with this shift, it is precisely the enigma that emerges, an Otherness within the big Other itself. Suffice it to recall the "translation" of the desire of the mother into the Name-of-the-Father. Lacan's name for the enigmatic message is the desire of the mother—the unfathomable desire the child discerns in maternal caressing. The trademark of misleading "introductions to Lacan" is to conceive of the ensuing symbolic paternal function as the intruder that disturbs the imaginary symbiotic bliss of the mother-child dyad, introducing into it the order of (symbolic) prohibitions (i.e., order as such). Against this misperception, one should insist that "father" is, for Lacan, not the name of a traumatic intrusion but the *solution* to the deadlock of such an intrusion, the answer to the enigma. The enigma, of course, is the enigma of (m)other's desire (What does she effectively want, above and beyond *me,* since I am obviously not enough for her?). "Father" is the *answer* to this enigma, the *symbolization* of this deadlock. In this precise sense, "father" is, according to Lacan's account of the paternal function, a translation or a symptom: a compromise solution that alleviates the unbearable anxiety of directly confronting the void of the other's desire.[108] The fundamental thrust of the entirety of Lacan's later teaching is that, today, this solution no longer works—the Name-of-the-Father is no longer the symptom/synthom that holds together the social link.[109] The political consequences of this insight are capital: any possible idea of revolutionary undermining has to break totally with the problematic of "anti-Oedipal revolt."

RIS

This devaluation of the Symbolic does not involve the shift toward some fetishized "Real in itself." Shifts in Lacan's thought should be taken into account here. The Lacan of the early 1950s was Hegelian (under the influence of Alexandre Kojève and Jean Hyppolite, of course), often directly

---

[108] Lacan's counterargument to Laplanche would have been that there is something missing in the latter's account: *why* does the small child get caught in the enigma of/in the Other? It is not enough to evoke here the precocious birth and the child's helplessness. For this gap to appear, for the parental gestures to appear as an enigmatic message—a message that is an enigma also for the parents themselves—the symbolic order must already be here.

[109] Far from endorsing Oedipus as the ultimate explanatory matrix, Lacan dismisses it as itself being a symptom to be interpreted: "I told you that the Oedipus complex is Freud's dream. As every dream, it needs to be interpreted" (Jacques Lacan, *Le séminaire, livre XVII: L'envers de la psychanalyse*, p. 159).

designating the analyst as the figure of the Hegelian philosopher, the work of analysis as following the Hegelian "cunning of reason," the end of analysis as "absolute knowledge," the mediation of all particular content in the universal symbolic medium, and so forth; in clear contrast, the "Lacan of the Real" asserts some traumatic core of the Real that forever resists being integrated into the Symbolic—and he does this by way of linking the Freudian *das Ding* with the Kantian Thing-in-itself.[110] We can clearly discern here the contours of the Lacan of symbolic castration: the Thing is prohibited, and this prohibition, far from thwarting desire, sustains it. In short, the symbolic order functions like Kant's transcendental screen, through which reality is rendered accessible and which, nonetheless, simultaneously prevents our direct access to it.

However, a closer reading reveals that, in the last decade and a half of his teaching (starting with *Seminar XI*), Lacan struggled to overcome this Kantian horizon—the clearest indication of it is his reactualization of the concept of drive. Drive functions beyond symbolic castration, as an inherent detour, topological twist, of the Real itself—and, Lacan's path from desire to drive is the path from Kant to Hegel. This shift in late Lacan from the "transcendental" logic (symbolic castration as the ultimate horizon of our experience, emptying the place of the Thing and thus opening up the space for our desire) to the dimension "beyond castration" (i.e., to a position that claims that, "beyond castration," there is more than the abyss of the Night of the Thing that swallows us), also has direct political consequences: the "transcendental" Lacan is obviously the "Lacan of democracy" (the empty place of Power for whose temporary occupancy multiple political subjects compete, against the "totalitarian" subject who claims to act directly on behalf of the Other's *jouissance*), while the Lacan "beyond castration" points toward a postdemocratic politics. There are thus three phases in the relationship of Lacan toward the tension between Kant and Hegel: from the universal-Hegelian self-mediation in the totality of the Symbolic, he passes to the Kantian notion of the transcendent Thing that resists this mediation, and then, in an additional twist, he transposes the gap that separates all signifying traces from the Otherness into the immanence itself, as its inherent cut.

One should thus focus on the way the three terms of the triad Real-Imaginary-Symbolic are inherently interwoven: the entire triad reflects itself within each of its three elements. There are three modalities of the Real: the "real Real" (the horrifying Thing, the primordial object, from Irma's throat to the Alien), the "symbolic Real" (the real as consistency:

---

[110] It was Bernard Baas who articulated in detail such a Kantian reading of Lacan. See Bernard Baas, *De la chose à l'objet* (Leuven: Peeters, 1998).

the signifier reduced to a senseless formula, like the quantum physics formulas that can no longer be translated back into, or related to, the everyday experience of our life-world), and the "imaginary Real" (the mysterious *je ne sais quoi*, the unfathomable "something" on account of which the sublime dimension shines through an ordinary object). The Real is thus effectively all three dimensions at the same time: the abyssal vortex that ruins every consistent structure, the mathematized consistent structure of reality, the fragile pure appearance. And, in a strictly homologous way, there are three modalities of the Symbolic: the real (the signifier reduced to a senseless formula), the imaginary (the Jungian "symbols"), and the symbolic (speech, meaningful language). There are also three modalities of the Imaginary: the real (fantasy, which is precisely an imaginary scenario occupying the place of the Real), the imaginary (the image as such in its fundamental function of a decoy), and the symbolic (again, the Jungian "symbols" or New Age archetypes). Far from being reduced to the traumatic void of the Thing resisting symbolization, the Lacanian Real thus also designates the senseless symbolic consistency (of the "matheme"), as well as the pure appearance irreducible to its causes ("the real of an illusion"). Consequently, Lacan not only supplements the Real as the void of the absent cause with the Real as consistency but he also he adds a third term, namely, that of the Real as pure appearing, which is also operative in Badiou in the guise of what he calls the "minimal difference" that arises when we subtract all fake particular differences, from the minimal "pure" difference between figure and background in Malevich's *White Square on Black Surface* up to the unfathomable minimal difference between Christ and other men.

In his *Le siècle*,[111] Badiou deploys two modes of what he calls the "passion of the Real" as the defining passion of the twentieth century: that of "purification" (of violently discarding the deceiving layers of false reality to arrive at the kernel of the real) and that of "subtraction" (of isolating the minimal difference that becomes palpable in the symptomal point of the existing order of reality). Is it not, then, that we should supplement Badiou's two passions of the Real (the passion of purification and the passion of subtraction) with that of scientific-theoretical *formalization* as the third approach to the Real? The Real can be isolated through violent purification, the shedding away of false layers of deceptive reality; it can be isolated as the singular universal that marks the minimal difference; and, it can also be isolated in the guise of a formalization that renders the subjectless "knowledge in the Real." It is easy to discern here again the triad of Real, Imaginary, Symbolic: the Real attained through violent

---

[111] See Alain Badiou, *Le siècle* (Paris: Editions du Seuil, forthcoming.

purification, the Imaginary of the minimal difference, and the Symbolic of the pure formal matrix.

The political consequences of this deadlock are crucial. The limitation of Badiou is nowhere more perceptible than in his positive political program, which can be summed as unconditional fidelity to the "axiom of equality": statements that contradict this axiom (like any linking of political rights to belonging to a certain race or ethnic group) should be rendered impossible, publicly unutterable, this axiom should consequently be applied to the rights of immigrant workers, women. . . . However, is this axiom not much closer to Jacobin revolutionary radicalism than to marxism? Did Marx not claim again and again that the whole topic of equality is a bourgeois ideological topic par excellence? The opposition between formal equality and factual inequality, the way the very form of equality sustains the inequality of exploitation, is at the very core of the market logic, and the way toward its overcoming does not lead through "true equality" but through suspending the underlying conditions of this tension between equality and inequality, namely, the market economy. And is not this insight today more actual than ever? Does globalization not mean, among other things, that workers all around the world are progressively "equalized," which is why multinational capital, far from being racist and sectarian, happily asserts and practices the equality of, say, an Indonesian and an American worker.

In *Le siècle,* Badiou seems to oscillate between the plea for a direct fidelity to the twentieth-century "passion of the Real" and the prospect of passing from the politics of purification to the politics of subtraction. While he makes it fully clear that the horrors of the twentieth century, from the Holocaust to gulag, are a necessary outcome of the purification-mode of the "passion of the Real," and while he admits that protests against it are fully legitimate (see his admiration for Varlam Shalamov's *Kolyma Tales*), he nonetheless stops short of renouncing it. Why? Because *the consequent following of the logic of subtraction would have forced him to abandon the very frame of the opposition between Being and Event.* Within the logic of subtraction, the Event is not external to the order of Being but located in the "minimal difference" inherent to the order of Being itself. Here, the parallel is strict between Badiou's two versions of the "passion of the Real" and the two main versions of the Real in Lacan: the Real as the destructive vortex, the inaccessible/impossible hard kernel that we cannot approach too much (if we get too close to it, we get burned, as in Nikita Mikhalkov's *Burnt by the Sun,* the movie about a Soviet hero-general caught in a Stalinist purge and "burnt by the sun" of the Russian Revolution), and the Real as the pure *Schein* of a minimal difference, as another dimension that shines through between the gaps of the inconsistent reality.

If Badiou were to accomplish this step, he would, perhaps, choose to conceive of the twenty-first century as the displaced repetition of the twentieth century. After the (self)destructive climax of the logic of purification, the passion of the Real should be reinvented as the politics of subtraction. There is a necessity in this blunder: subtraction is possible only after the fiasco of purification, as its repetition, in which the "passion of the Real" is sublated, freed of its (self)destructive potential. In the absence of this step, Badiou is left with only two options: either to remain faithful to the destructive ethics of purification, or to take refuge in the Kantian distinction between a normative regulative Ideal and the constituted order of reality—say, to claim that the Stalinist *désastre* occurs, that the (self)destructive violence explodes, when the gap that forever separates the Event from the order of Being is closed, when the Truth-Event is posited as fully realized in the order of Being.

Along these lines, Badiou recently[112] proposed as (one of) the definition(s) of Evil: the total *forcing of the Unnameable,* the accomplished naming of it, the dream of total Nomination ("everything can be named within the field of the given generic truth procedure")—the fiction (the Kantian regulative Idea?) of the accomplished truth-procedure is taken for reality (it starts to function as constitutive). According to Badiou, what such forcing obliterates is the inherent limitation of the generic truth-procedure (its undecidability, indiscernability . . .): the accomplished truth destroys itself; the accomplished political truth turns into totalitarianism. The ethics of Truth is thus the ethics of the respect for the unnameable Real that cannot be forced.[113] However, the problem here is how to avoid the Kantian reading of this limitation. Although Badiou rejects the ontological-transcendental status of finitude as the ultimate horizon of our existence, is his limitation of truth-procedure ultimately not grounded in the fact that it is finite? Significantly, Badiou, the great critic of the notion of totalitarianism, resorts here to this notion in a way very similar to the Kantian liberal critics of the "Hegelian totalitarianism" a subject, the operator of the infinite truth-procedure, who, in an act of pure decision or choice, proclaims the Event as the starting point of reference of a truth-procedure (statements like "I love you," "Christ has arisen from the dead"). So, although Badiou subordinates subjectivity to the infinite truth-procedure, the place of this procedure is

---

[112] At a conference for the European Graduate School in Saas Fee, August 2002.

[113] It also seems problematic to conceive of "Stalinism" as a too radical "forcing" of the order of being (the existing society). The paradox of the 1928 "Stalinist revolution" was rather that, in all its brutal radicality, *it was not radical enough* in effectively transforming the social substance. Its brutal destructiveness has to be read as an impotent *passage à l'acte.* Far from simply standing for a total forcing of the unnameable Real on behalf of the Truth, the Stalinist "totalitarianism" instead designates the attitude of absolutely ruthless "pragmatism," of manipulating and sacrificing all "principles" on behalf of maintaining power.

silently constrained by the subject's finitude. And, does Badiou, *the* anti-Levinas, with this topic of the respect for the unnameable, not come dangerously close precisely to the Levinasian notion of the respect for Otherness—the notion that is, against all appearances, totally inoperative at the political level? Recall the well-known fiasco of Levinas when, a week after the Sabra and Shatila massacres in Beirut, he participated in a radio broadcast with Shlomo Malka and Alain Finkelkraut. Malka asked him the obvious "Levinasian" question: "Emmanuel Levinas, you are the philosopher of the 'other.' Isn't history, isn't politics the very site of the encounter with the 'other,' and for the Israeli, isn't the 'other' above all the Palestinian?" To this, Levinas answered:

> My definition of the other is completely different. The other is the neighbor, who is not necessary kin, but who can be. And in that sense, if you're for the other, you're for the neighbor. But if your neighbor attacks another neighbor or treats him unjustly, what can you do? Then alterity takes on another character, in alterity we can find an enemy, or at least then we are faced with the problem of knowing who is right and who is wrong, who is just and who is unjust. There are people who are wrong.[114]

The problem with these lines is not their potential Zionist anti-Palestinian attitude but, on the contrary, the unexpected shift from high theory to vulgar commonsensical reflections. What Levinas is basically saying is that, as a principle, respect for alterity is unconditional (the highest sort of respect), but, when faced with a concrete other, one should nonetheless see if he is a friend or an enemy. In short, in practical politics, the respect for alterity strictly *means nothing*. No wonder, then, that Levinas also perceived alterity as a radical strangeness posing a threat, a point at which hospitality is suspended. This is clear from the following passage about the "yellow peril" from what is arguably his weirdest text, "The Russo-Chinese Debate and the Dialectic" (1960), a comment on the Soviet-Chinese conflict:

> The yellow peril! It is not racial, it is spiritual. It does not involve inferior values; it involves a radical strangeness, a stranger to the weight of its past, from where there does not filter any familiar voice or inflection, a lunar or Martian past.[115]

Does this not recall Heidegger's insistence, throughout the 1930s, that the main task of Western thought today is to defend the Greek breakthrough, the founding gesture of the "West," the overcoming of the prephilosophical, mythical, "Asiatic" universe, to struggle against the renewed "Asiatic" threat—the greatest opposite of the West is "the mythical

---

[114] Emmunuel Levinas, *The Levinas Reader* (Oxford: Blackwell, 1989), p. 294.
[115] Emmanuel Levinas, *Les imprèvus de l'histoire* (Saint Clément: Fata Morgana, 1994), p. 172.

in general and the Asiatic in particular"?[116] Back to Badiou: what all this means is that there is a Kantian problem with Badiou that is grounded in his dualism of Being and Event and that has to be surpassed. The only way out of this predicament is to assert that the unnameable Real is not an external limitation but an *absolutely inherent* limitation. Truth is a generic procedure that cannot comprise its own concept-name which would totalize it (as Lacan puts it, "there is no meta-language," or, as Heidegger puts it, "the name for a name is always lacking"—and this lack, far from being a limitation of language, is its positive condition, that is, it is only because through this lack that we have language). So, like the Lacanian Real that is not external to the Symbolic but makes it non-all from within (as Laclau explains it, in an antagonism, the external limit coincides with the internal one), the unnameable is inherent to the domain of names. (This is why, for Badiou as for Heidegger, poetry is the experience/articulation of the limits of the potency of language, of the limits of what we can force through and with language.) *This* and only this is the proper passage from Kant to Hegel: not the passage from limited/incomplete to full/completed nomination ("absolute knowledge") but the passage of the very limit of nomination from the exterior to the interior.

The materialist solution is thus that the Event is *nothing but* its own inscription into the order of Being, a cut/rupture in the order of Being on account of which Being cannot ever form a consistent All. There is no Beyond of Being that inscribes itself into the order of Being. There "is" nothing but the order of Being. One should recall here yet again the paradox of Einstein's general theory of relativity, in which matter does not curve space but is an effect of space's own curvature. An Event does not curve the space of Being through its inscription into it: on the contrary, an Event is *nothing but* this curvature of the space of Being. "All there is" is the interstice, the nonself-coincidence, of Being, namely, the ontological nonclosure of the order of Being. What this means at the ontological level is that, ultimately, one should reject Badiou's notion of mathematics (the theory of pure multiplicity) as the only consistent ontology (science of Being): if mathematics is ontology, then, to account for the *gap* between Being and Event, one either remains stuck in dualism *or* one has to dismiss the Event as an ultimately illusory local occurrence within the encompassing order of Being. Against this notion of multiplicity, one should assert as the ultimate ontological given the gap that separates the One from within.

---

[116] Martin Heidegger, *Schelling's Treatise on Human Freedom* (Athens: Ohio University Press, 1985), p. 146.

Consequences

1

SCIENCE: COGNITIVISM WITH FREUD

"Autopoiesis"

The central problem of Deleuze, that of the emergence of the New, is deeply Kantian-Hegelian. It is related to the question "How is a free act possible within the causal network of material interdependences?", because something really New can emerge only if the determinative power of the linear causal chain is not complete. Here is Mario Bunge's concise critical formulation of a "world running on a strictly causal pattern":

> If the joint action of several causes is always an external juxtaposition, a superposition, and in no case a synthesis having traits of its own, and if the hypothetical patients on which the causal agents act are passive things incapable of spontaneity or self-activity—incapable, in short, of adding something of their own to the causal bond—then it follows that, in a sense, *effects preexist in their causes.* According to this extreme but consistent doctrine on the nature of causation, *only old things come out of change;* processes can give rise to objects new in number or new in some quantitative aspects, not however new in kind, or, again, no new qualities can emerge.[1]

This bring us to Deleuze's fundamental paradox: the implication of his absolute immanentism, of his rejection of any transcendence, is precisely that an effect can transcend its cause, or—another aspect of the same problematic—that relations are external to the objects that relate to each other (recall Deleuze's reading of Hitchcock!). This externality of relations is grounded in the fact that, in a set of elements, the number of subsets we can form is larger than the number of the elements

[1] Mario Bunge, *Causality and Modern Science* (New York: Dover Press, 1979), p. 203.

themselves. And the most succinct definition of the excessive element, the "dark precursor," is precisely that of a pseudo element that, within the multitude of elements, holds the place of relations. Say, according to Fredric Jameson's reading of *Wuthering Heights,* Heathcliff is not one among the novel's characters but a kind of zero-element, a purely structural function of the "vanishing mediator," a mechanism for mediating the two series, that of the old organic-patriarchal social relations and that of the modern capitalist relations, a point of passage between the two:

> Heathcliff can no longer be considered the hero or the protagonist in any sense of the word. He is rather, from the very beginning, . . . something like a mediator or a catalyst, designed to restore the fortunes and to rejuvenate the anemic temperament of the two families.[2]

The Deleuzian excess of relations is thus the space of freedom as that of *reflexive* relations, of relating to relations—the excess over the linear network of causal relations, the way the subject relates to its conditions and causes (assuming or rejecting them). Already in Kant I am determined by causes, but I retroactively determine which causes will determine me. In short, does not Deleuze implicitly rely here on what is usually referred to as the Kantian "incorporation thesis"? We subjects are passively affected by pathological objects and motivations; but, in a reflexive way, we ourselves have the minimal power to accept (or reject) being affected in this way. Or, to risk a Deleuze-Hegelian formulation, the subject is a fold of reflexivity by means of which I retroactively determine the causes allowed to determine me, or, at least, the *mode* of this linear determination. "Freedom" is thus inherently retroactive. At its most elementary, it is not simply a free act that, out of nowhere, starts a new causal link, but rather a retroactive act of endorsing which link/sequence of necessities will determine me. Here, one should add a Hegelian twist to Spinoza: freedom is not simply "recognized/known necessity" but recognized/assumed necessity, the necessity constituted/actualized through this recognition. This excess of the effect over its causes thus also means that the effect is retroactively the cause of its cause—this temporal loop is the minimal structure of life (on this point, see the work of Francisco Varela). Recall as well Borges's precise formulation of the relationship between Kafka and the multitude of his precursors, from old Chinese authors to Robert Browning:

> Kafka's idiosyncrasy, in greater or lesser degree, is present in each of these writings, but if Kafka had not written we would not perceive it; that is to say, it would not exist. . . . Each writer *creates* his precursors. His work modifies our conception of the past, as it will modify the future.[3]

---

[2] Fredric Jameson, *The Political Unconscious* (London: Routledge, 2002), pp. 113–14.
[3] Jorge Luis Borges, *Other Inquisitions: 1937–52* (New York: Washington Square Press, 1966), p. 113.

The properly dialectical solution of the dilemma of "Is it really there, in the source, or did we only read it into the source?" is thus that it is there, but we can only perceive and state this retroactively, from today's perspective, and this retroactive causality, exerted by the effect itself upon its causes, is the minimal sine qua non of freedom. Is it not that, without this freedom, the effects would, in a way, not only preexist *in* their causes but also directly *preexist* their causes? That is to say, without the excess/gap between cause and effect, the effect would preexist its cause in the sense that it would already be given in advance of its cause, regulating the deployment of the causal link as its hidden telos—teleology is the truth of linear mechanical causality (as Hegel put it). Going even a step further, one should paradoxically claim that this assertion of the excess of the effect over its cause, of the possibility of freedom, is the fundamental assertion of Deleuze's *materialism*. That is to say, the point is not just that there is an immaterial excess over the material reality of multiple bodies but that this excess is immanent to the level of the bodies themselves. If we subtract this immaterial excess, we do not get "pure reductionist materialism" but instead get a covert idealism. No wonder that Descartes, the first to formulate the tenets of modern scientific materialism, was also the first to formulate the basic modern idealist principle of subjectivity: "There is a fully constituted material reality of bodies and nothing else" is effectively an *idealist* position.

It is interesting to note how the debate on "supervenient causality" in brain sciences echoes the Deleuzian theme of quasi cause. Was it not already Deleuze himself who linked the Sense-Event to the system-theory notion of emergent qualities? Is not the Sense-Event something that *emerges* out of the complex network of corporeal causes?[4] Of course, the following is the key question here: is the status of consciousness purely epiphenomenal from the causal standpoint or does it display a causality of its own? It would be interesting to confront Deleuze with these naive questions: is the level of Sense-Event just a sterile effect, a theater of shadows? Does it somehow affect the level of the corporeal network of causes or can this latter level be described without regard for the flow of Sense?

When we say that consciousness supervenes or, more strongly, that it emerges, does this mean that its own specific causal power can also affect the "lower" levels out of which it emerged? Or, to quote Hasker, the notion of "downward" causal influence means that "the behavior of 'lower' levels—that is, of the components of which the 'higher-level' structure consists—is different than it would otherwise be, because of

[4] Is not the term "emergent property" all too often used as a pseudo concept, as a category with an entirely negative content—it merely names our ignorance? We somehow see that, without any external help or intervention, order emerges out of a chaotic interaction, and, without knowing how this occurs, we call it "emergent property."

the influence of the new property that emerges in consequence of the higher-level organisation."[5] Let us say that I perform certain physical gestures (raising my hand, etc.) as the result of my decision to greet a friend. Can this physical gesture also be fully causally explained at the "lower" level of the physical interaction of the components of my body, in the abstraction of the "higher" level of my conscious intentions?

Underlying all these considerations is the ultimate difficulty of the notion of organism: if we are effectively to account for the autonomous "quasi" causality of the higher level, it should be a minimally *retroactive* causality, a self-relating causality that "runs backward" in time, or, as Hegel would have put it, the act of "positing the presuppositions." As Kant already knew, freedom does not mean simply a cause that supplements material causes but means a reflexive cause that determines which (material) causes will determine me. Freedom means that I am never entirely a victim of circumstances: I always dispose of a minimum of freedom to determine which circumstances will determine me (again, the "incorporation thesis").[6]

The solution lies precisely in the notion of the noncompleteness of physical causality: freedom retroactively determines the causal chain that comes to determine me, and this minimal space of choice is sustained by the inherent indeterminacy of the physical processes themselves. In a substantial sense, freedom means, of course, that the causal role of consciousness is not purely transitive, that it can "cause things it isn't caused to cause,"[7] that, as Kant himself put it, it can start a new causal line/chain ex nihilo. However, this "nihilo" is located in physical reality itself, as its causal incompleteness. The big argument of those who want to undermine materialism is "why the physical isn't closed": they aim to demonstrate that, for a priori reasons, the chain of physical causes is not complete, self-enclosed, all-explaining, namely, that there must be room for another mode of causality. Here, however, a reference to Lacan's logic of "non-All" could be of some help. What if we read the incompleteness of the (physical) causal links as the obverse of the fact that there is no exception to them, no other causality? And, what if, on the contrary, we conceive the completeness/closure of the physical as relying on, as involving, a metaphysical exception, a divine or spiritual ground? It is the gap in physical causality as such that opens up the space of freedom, without being filled with another positive causality—as Deleuze expressed it, the only causality "beyond and above" the corporeal one is that of the immaterial quasi cause.

[5] William Hasker, *The Emergent Self* (Ithaca, N.Y.: Cornell University Press, 1999), p. 175.
[6] See Henry Allison, *Kant's Theory of Freedom* (Cambridge: Cambridge University Press, 1990).
[7] William Hasker, op. cit., p. 177.

When Chalmers writes in his argument against the reductive explanation of consciousness that "even if we knew every last detail about the physics of the universe—the configuration, causation, and evolution among all the fields and particles in the spatio-temporal manifold—*that* information would not lead us to postulate the existence of conscious experience,"[8] he commits the standard Kantian mistake: such a total knowledge is strictly nonsensical, epistemologically *and* ontologically. His reasoning is the obverse of the vulgar determinist notion articulated in marxism by Bukharin, who wrote that, if we were to know the entirety of physical reality, we would also be able to predict precisely the emergence of a revolution. More generally, this line of reasoning—consciousness as an excess/surplus over physical totality—is misleading since it has to evoke a meaningless hyperbole. When we imagine the Whole of reality, there is no longer any place for consciousness (and subjectivity). There are, as we have already seen, only two options left open here: either subjectivity is an illusion or reality is *in itself* (not only epistemologically) not-All.

In one of the unexpected encounters of contemporary philosophy with Hegel, the "Christian materialist" Peter van Inwagen developed the idea that material objects like automobiles, chairs, computers, and so forth simply *do not exist*. Say, a chair is not effectively, for itself, a chair—all we have is a collection of "simples" (i.e., more elementary objects "arranged chairwise"); so, although a chair functions as a chair, it is composed of a multitude (wood pieces, nails, cushions, etc.) that are, in themselves, totally indifferent toward this arrangement (there is, stricto sensu, no "whole" a nail is here a part of). It is only with organisms that we have a Whole. Here, the unity is minimally "for itself"; parts effectively interact.[9] As it was developed already by Lynn Margulis, the elementary form of life, a cell, is characterized precisely by such a minimum of self-relating, a minimum exclusively through which the limit between Inside and Outside that characterize an organism can emerge. And, as Hegel put it, thought is only a further development of this For-itself.

In biology, for instance, we have, at the level of reality, only bodily interacting. "Life proper" emerges only at the minimally "ideal" level, as an immaterial event that provides the form of unity of the living body as the "same" in the incessant change of its material components. The basic problem of evolutionary cognitivism—that of the emergence of the ideal life-pattern—is none other than the old metaphysical enigma of the relationship between chaos and order, between the Multiple and

8 David Chalmers, *The Conscious Mind* (Oxford: Oxford University Press, 1996), p. 101.
9 Peter van Inwagen, *Material Beings* (Ithaca, N.Y.: Cornell University Press, 1990).

the One, between parts and their whole. How can we get "order for free," that is, how can order emerge out of initial disorder? How can we account for a whole that is larger than the mere sum of its parts? How can a One with a distinct self-identity emerge out of the interaction of its multiple constituents? A series of contemporary researchers, from Lynn Margulis to Francisco Varela, assert that the true problem is not how an organism and its environs interact or connect but, rather, the opposite one: how does a distinct self-identical organism emerge out of its environs? How does a cell form the membrane that separates its inside from its outside? The true problem is thus not how an organism adapts to its environs but how it is that there is something, a distinct entity, that must adapt itself in the first place. And, it is here, at this crucial point, that today's biological language starts to resemble, quite uncannily, the language of Hegel. When Varela, for example, explains his notion of autopoiesis, he repeats, almost verbatim, the Hegelian notion of life as a teleological, self-organizing entity. His central notion, that of a loop or bootstrap, points toward the Hegelian *Setzung der Voraussetzungen:*

> Autopoiesis attempts to define the uniqueness of the emergence that pro-
> duces life in its fundamental cellular form. It's specific to the cellular level.
> There's a circular or network process that engenders a paradox: a self-
> organizing network of biochemical reactions produces molecules, which do
> something specific and unique: they create a boundary, a membrane, which
> constrains the network that has produced the constituents of the membrane.
> This is a logical bootstrap, a loop: a network produces entities that create a
> boundary, which constrains the network that produces the boundary. This
> bootstrap is precisely what's unique about cells. A self-distinguishing entity
> exists when the bootstrap is completed. This entity has produced its own
> boundary. It doesn't require an external agent to notice it, or to say, "I'm
> here." It is, by itself, a self-distinction. It bootstraps itself out of a soup of
> chemistry and physics.[10]

The conclusion to be drawn is thus that the only way to account for the emergence of the distinction between the "inside" and "outside" constitutive of a living organism is to posit a kind of self-reflexive reversal by means of which, to put it in Hegelese, the One of an organism as a Whole retroactively "posits" as its result, as that which it dominates and regulates, the set of its own causes (i.e., the very multiple process out of which it emerged). In this way—and only in this way—an organism no longer is limited by external conditions but is fundamentally self-limited. Again, as Hegel would have articulated it, life emerges when the external

---

[10] Francisco Varela, "The Emergent Self," in *The Third Culture*, edited by John Brockman (New York: Simon and Schuster, 1996), p. 212.

limitation (of an entity by its environs) turns into self-limitation. This brings us back to the problem of infinity: for Hegel, true infinity does not stand for limitless expansion but stands for active self-limitation (self-determination) in contrast to being-determined-by-the-other. In this precise sense, life (even at its most elementary as a living cell) is the basic form of true infinity since it already involves the minimal loop by means of which a process no longer is simply determined by the Outside of its environs but is itself able to (over)determine the mode of this determination and thus "posits its presuppositions." Infinity acquires its first actual existence the moment a cell's membrane starts to functions as a self-boundary. So, when Hegel includes minerals in the category of "life," as the lowest form of organisms, does he not anticipate Margulis, who also insists on forms of life preceding vegetable and animal life? The further key fact is that we thus obtain a minimum of ideality. A property emerges that is purely virtual and relational, with no substantial identity:

> My sense of self exists because it gives me an interface with the world. I'm "me" for interactions, but my "I" doesn't substantially exist, in the sense that it can't be localized anywhere.... An emergent property, which is produced by an underlying network, is a coherent condition that allows the system in which it exists to interface at that level—that is, with other selves or identities of the same kind. You can never say, "This property is here; it's in this component." In the case of autopoiesis, you can't say that life—the condition of being self-produced—is in this molecule, or in the DNA, or in the cellular membrane, or in the protein. Life is in the configuration and in the dynamical pattern, which is what embodies it as an emergent property.[11]

Here we encounter the minimum of "idealism" that defines the notion of Self. A Self is precisely an entity without any substantial density, without any hard kernel that would guarantee its consistency. If we penetrate the surface of an organism and look deeper and deeper into it, we never encounter some central controlling element that would be its Self, secretly pulling the strings of its organs. The consistency of the Self is thus purely virtual; it is as if it were an Inside that appears only when viewed from the Outside, on the interface-screen—the moment we penetrate the interface and endeavor to grasp the Self "substantially," as it is "in itself," it disappears like sand between our fingers. The materialist reductionists who claim "there really is no self" are thus right, but they nonetheless miss the point. At the level of material reality (inclusive of the psychological reality of "inner experience"), there effectively is no Self. The Self is not the "inner kernel" of an organism but a surface-effect. A "true"

[11] Varela, op. cit., pp. 215–16.

human Self functions, in a sense, like a computer screen: what is "behind" it is nothing but a network of "selfless" neuronal machinery.

Memes, Memes Everywhere

In the 1990s, a Japanese toy called tamagochi was very popular. It reduced the other with whom we communicate (usually a pet animal) to a purely virtual presence on a screen. The game played with it involves acting as if there is a real, living creature behind the screen—we get excited, cry for it, although we know very well that there is nothing behind, just a meaningless digital network. If we take seriously what we just said, we cannot avoid the conclusion that the Other Person with whom we communicate is ultimately also a kind of tamagochi. When we communicate with another subject, we get signals from him, we observe his face as a screen, but, not only do we, partners in communication, never get to know what is "behind the screen"; the same goes for the concerned subject himself (i.e., the subject does not know what lies behind the screen of his very own (self)consciousness, what kind of a Thing he is in the Real). (Self)consciousness is a surface-screen that produces the effect of "depth," of a dimension beneath it. And yet, this dimension is accessible only from the standpoint of the surface, as a kind of surface-effect: if we effectively reach behind the screen, the very effect of the "depth of a person" dissolves. What we are left with is just a set of meaningless processes that are neuronal, biochemical, and so forth. For that reason, the usual polemics about the respective roles of "genes versus environment" (of biology versus cultural influence, of nature versus nurture) in the formation of the subject misses the key dimension, namely, that of the *interface* that both connects and distinguishes the two. The "subject" emerges when the "membrane," the surface that delimits the Inside from the Outside—instead of being just a passive medium of their interaction—starts to function as their active mediator.

The conclusion is then that, even if science defines and starts to manipulate the human genome, this will not enable it to dominate and manipulate human subjectivity. What makes me "unique" is neither my genetic formula nor the way my dispositions were developed due to the influence of the environment but the unique self-relationship emerging out of the interaction between the two. More precisely, even the word "interaction" is not quite adequate here, insofar as it still implies the mutual influence of two given sets of positive conditions (genes and environment), thus failing to cover the crucial feature of *Selbst-Beziehung* (the self-referential loop due to which, in the way I relate to my environment, I never reach the "zero-level" of being passively influenced by it, since, instead, I always-already relate to myself in relating to it, that is, I always-already, with a minimum of "freedom," determine in advance the way I will be determined by the environment, up to the most elementary level of sensible perceptions). The way I "see myself," the imaginary and symbolic features that constitute my "self-image" (or, even more fundamentally, the fantasy that provides the ultimate coordinates of my being), is neither in the genes nor imposed by the environment but in the unique way each subject relates to himself, "chooses himself," in relationship to his environs, as well as to (what he perceives as) his "nature."

We are thus dealing with a kind of "bootstrap" mechanism that cannot be reduced to the interaction of myself as a biological entity and my environment: a third mediating agency emerges (the subject, precisely), that has no positive substantial Being since, in a way, its status is purely "performative" (i.e., it is a kind of self-inflamed flame, nothing but the outcome of its activity—what Fichte called a *Tathandlung*, the pure act of self-referential *Selbst-Setzung*). Yes, I emerge through the interaction between my biological bodily base and my environs—but, what both my environs and my bodily base are is always "mediated" by my activity. It is interesting to note how today's most advanced cognitive scientists take over (or, rather, develop out of their own research) this motif of minimal self-reference that the great German Idealists were trying to formulate in terms of "transcendental spontaneity." So, in the case of human clones (or, already today, of identical twins), what accounts for the uniqueness of each of them is not simply that they were exposed to different environments but the way that each of them formed a unique structure of self-reference out of the interaction between his genetic substance and his environment.

The Deleuzian topic of pseudo cause can thus be correlated to the Hegelian notion of the (retroactive) positing of presuppositions: the direct causality is that of the real interaction of bodies, whereas the pseudo causality is that of retroactively positing the agent's presuppositions, of ideally assuming what is already imposed on the agent.[12] And what if this also accounts for the emergence of the Subject as a free/autonomous agent? The only "real" causality occurs at the bodily level of interacting multitudes, while the Subject acts as a "pseudo cause" that creates events in an autonomous way—again, Deleuze here comes unexpectedly close to Hegel. In the modern sciences, this closed circle of the self-referential "positing [of] the presuppositions," which Hegel already perceived as the fundamental characteristic of a living entity, is designated

---

[12] Compare this with Dupuy's distinction between the linear historical causality and the outbreak of the New that retroactively grounds its own possibility. See Jean-Pierre Dupuy, *Pour un catastrophisme éclairé* (Paris: Editions du Seuil, 2002).

as "autopoiesis": in a kind of retroactive loop, the result (the living entity) generates the very material conditions that engender and sustain it. In the tradition of German Idealism, the living organism's relation to its external other is always-already its self-relationship (i.e., each organism "posits" its presupposed environment).

The problem with this autopoietic notion of life, elaborated by Maturana and Varela in their classic *Autopoiesis and Cognition*,[13] does not reside in the question "Does this notion of autopoiesis effectively overcome the mechanistic paradigm?" but, rather, in the question "how are we to pass from this self-enclosed loop of Life to (Self)Consciousness?" (Self)Consciousness is also reflexive, self-relating in its relationship to an Other. However, this reflexivity is thoroughly different from the organism's self-enclosure. A (self)conscious living being displays what Hegel calls the infinite power of Understanding, of abstract (and abstracting) thought—it is able, in its thoughts, to *tear apart* the organic Whole of Life, to submit it to a mortifying analysis, to reduce the organism to its isolated elements. (Self)Consciousness thus *reintroduces the dimension of DEATH into organic Life:* language itself is a mortifying "mechanism" that colonizes the Organism. (This, according to Lacan, is what Freud was after in his hypothesis on the "death drive.") It was (again) already Hegel who formulated this tension (among other places) at the beginning of the chapter on Self-Consciousness in his *Phenomenology of Spirit,* in which he opposed the two forms of "Life" qua self-relating through relating to the Other: (organic-biological) *life* and (*self*)*consciousness.* The true problem is not (only) how to pass from preorganic matter to life but how life itself can break its autopoietic closure and ex-statically start to relate to its external Other (where this ex-static openness can also turn into the mortifying objectivization of Understanding). The problem is not Life but the Death-in-Life ("tarrying with the negative") of the speaking organism.

Within the history of biology, this topic of autopoiesis is part of the "idealist" tendency of *hylozoism:* everything that exists, the whole of nature, is alive—it suffers and enjoys. There is no death in this universe; what happens in the case of "death" is just that a particular coordination of living elements disintegrates, whereas Life goes on, both the Life of the Whole and the life of the elementary constituents of reality. (The Sadean "absolute crime" aims at destroying precisely this second life that survives biological death.)[14] We find this position from Aristotle (his notion of

---

[13] See Humberto R. Maturana and Francisco J. Varela, *Autopoiesis and Cognition: The Realization of the Living* (Dordrecht: D. Reidel, 1980).

[14] I rely here on Jacques-Alain Miller, "Lacanian Biology and the Event of the Body," *Lacanian Ink* 18 (2001): 6–29.

soul as the One-Form of the body) and traditional Stoicism through Denis Diderot (for whom even stones feel pain; it's just that we don't hear them—reminding us of the ingenious Patricia Highsmith short story about a woman who was able to hear the trees shouting when being cut down) and the Schellingian Romantic notion of the World-Soul, up to the whole panoply of today's theories, from the notion of Gaia (Earth as a living organism) to Deleuze, the last great philosopher of the One, the "body without organs" that thrives in the multitude of its modalities. One should also add to this series thinkers as different as Francisco Varela, Maurice Merleau-Ponty, and Heidegger, who all search for the unity of body and subject, the point at which the subject directly "is" his or her body.

Against this tradition stands the Cartesian tradition to which Lacan fully subscribes: the body exists in the order of *having*—*I am not* my body, *I have* it, and this gap renders possible the gnostic dream of Virtual Reality in which I will be able to shift from one to another virtual body. For Lacan, the key implication of the Cartesian reduction of the body to *res extensa* is that *jouissance* is evacuated from bodies, in contrast to hylozoism, in which the body *enjoys itself*: "ça jouit," as Lacan and Deleuze put it. In today's science and technology, a "body in pieces" is emerging, a composite of replaceable organs (pacemakers, artificial limbs, transposed skin, heart, liver, and other transplants—up to the prospect of genetically cultivated reserve organs). This trend culminates in today's biogenetics: the lesson of the genome project is that the true center of a living body is not its Soul but its genetic algorithm. It was already Weismann, one of Freud's key references, who, more than one hundred years ago, established the distinction between an organism's "mortal" and "immortal" parts: its "soma," the external body-envelope that grows and disintegrates, and the "germ-cells," the genetic component that reproduces itself, remaining the same from one to another generation. Richard Dawkins provided the ultimate formula of this distinction with his notion of the "the selfish gene": it is not that individual organisms use their genes to replicate themselves; it is, on the contrary, individual organisms that are the means for the genes to reproduce themselves.

The properly *materialist* problem is, How does *subjectivity* emerge in this reproductive cycle of genes? The line from germ to genome radicalizes the notion of the body within a body, of the real "immortal" body persisting, reproducing itself, through the generation and corruption of passing mortal bodies. The Lacanian subject is neither the organic Form-Soul-One of the body, nor the germ-genome, the body within the body. The emergence of subjectivity introduces a complication here. Richard Dawkins tried to elaborate a parallel between genes and memes—in the same way bodies are just means for the reproduction of genes, individuals are just means for the propagation, for the reproduction and expansion, of memes qua elementary units of meaning.[15] The problem here is that, with the symbolic order, the passing individual is not just S, the soma, the disposable envelope, but $, the barred subject, the self-relating negativity that perverts/inverts the natural order, introducing a radical "pathological" imbalance. It is the individual who uses the memes for his or her own purposes. "Memes" (the symbolic tradition) are a secondary attempt to reintroduce a kind of stability and order, to reestablish the proper subordination of the particular to the universal, that was disturbed by the emergence of subjectivity: "subject" is the mortal vanishing accident that posits itself as an infinite end-in-itself.

One should be careful not to miss the specific level of the notion of memes. A "meme" spreads neither because of its actual beneficial effects upon its bearers (say, those who adopt it are more successful in life and thus gain an upper hand in the struggle for survival) nor because of its characteristics that make it subjectively attractive to its bearers (one would naturally tend to give privilege to the idea that promises happiness over the idea that promises nothing but misery and renunciation). Like a computer virus, the meme proliferates simply by programming its own retransmission. Recall the classic example of two missionaries working in a politically stable and opulent country. One says, "The end is near—repent or you will suffer immensely," whereas the other's message is just to enjoy a happy life. Although the second one's message is much more attractive and beneficent, the first one will win—why? Because, if you really believe that the end is near, you will exert a tremendous effort to convert as many people as possible, whereas the other belief does not require such an extreme engagement in proselytizing. What is so unsettling about this notion is that we, humans endowed with mind, will, and an experience of meaning, are nonetheless unwitting victims of a "thought contagion"[16] that operates blindly, spreading itself like a computer virus. No wonder that, when talking about memes, Dennett regularly resorts to the same metaphors as Lacan apropos of language: in both cases, we are dealing with a parasite that penetrates and occupies the human individual, using it for its own purposes. And, effectively, does "memetics" not (re)discover the notion of a specific symbolic level that operates outside (and, consequently, cannot be reduced to) the standard couple of objective biological facts (beneficent "real" effects) and subjective experience (the attraction of the meaning of a meme)? In a

[15] See Richard Dawkins, *The Selfish Gene* (Oxford: Oxford University Press, 1989).
[16] See Aaron Lynch, *Thought Contagion* (New York: Basic Books, 1996).

liminal case, an idea can spread even if, in the long term, it brings only destruction to its bearers and is even experienced as unattractive.

Is there not a surprising parallel between this notion of memes and the Marxist-Hegelian notion of alienation? In the same way memes, misperceived by us, subjects, as means of our communication, effectively run the show (they use *us* to reproduce and multiply themselves), productive forces, which appear to us as means to satisfy our needs and desires, effectively run the show. The true aim of the process, its end-in-itself, is the development of the productive forces, and the satisfaction of our needs and desires (i.e., what appears to us as the goal) is effectively just the means for the development of the productive forces. This reversal, unbearable to our narcissism, is paradigmatic of modern science, of its production of knowledge that is, in a way, too traumatic to be incorporated into the beliefs which structure our daily lives. Already, quantum physics can no longer be "understood" (its results cannot be integrated into our everyday view of reality). The same goes for biogenetics. Although we accept its truth, we simultaneously maintain toward it the attitude of fetishist disavowal. We refuse to believe *not in a religious doctrine beyond scientific knowledge but in what scientific knowledge itself is telling us about ourselves.*

Against Hyphen-Ethics

What is false with today's discussion concerning the "ethical consequences of biogenetics" (along with similar matters) is that it is rapidly turning into what Germans call *Bindenstrich-Ethik,* the ethics of the hyphen—technology-ethics, environment-ethics, and so on. This ethics does have a role to play, a role homologous to that of the "provisional ethic" Descartes mentions at the beginning of his *Discourse on Method.* When we engage on a new path, full of dangers and shattering new insights, we need to stick to old established rules as a practical guide for our daily lives, although we are well aware that the new insights will compel us to provide a fresh foundation for our entire ethical edifice (in Descartes's case, this new foundation was provided by Kant, in his ethics of subjective autonomy). Today we are in the same predicament: the "provisional ethics" cannot replace the need for a thorough reflection of the emerging New.

In short, what gets lost here, in this hyphen-ethics, is simply ethics as such. The problem is not that universal ethics gets dissolved in particular topics but, on the contrary, that particular scientific breakthroughs are directly confronted with the old humanist "values" (say, how biogenetics affects our sense of dignity and autonomy). This, then, is the choice we are confronting today: either we choose the typically postmodern stance of reticence (let's not go to the end, let's keep a proper distance toward the scientific Thing so that this Thing will not draw us into its black hole, destroying all our moral and human notions), or we dare to "tarry with the negative (*das Verweilen beim Negativen*)," that is, we dare to fully assume the consequences of scientific modernity, with the wager that "our Mind is a genome" will also function as an infinite judgment.

The main consequence of the scientific breakthroughs in biogenetics is the end of nature. Once we know the rules of its construction, natural organisms are transformed into objects amenable to manipulation. Nature, human and inhuman, is thus "desubstantialized," deprived of its impenetrable density, of what Heidegger called "earth." Biogenetics, with its reduction of the human psyche itself to an object of technological manipulation, is therefore effectively a kind of empirical instantiation of what Heidegger perceived as the "danger" inherent to modern technology. Crucial here is the interdependence of man and nature: by reducing man to just another natural object whose properties can be manipulated, what we lose is not (only) humanity but *nature itself*. In this sense, Francis Fukuyama is right. Humanity itself relies on some notion of "human nature" as what we inherited and was simply given to us, the impenetrable dimension in/of ourselves into which we are born/thrown. The paradox is thus that that there is man only insofar as there is impenetrable inhuman nature (Heidegger's "earth").

How, then, do we react to this threat? Recall the well-known case of Huntington's disease. The gene directly responsible for it was isolated, and each of us can learn precisely not only if he will get Huntington's but also when he will get it. It depends on a genetic transcription mistake, the stuttering repetition of the "word" CAG in the middle of this gene. The age at which the madness will appear depends strictly and implacably on the number of repetitions of CAG in one place in this gene (if there are forty repetitions, you will get the first symptoms at fifty-nine, if forty-one, at fifty-four, if fifty, at twenty-seven . . .). Good living, bodily fitness, the best medicine, healthy food, as well as family love and support can do nothing about it: "It is pure fatalism, undiluted by environmental variability."[17] There are, as yet, no cures; we can do nothing about it. So, what should we do when we know that we can submit ourselves to testing and thus acquire a knowledge that, if positive, tells us exactly when we will go mad and die? Can one imagine a clearer situation of "traversing the fantasy" and being confronted with the utterly meaningless Real of a contingency determining our life? No wonder

[17] Matt Ridley, *Genome* (New York: Perennial, 2000), p. 64.

that the majority of people (including the scientist who identified this gene) choose ignorance. This ignorance is not simply negative, since its void opens up the place for fantasizing. Furthermore, with the prospect of biogenetic interventions opened up by the access to the genome, the species freely changes/redefines *itself*, its own coordinates; the access to the genome effectively emancipates humankind from the constraints of a finite species, from its enslavement to the "selfish genes." This emancipation, however, comes at a price. During a talk in Marburg, Habermas repeated his warnings against biogenetic manipulations with humans:

> With interventions into man's genetic inheritance, the domination over nature reverts into an act of taking-control-over-oneself, which changes our generic-ethical self-understanding and can disturb the necessary conditions for an autonomous way of life and universalistic understanding of morals.[18]

Habermas sees two threats lurking here. First, such interventions blur the borderline between what we made and what grew up spontaneously, thereby affecting the individual's self-understanding. How will an adolescent react upon learning that his "spontaneous" (say, aggressive or peaceful) dispositions are the result of others' intentional intervention into his genetic code? Will this not undermine the very heart of his identity as a person, namely, the notion that we develop our moral identity through *Bildung*, the painful struggle to form/educate one's natural dispositions? Ultimately, the prospect of direct biogenetic interventions renders the very notion of education meaningless. Second, at the intersubjective level, such biogenetic interventions will give birth to asymmetrical relations between those who are "spontaneously" human and those whose characteristics were artificially manipulated: some people will appear as privileged creators of others. At the most elementary level, this affects our sexual identity. What is at stake here is not only the possibility of parents choosing the sex of their offspring but also the status of sex-changing operations. Up until now, it was possible to justify them by evoking the gap between one's biological and one's psychic sexual identity. When a biological man experiences himself as a woman trapped in a man's body, why shouldn't (s)he be allowed to change her biological sex and thus introduce balance into her sexual and emotional life? However, the prospect of biogenetic manipulation opens up the much more radical possibility of manipulating psychic identity itself.

Although this argumentation is impeccable in its simplicity, there is one big problem with it: does the very fact of the possibility of biogenetic manipulations not retroactively change the self-understanding of ourselves as "natural" beings, in the sense that we now experience our

[18] Quoted from Thorsten Jantschek, "Ein ausgezehrter Hase," *Die Zeit*, 5 July 2001, Feuilleton, p. 26.

"natural" dispositions themselves as something "mediated," not simply as something immediately given but as something that can be in principle manipulated (and is thus simply contingent)? The key point here is that there is no return to the preceding naive immediacy. Once we *know* that our natural dispositions depend on blind genetic contingency, every stubborn sticking to these dispositions is as fake as sticking to old "organic" mores in a modern universe. So, basically, what Habermas is saying is although we now know that our dispositions depend on meaningless genetic contingency, let us pretend and act as if this is not the case so that we can maintain our sense of dignity and autonomy. The paradox is here that autonomy can only be maintained by prohibiting access to the blind natural contingency that determines us, that is, ultimately, by *limiting* our autonomy and freedom of scientific intervention. (Although, at some radical level, autonomy *is* linked to contingency; there is something humiliating in knowing exactly when I will die. Back in the 1950s, there was a death-row prisoner in the United States who, from the scarce materials at his disposal [metal pipes of his bed, the chemicals of the playing cards colors, etc.] improvised a gun that, every night, he aimed at his head. The gun was constructed so that the prisoner did not know when, exactly, it would fire off and kill him. When it happened, he died suddenly and of his own hand, thus asserting the minimum of his autonomy.) Is this not a new version of the old conservative argument that, if we are to retain our moral dignity, it is better not to know certain things? Again, Habermas's logic is here: since the results of science pose a threat to our (predominant notion of) autonomy and freedom, one should curtail science. The price we pay for this solution is the fetishist split between science and ethics ("I know very well what science claims, but, nonetheless, in order to retain [the appearance of] my autonomy, I choose to ignore it and act as if I don't know it"). This prevents us from confronting the true question: *how do these new conditions compel us to transform and reinvent the very notions of freedom, autonomy, and ethical responsibility?*

However, what about the possible Catholic counterargument according to which the true danger is not our effective reduction to nonspiritual entities but the very fact that, in biogenetics, *we—men—treat ourselves as such.* In other words, the point is not that we have or we do not have an immortal soul, and so forth—of course we do—but that, in engaging with biogenetics, we lose the awareness of this status and treat ourselves as if we are merely biological organisms. This only displaces the problem: would not, if such is the case, Catholic believers be the ideal subjects to engage fully in biogenetic manipulations since they would be completely aware that they are dealing only with the material aspect of human existence, not with the very spiritual kernel of man? In short, they should be allowed to do whatever they want in biogenetics since their faith in the human soul, in a transcendent spiritual dimension, would protect them from reducing man to the object of their scientific manipulations. Our question thus returns with a vengeance: if men have an immortal soul or an autonomous spiritual dimension, why, then, fear biogenetic manipulations?

The further religious counterargument is that, with the soul as independent of the body (brain), our body is its God-created instrument, namely, the way the soul expresses itself in this world. So, if we mess with its basic structure too much, we may disturb a precise structure created by God as a receptacle for our soul, thus obfuscating the soul's expression (in the same way that radio is just an instrument for receiving waves and thereby rendering audible the transmitted message—if we mess with it too much, the transmission no longer works). However, this counterargument is also ambiguous: if we can understand the way the instrument works, why should we abstain from improving it?

From the psychoanalytic standpoint, the core of the problem resides in the autonomy of the symbolic order. Suppose I am impotent because of some unresolved blockade in my symbolic universe, and I take Viagra instead of "educating" myself through the work of resolving the symbolic hindrance/inhibition. The solution works: I am again able to perform sexually. But the problem remains: how will the symbolic blockade itself be affected by this solution? How will the solution be "subjectivized"? The situation here is thoroughly undecidable; the solution will not be experienced as the result of the symbolic working through of the blockade. As such, it can unblock the symbolic obstacle itself, compelling me to accept its utter meaninglessness, or it can generate a psychotic twist, causing the return of the obstacle at some more fundamental psychotic level (say, I am pushed into a paranoiac attitude, experiencing myself as exposed to the caprice of some master whose interventions can decide my destiny). There is always a symbolic price to be paid for such "unearned" solutions. And, mutatis mutandis, the same goes for the attempts to fight crime through direct biochemical or biogenetic intervention. When one fights crime by submitting the criminals to biochemical treatment, compelling them to take medications against excessive aggression, one leaves intact the social mechanisms that triggered these potentials for aggression in the individuals.

In his *Kinds of Minds,* Dennett reports on the "Capgras delusion": "the sufferer's conviction that a close acquaintance (usually a loved one) has been replaced by an impostor who looks like (and sounds like and acts like) the genuine companion, who has mysteriously disappeared."[19]

[19] Daniel Dennett, *Kinds of Minds* (London: Phoenix, 1996), p. 148.

The sufferers sometimes go so far as to murder their spouses, who they consider to be impostors. Dennett sees the solution of this enigmatic mental illness in the hypothesis elaborated by Andrew Young apropos of "prosopagnosia" (people who cannot recognize familiar human faces: say, they cannot identify their closest friends until they hear them speak). However, when they are shown photographs of anonymous people, celebrities, and their close friends, they show a heightened galvanic skin response when they are shown a person they know, although they claim not to recognize them. So, something in them nonetheless *did* recognize them. Young's conclusion is that there must be (at least) two different systems of identifying a face in our psyche: the overt, conscious face-recognition system and the covert system, which normally provides a reassuring vote of agreement. In the case of prosopagnosia, the overt system is impaired while the covert system continues to function. What if, then, in the case of Capgras delusion, we have the opposite malfunctioning? The overt face-recognition functions normally, but it lacks the covert vote of agreement—and, logically, the result is thus experienced as "although this person looks and acts exactly like my wife, *something is missing,* she must be an impostor!" Do we not encounter here the gap between the series of positive properties and the mysterious *je ne sais quoi* that accounts for the person's self-identity beyond all positive properties (what Lacan calls *objet petit a,* something "in you more than yourself")? There is, however, one problem with Dennett's and Young's explanation: it is not *all* faces that provoke this paranoiac reaction but just *one* close acquaintance, usually a loved one. How, without a reference to inherent psychological dynamics, can we account for this *selective* malfunctioning of the covert system that is not suspended in general but only when it confronts *one* beloved face?

Another lesson of psychoanalysis here is that, contrary to the notion that curiosity is inborn and innate in humans (there is, deep within each of us, a *Wissenstrieb,* a drive to know), the spontaneous attitude of a human being is that of "I don't want to know about it." The fundamental desire is the desire *not* to know too much. Every true progress in knowledge has to be brought about by a painful struggle against our spontaneous propensities. Let's, for a moment, return to Huntington's disease. If there is, in my family, a history of this disease, should I take the test that will tell me if (and when) I will inexorably get the disease? If I cannot bear the prospect of knowing when I will die, the (more fantasmatic than realistic) ideal solution may seem to be the following one. I authorize another person or institution whom I trust completely to test me and *not to tell me the result,* only to kill me unexpectedly and painlessly in my sleep just before the onslaught of the fatal illness (assuming the result to be positive). However, the problem with this solution is that *I know that the Other knows* (the truth about my illness), and this ruins everything, exposing me to horrifying, gnawing suspicion. Is, then, the ideal solution the opposite one: if I suspect that my child may have the disease, I test him *without him knowing it* and then kill him painlessly just before the onslaught? The ultimate fantasy here would be that of an anonymous state institution doing this for all of us without our knowledge. But, again, the question pops up: do we know about it (that the other knows) or not? The way toward a perfect totalitarian society is open. What is false here is the underlying premise: the notion that the ultimate ethical duty is that of protecting the Other from pain, of keeping him in protective ignorance.

After we learn some bad news, we would prefer *not* to know it, but we cannot go back—once we know we know it, there is no return to innocent ignorance. The most recent case of this is provided by bio-genetics. When we learn to manipulate even our psychic properties, this, of course, demystifies our perception of "human nature," undermining our sense of personal dignity. However, the preceding ignorance appears as blessed only from the perspective of this knowledge; in other words, it is only after losing this blessed ignorance that we learn how blessed we were. It is similar with the celebration, in movies and narratives, of a lone hero who accomplishes his sacrificial act for the good of others unseen, without others being aware of it. Although people around him ignore him or even laugh at him, he is deeply satisfied in and with himself—or is he? Is it not, rather, that he did it for the big Other who appears precisely at this point at which there are no "real" others to take note of him? In other words, does not the satisfaction he gets emerge from the imagined gaze that observes him? This big Other is eventually embodied in us, spectators—as if the hero knows he is part of a film (or, at least, part of a story). (The concept of the big Other, with its ambiguous virtual status, is, in itself, a compromise, the avoidance of both terms of the alternative confronts us, or to quote Arthur Clark: "Either we are alone in the universe [with no other intelligent beings out there], or we are not alone. Both possibilities are equally terrifying." The big Other is thus something in-between, enabling us to have our cake and eat it too. There is no real Other out there, but there is nonetheless the fiction of the big Other that enables us to avoid the horror of being alone.) Recall, also, the well-known paradox of the choice a group of four military commandos has to make: if all of them participate in a dangerous action, they have a 50 percent chance of getting killed; if only one of them (chosen by a lottery) does it, he will be killed for sure, so the chance of survival is 25 percent. Although the rational strategy is to chose the second option (which involves a 100 percent greater survival chance than the first one), a large majority of people would choose the first option: although I have a greater chance of getting killed, the outcome is open until the end (i.e., I can retain my hope the entire time, never taking the risk of finding myself in a position in which I know for sure that I will soon die). What all of these three cases share is the temporality in which the choice is not simply a choice among different possibilities: the act of choice changes its own terms.

So, back to our basic point: it is not so much that, with biogenetics, we lose our freedom and dignity. Rather, we experience that *we never had them in the first place.* If, today, we already have "therapies that blur the line between what we achieve on our own and what we achieve because of the levels of various chemicals in our brains,"[20] does not the very efficiency of these therapies imply that "what we achieve on our own" also depends on *different* "levels of various chemicals in our brains"? Hence, it is not that, to quote Tom Wolfe's famous title, we are told "Sorry, but Your Soul Just Died"—what we are effectively told is that we never had a soul in the first place. If the claims of biogenetics hold, then the choice we are confronting today is not between human dignity and the "posthuman" technological generation of individuals but between clinging to the *illusion* of dignity and accepting the *reality* of what we are. Thus, when Francis Fukuyama states that "the desire for recognition has a biological basis and that that basis is related to levels of serotonin in the brain,"[21] does not our very awareness of this fact undermine the feeling of dignity that comes from being recognized by others? One cannot have it on both levels simultaneously. One can have it only at the price of a fetishist disavowal: "Although I know very well that my self-esteem depends on serotonin, I nonetheless enjoy it." On the following page, Fukuyama deploys the matrix of the three levels of achieving self-esteem:

> The normal, and morally acceptable, way of overcoming low self-esteem was to struggle with oneself and with others, to work hard, to endure sometimes painful sacrifices, and finally to rise and be seen as having done so. The problem with self-esteem as it is understood in American pop psychology is that it becomes an entitlement, something everyone needs to have whether it is deserved or not. This devalues self-esteem and makes the quest for it self-defeating.
>
> But now along comes the American pharmaceutical industry, which through drugs like Zoloft and Prozac can provide self-esteem in a bottle by elevating brain serotonin.[22]

[20] Francis Fukuyama, *Our Posthuman Future* (London: Profile Books, 2002), p. 8.
[21] Fukuyama, op. cit., p. 45.
[22] Fukuyama, op. cit., p. 46.

The difference between the second and third options is much more uncanny than it may initially appear to be: they are not "fake" in the same way. When I get self-esteem because society agrees that I am entitled to it and provides the recognition of my peers, this effectively is a self-defeating, performative paradox; however, when I get it through drugs, I get "the real thing." Let us imagine the following scenario: I participate in a quiz competition; instead of the hard process of learning, I enhance my memory with drugs. However, my self-esteem, which I get by way of winning the competition, is still based on the real achievement, that is, I really performed better than my colleague, who spent many nights trying to learn all the relevant data about the quiz topic. The obvious intuitive counterargument here is that it is only my competitor who has the right to be truly proud because his result was the outcome of hard work and painful dedication. However, is there not something inherently humiliating and patronizing in such a stance, as when we say to a mentally impaired person who successfully weaves the proverbial basket "You should be proud of what you did"? Even more, is it not that, say, we perceive it as justified when someone, with a breathtaking natural talent for singing, takes pride in his performance, although we are aware that his singing is based more on his talent than on his effort and training (the old Mozart-Salieri problem—Salieri's envy at how Mozart, composing with ease, produced superior works to those of Salieri, despite the latter's excruciating effort and dedication)? And yet, if I were to improve my singing through a drug, I would be denied the esteem (with the exception of the situation in which I would put great effort into inventing such a drug and then testing it on myself). It is thus not simply hard work and struggle versus the help of a drug. The point is, rather, that hard work as well as natural talent are considered "part of me," of my Self, whereas drug enhancement results from an external manipulation. And, again, this brings us back to the same problem: once we *know* that my "natural talent" depends on some chemicals in my brain, does it really matter, morally, if I got it from "outside" or from natural birth? To complicate things even further: what if my willingness itself to engage in inner struggle, discipline, and hard work depends on some chemicals? So, what if, to win a quiz competition, I do not take directly a drug that enhances my memory but "merely" a drug that strengthens my resolve and dedication? Is this still "cheating"? And, the final (but crucial) twist: is the self-esteem that I gain through "real" achievements really a priori deserved? Is it not that, on account (not only of social injustice, but) of the gap between the level of real achievements and their recognition in a symbolic public ritual, recognition *adds something* to "real performance"? Long ago, Lacan emphasized why, even when we know how we scored, there is a minimal gap between this objective knowledge and its performative proclamation bestowing on us a title. The problem with drugs is thus not simply that they generate an undeserved self-esteem, a self-esteem not grounded in our "real achievements," but, more paradoxically, that they deprive us of the satisfaction provided by the *intersubjective symbolic ritual.*

Why, then, did Fukuyama pass from the end-of-history defense of liberal democracy to the threat posed by brain sciences? In a first approach, the answer seems easy. The biogenetic threat is a new, much more radical, version of the "end of history," which undermines the very foundations of liberal democracy. The new scientific and technological developments potentially render obsolete the free and autonomous liberal-democratic subject. There is, however, a deeper reason for Fukuyama's turn to the brain sciences, a reason that directly concerns his political vision. It is as if the prospect of biogenetic manipulations forced Fukuyama to take note of the dark obverse of his idealized image of liberal democracy. All of a sudden, apropos the biogenetic threat, he is compelled to affirm all of the things that magically vanished from his liberal-democratic utopia. The prospect of biogenetic interventions and other forms of brain manipulations opens up the dark prospects of corporations misusing the free market to manipulate people and to engage in terrifying medical experiments, of rich people breeding their offspring as a special race with superior mental and physical capacities (thus instigating a new class warfare), and similar nightmarish scenarios. It is clear to Fukuyama that the only way to limit this danger is to reassert a strong state control of the market and to develop new forms of democratic political will.[23]

While agreeing with all of this, one is tempted to add the following: *do we not need these measures also independently of the biogenetic threat, just in order to control the terrifying potentials of the global market economy itself?* Maybe the problem is not biogenetics as such but, rather, the social context of power relations within which it functions. What makes biogenetics dangerous is the way its use is determined by the interests of corporate capital and of the state agencies tempted to rely on it in order to increase their control of the population—the problem is ultimately not "ethical" but economico political. The difficulty with Fukuyama is thus double: his argumentation is, at one and the same time, too abstract and too concrete. He fails to question the full philosophical implications of the new brain sciences and related technologies, *and* he fails to locate these sciences and technologies in their antagonistic socioeconomic context.

---

[23] While it is easy to make fun of Francis Fukuyama's obvious simplifications, there is nonetheless something refreshing about him. In our intellectual space full of false protesters, here we finally have a fully pledged *apologist for the existing order.* No wonder his work often unexpectedly touches on a grain of truth.

What Fukuyama does not grasp (and what a true Hegelian *should* have grasped) is the necessary link between the two "ends of history," the necessary passage from the one to the other. The liberal-democratic "end of history" immediately turns into its opposite since, in the very hour of its triumph, it starts to lose its very foundation, the liberal-democratic subject itself.

So, what would Hegel have said apropos the genome project and biogenetic interventions? Whatever his reaction, it would definitely not have been to shirk away out of fear, preferring ignorance to risk. From a proper Hegelian perspective, one has to go through this thorough self-objectivization, since it is only through it that the subject as pure form—the pure form of the subject—emerges, as the point *from which* I can apprehend with horror how "that's me," that genetic formula. In short, would not Hegel rejoice at "Thou art genome!" at this shattering new version of the old "Thou art that!" as the ultimate example of the infinite judgment, completing the series of "the spirit is a bone" and "the Self is money"? The confrontation with the meaningless Real of the genome thus obliterates the fantasy-screen through which I perceive reality: in the formula of the genome, I am compelled to directly access the Real. Contrary to Habermas, one should assert the ethical *necessity* of assuming the full genome objectivization: this reduction of my substantial being to the senseless genome formula obliterates the fantasmatic *étoffe du moi*, the stuff of which our egos are made, thereby reducing me to the pure subject: faced with the genome, I am nothing, *and this nothing is the subject itself.*

The "postsecular" striving to formulate the "limits of disenchantment" all too quickly accepts the premise that the inherent logic of Enlightenment ends up in the total scientific self-objectivization of humanity, in the transformation of humans into available objects of scientific manipulation, so that the only way to retain human dignity is to salvage religious legacy by way of translating it into a modern idiom. Against this temptation, it is crucial to insist to the end in the project of Enlightenment. Enlightenment remains an "unfinished project" that has to be brought to its end, and this end is *not* the total scientific self-objectivization but—this wager has to be taken—a new figure of freedom that will emerge when we follow the logic of science to the end.

Cognitive Closure?

Are we ready to assume this "infinite judgment"? The cover story of *Newsweek* from May 7, 2001 ("Religion and the Brain") reports on the latest successes of "neurotheologians," who can identify the brain processes that accompany intense religious experiences: say, when a subject experiences herself as timeless and infinite, part of the cosmic All, delivered of the constraints of her Self, the region of her brain that processes information about space, time, and the orientation of the body in space "goes dark"; in the blocking of the sensory inputs that occurs during intense meditative concentration, the brain has no choice but to perceive the self as endless and intimately interwoven with everyone and everything. The same goes for visions: they clearly correspond to abnormal bursts of electrical activity in the temporal lobes (the "temporal-lobe epilepsy"), and so on. The report tries to conclude on a more open-ended note. Of course, everything we experience also exists as a neurological activity. However, this in no way resolves the question of causality. For instance, when we eat an apple, we also experience the satisfaction of its good taste as a neuronal activity, but this in no way affects the fact that the apple was really out there and caused our activity. In the same fashion, it is totally undecided whether our brain wiring creates (our experience of) God or whether God created our brain wiring. Furthermore, religion cannot be reduced to an inner psychic (mystical or otherwise) experience. It is (also) a matter of belief in certain (propositional) truths, of our ethical stance and practical activity—what matters for a Jew is following the Law, not your thoughts and experiences while you are doing it.

However, this easy way out conceals a deeper deadlock. The question of causality seems relatively simple to resolve. What if we (the experimenting doctor) directly intervene in the appropriate parts of the brain, causing the brain activity in question? If, during this activity of ours, the subject "experiences the divine dimension," does this not provide a conclusive answer? And does the same not hold for the second counterargument? If we bombard the subject with religious doctrines plus submit him to the appropriate electrical or chemical stimuli, and then get a person who acts, thinks, and feels as a deeply religious person, does this also not resolve the dilemma? Furthermore, the comparison with the apple is inappropriate for the same reason; long ago, Hegel criticized Kant, who, in his derision of the ontological proof of God, claimed that the notion of one hundred talers is not the same as having the actual one hundred talers in our pocket: the point is precisely that we are talking about *God,* an infinite Entity supposed to exists outside our ordinary reality, not about apples or talers. However, the problem here is more complex since, as McGinn was right to point out, to know consciousness would be to know the intersection of brain and mind, the physical/biological process that directly "is" thought/awareness (not just its bodily correlative, "what goes on in the brain while we think") and the thought that directly "is" a physical process (in the sense of "H_2O is water"):

> The unknown properties of the brain that allow consciousness to emerge from it thus overlap with the hidden aspects of consciousness that allow it to be embodied in the brain. The principle of emergence coincides with the principle of embodiment. . . . The unknown properties of the brain that explain consciousness *are* the aspects of consciousness that lie hidden from view. It is not that these two areas of ignorance are unrelated to each other; on the contrary, they are the *same* area of ignorance.[24]

What if this is impossible not only in the sense of cognitive closure but, over and above this, in the sense that awareness itself is *defined* by the distance toward its bodily correlative (i.e., subject is $ — it eludes what it is as object)? If I were to know directly what I am as a body, in objective reality, as a "thing that thinks" (Kant), I would no longer be thinking in the human sense (the only one accessible to us)—*and* reality itself would no longer be reality. This closure is thus not merely cognitive; it ontologically constitutes thought-awareness-consciousness.[25] These paradoxes bring us to the notorious zombie-problem in today's cognitive sciences, perhaps the ultimate proof of Lacan's thesis that consciousness itself has the status of an object:

> [A] zombie is or would be a human being who exhibits perfectly natural, alert, loquacious, vivacious behavior but is in fact not conscious at all, but rather some sort of automaton. The whole point of the philosopher's notion of zombie is that you can't tell a zombie from a normal person by examining external behavior. Since that is all we ever get to see of our friends and neighbors, *some of your best friends may be zombies.*[26]

This notion of a zombie was proposed in order to reject behaviorist-reductionist constructions of human mind: they can construct an entity that looks and acts like a human being, which has all phenomenal properties of a human being, yet it nonetheless does not have what we intuitively grasp as "consciousness" or "self-awareness." The problem, of course, is that it is impossible to pin down consciousness to a specific, observable, empirical property. The two series of behavior (the human being's and the zombie's) might be, for all practical purposes, indistinguishable, and yet the elusive difference is nonetheless crucial (the elusive X that accounts for the difference being the Lacanian *objet petit a*). On closer

---

[24] Colin McGinn, *The Mysterious Flame* (New York: Basic Books, 1999), pp. 155–56.
[25] Furthermore, is McGinn not engaged in the Cartesian search for a new version of pineal gland? What if the mysterious "C" ingredient is not a localized particular ingredient to be *added* to the brain as we know it, but purely structural, a topological twist?
[26] Daniel C. Dennett, *Consciousness Explained* (New York: Little, Brown, 1991), p. 73.

inspection, the opposition of a "normal" human being with "inner experience" and a zombie is even more paradoxical than it may appear. When we claim that a zombie does not feel anything, even if it thinks and acts as if it does (there is nothing it is like to be *it*), who is here deceived: we, external observers, or the zombie itself? If it is the outside observers who, when observing a zombie's behavior, cannot distinguish it from human behavior, why, then, would a zombie imitate inner life, acting for the observer *as if* he has one? If, on the other hand, a zombie deceives *itself*, then,

> to the extent that "seemings" of your own phenomenal states are constituted by self-ascriptive judgements, beliefs, thoughts, memories, expectations, and so forth about those states (and no doubt there is a significant extent to which such seemings are so constituted), it would be warranted to say that your inner life would continue to *seem* the same to you, despite the fact that you would cease to have any genuine phenomenal states once you turned into a zombie. Put differently, according to the zombie hypothesis, you would now be "hallucinating" your own phenomenology.[27]

But, how, then, are we to distinguish seeming from seeming of seeming? Can a state *seem to me to seem*? Is this position not a nonsensical one, vulnerable to Dennett's classical reproach bearing upon a senseless distinction between how things (really) appear to me and how they appear to appear to me? Is not the necessary result that of Dennett: there are just fragmentary, secondary "seemings," and what is beyond is just a neuronal mechanism? However, what about the opposite radical conclusion, namely, that every seeming is a seeming of seeming—that seeming is, in its very concept, split, reflexive, in the same way Kierkegaard claimed that we cannot ever be sure that we believe—we only believe that we believe? Consequently, is it not that the ontological split introduced by the emergence of seeming is never simply between appearance and reality but also always inherent to seeming itself? The Hegelian thesis here is not only that the way things appear is inherent to what they are, that appearance is essential—one should add to it that essence itself is inherent to appearance, reflected in the split of appearances. The true enigma is not what things "really are" but how they *"really seem* to me." This points toward the Lacanian notion of fantasy. The conclusion is thus a clear and unambiguous one: we all *are* zombies who are not aware of it, who are self-deceived into perceiving themselves as self-aware.

What, then, about the standard philosophical argument against psychoanalysis, according to which, by way of passing directly to the

---

[27] Guven Guzeldere, "Introduction: The Many Faces of Consciousness," in *The Nature of Consciousness,* edited by Ned Block, Owen Flanagan, and Guven Guzeldere (Cambridge, Mass.: MIT Press, 1997), p. 44.

Unconscious, Freud fails to provide a proper theory of what consciousness itself is? Is it not that—far from designating two opposed poles at the same level or internal to the same notional field, with innumerable intermediate states (confused half-awareness, etc.)—consciousness and the Unconscious are *thoroughly incommensurable.* At the level of consciousness, one simply cannot imagine the Freudian unconscious (what one *can* imagine is the *Lebensphilosophie* "unconscious" of deep "irrational" instincts). And is the Unconscious not so much external to conciousness as, rather, indifferent to it, functioning at a different level? However, before conceding this point too hastily, one should take a closer look at the Freudian opposition of consciousness and memory, the idea that what does not become conscious gets inscribed into a memory trace. Is not the consequence of this thesis that consciousness is, at its most fundamental, a defense-formation, a mode of repression: we become conscious of something so that we can directly forget it, so that it does not inscribe itself into memory and continue to haunt us? The task here would be to connect this Freudian thesis to the cognitivist "Hegelian" insight into the fundamentally "reductionist" function of consciousness. The link between consciousness and complexity resides not in the fact that "when things become too complex, consciousness has to enter" but, on the contrary, that consciousness is the medium of the radical *simplification* of complexity. Consciousness is the medium of "abstraction" par excellence, of the reduction of its object to a couple of simple features.

Do Benjamin Libet's (deservedly) famous experiments not point in this same direction? What makes them so interesting is that, although the results are clear, it is not clear what they are arguments *for.*[28] It can be argued that they demonstrate how there is no free will: even before we consciously decide (say, to move a finger), the appropriate neuronal processes are already underway, which means that our conscious decision just takes note of what is already going on (adding its superfluously authorization to a fait accompli). On the other hand, consciousness does seem to have the veto power to stop this process already underway, so there seems to be at least the freedom to *block* our spontaneous decisions. And yet, what if our very ability to veto the automatic decision is again conditioned by some "blind" neuronal processes? There is, however, a third, more radical option. What if, prior to our conscious decision, there already was an *unconscious* decision that triggered the "automatic" neuronal process itself? Prior to Freud, Schelling developed the notion that the basic free decisions made by us are unconscious. So, with regard

[28] See Benjamin Libet, "Unconscious Cerebral Initiative and the Role of Conscious Will in Voluntary Action," *The Behavioral and Brain Sciences* 8 (1985): 529–39; and Benjamin Libet, "Do We Have Free Will?" *Journal of Consciousness Studies* 1 (1999): 47–57.

to Libet's experiment, from the Freudian standpoint, the basic underlying problem is that of the status of the Unconscious: are there only conscious thoughts (my belated conscious decision to move a finger) and "blind" neuronal processes (the neuronal activity to move the finger), or is there also an unconscious "mental" process? And, what is the ontological status of this unconscious, if there indeed is one? Is it not that of a purely virtual symbolic order, of a pure logical *presupposition* (the decision *had to be made,* although it was never effectively made in real time)?

It is with regard to such questions that the cognitivist project seems unable to provide a materialist answer. It either denies them or takes refugee in a "dualist" idealist position. When Daniel Dennett almost compulsively varies the theme of how dangerous "Darwin's idea" is, one is tempted to raise the suspicion that his insistence conceals/reveals the opposite fear: what if Darwin's idea (the radical contingency of evolution, the emergence of intentionality and mind itself out of a blind process of genetic variations and selection) is the one whose message is pacifying (take it easy, there is no meaning or obligation in our lives . . .)? What if, in a Kierkegaardian way, the true "danger," the truly unbearable trauma, would be to accept that we *cannot* be reduced to an outcome of evolutionary adaptation, that there is a dimension eluding cognitivism? No wonder, then, that the most succinct definition of cognitivism is internalized behaviorism: a behaviorism of the interior (in the same way that, in contrast to a Jew, a Christian has to be "inwardly circumcised"). That is to say, does it not (re)apply the behaviorist reduction (a reduction to observable positive processes) to internal processes: mind is no longer a black box, but a computational machine?

It is because of this self-inflicted circumcision that many a cognitivist (from Pinker to McGinn) tries to account for the paradox of (self)consciousness by claiming that its inability to "know itself," to account for itself as an object in the world, is cosubstantial with consciousness itself, its inherent constituent. (Pinker offers a more scientific evolutionist version—consciousness did not emerge with the aim to understand/explain itself but emerged with other evolutionary functions, while McGinn offers a more purely theoretical version of why consciousness is necessarily an enigma to itself.) What we get here is nothing less than the evolutionary biological explanation of the emergence of metaphysics. However, a Heideggerian counterquestion, issuing from the framework of *Being and Time,* immediately pops up here: is it not that, nonetheless, consciousness *necessarily* questions itself, asks itself the enigma it is a priori unable to answer? (As Heidegger himself puts it: *Dasein* is an entity that questions its own being.) How did *this* property emerge within the evolutionary logic? The point is not only that, *on top* of its adaptive functions (how to find one's way in the environs, etc.), consciousness is *also* bothered by enigmas having no evolutionary, adaptive function (humor, art, metaphysical questions). The (further and) crucial point is that this useless supplement, the compulsive fixation on problems that a priori cannot be solved, retroactively enables a true explosion of procedures (techniques, insights) with exuberant survival value—it is as if, to assert its priority over other living beings in the struggle for survival, the human animal has to forsake the struggle for survival itself and focus on other questions. Victory in the struggle for survival can be gained only as a by-product: if one focuses directly on the struggle for survival, one loses it. Only a being obsessed with impossible/unsolvable problems can make a breakthrough in possible knowledge. What this means is that, as Heidegger would have phrased it, in contrast to the animal struggle for survival, man's struggle is always-already experienced as the horizon of meaning for his existence. Developing technology, struggling for power, occurs within and as a certain disclosure of Being rather than being an immediate "fact of life."[29]

When McGinn claims that there is, in reality, nothing mysterious about how the brain generates consciousness (we humans are just forever cognitively closed to understanding this process in the same way the understanding of quantum mechanics lies beyond the cognitive capacities of monkeys), the irony here is double: not only do we incessantly *try* to understand conciousness, in clear contrast to monkeys (who do not care about quantum physics), but even humans themselves (and not only monkeys) cannot really understand quantum physics (in the strict sense of translating it into their horizon of meaning). This deadlock becomes clearly discernible in "The Meaning of Life," the last chapter of Steven Pinker's *How the Mind Works*,[30] a chapter dedicated to an evolutionary account of human activities which make no contribution to the adaptive success of the human animal, namely, art, the telling of jokes, and the questioning of the meaning of life (philosophy, religion).

Following McGinn, Pinker concludes that, "our minds lack the equipment to solve the major problems of philosophy,"[31] and emphasizes that there is nothing metaphysical in this "cognitive closure." It can and should be accounted for in strict evolutionary terms: "It is an observation about one organ of one species, equivalent to observing that cats are color-blind or that monkeys cannot learn long division. It does not justify religious or mystical beliefs but explains why they are futile."[32] Due to the way it emerged in the course of the evolution, humanity "owes its power to

---

[29] It is not only that, on the top of the struggle for survival men express also in "higher" entities; the struggle for survival itself is for man always a way of *understanding* his existence.

[30] See Steven Pinker, *How the Mind Works* (Harmondsworth, England: Penguin Books, 1998).

[31] Pinker, op. cit., pp. 562–63.

[32] Pinker, op. cit., p. 563.

its syntactic, compositional, combinatorial abilities"; as such, it was not made to grasp phenomena that are "peculiarly holistic and everywhere-at-once and nowhere-at-all and all-at-the-same-time";[33] "Our bafflement at the mysteries of the ages may have been the price we paid for a combinatorial mind that opened up a world of words and sentences."[34] Pinker lists three such phenomena: sentience, "I," and referring. Sentience is not a combination of brain events or computational states but an immediate experience; the "I" is not a combination of body parts or brain states or bits of information but "a unity of selfness over time, a single locus that is nowhere in particular. Free will is not a casual chain of events and states, by definition."[35] And, in the same way, although the combinatory nature of meaning is well explored, "the *core* of meaning—the simple act of referring to something—remains a puzzle, because it stands strangely apart from any causal connection between the thing referred to and the person referring."

However, if we claim that we are dealing here with the "mismatch between the very nature of these problems and the computational apparatus that natural selection has fitted us with,"[36] the true enigma is not the enigma of the meaning of life as such but, rather, *why does our mind persistently probe into the meaning of life in the first place*? If religion and philosophy are (in part, at least) "the application of mental tools to problems they were not designed to solve,"[37] how did this misapplication occur, and why is it so persistent? Note the Kantian background of this position: it was already Kant who claimed that the human mind is burdened by metaphysical questions that it a priori cannot answer. These questions cannot be suspended; they are part of our very human nature. And, since Hegel provided the elaborate critique of Kant, it would be interesting to reread these Kantian antinomies of today's cognitivism through Hegelian lenses.

"Little Jolts of Enjoyment"

When Pinker deals with art, he proposes the basic formula of this "misapplication":

> Some parts of the mind register the attainment of increments of fitness by giving us a sensation of pleasure. Other parts use a knowledge of cause and effect to bring about goals. Put them together and you get a mind

[33] Pinker, op. cit., p. 564.
[34] Pinker, op. cit., p. 565.
[35] Pinker, op. cit., p. 564.
[36] Pinker, op. cit., p. 565.
[37] Pinker, op. cit., p. 525.

that rises to a biologically pointless challenge: figuring out how to get at the pleasure circuits of the brain and deliver the little jolts of enjoyment without the inconvenience of wringing bona fide fitness increments from the harsh world.[38]

No wonder Pinker's first example of this short circuit is a rat caught in the vicious cycle of lethal enjoyment: "When a rat has access to a lever that sends electrical impulses to an electrode implanted in its medial forebrain bundle, it presses the lever furiously until it drops of exhaustion, forgoing opportunities to eat, drink, and have sex."[39] In short, the poor rat literally got her brain fucked out. This is how drugs work: by way of directly affecting our brain—what we get here is a "pure" aphrodisiac, not a means of stimulating our senses as instruments for providing pleasure to our brain but the direct stimulation of the pleasure centers in the brain itself. The next, more mediated step is to access the pleasure circuits "via the senses, which stimulate the circuits when they are in an environment that would have led to fitness in past generations."[40] In past generations, when the animal recognized a pattern in its environs enhancing its chance for survival (to get food, avoid danger, etc.), this recognition was signaled/accompanied by the experience of pleasure; now, the organism directly produces such patterns just to get pleasure. This matrix accounts for food, drink, and sexual pleasures—and even for art. The foundation of the aesthetic experience is the recognition of (symmetric, clear, etc.) sensual patterns that, originally, enabled us to orient ourselves in our environs.

Of course, the enigma here is *how does this short circuit come about?* How can the pleasure experience, which was originally a mere by-product of the goal-oriented activity aiming at our survival (i.e., a signal that this goal was achieved), turn into an aim-in-itself? The exemplary case here, of course, is that of sexuality: sexual pleasure, which originally signaled that the goal of procreation was achieved, becomes an aim-in-itself, so that the human animal spends large amounts of time pursuing this aim, planning it in all details, even directly blocking the original goal (through contraception). It is the Catholic attitude of allowing sex only for the goal of procreation that debases it to animal coupling.

The basic paradox here is that the specifically human dimension emerges precisely when what was originally a mere by-product is elevated into an autonomous aim: man is not more "reflexive"; on the contrary, man perceives as a direct goal what, for an animal, has no intrinsic value. In short, the zero-degree of "humanization" is not a further

[38] Pinker, op. cit., p. 524.
[39] Pinker, op. cit., p. 524.
[40] Pinker, op. cit., p. 524.

"mediation" of animal activity, its reinscription as a subordinated moment of a higher totality (say, we eat and procreate to develop higher spiritual potentials) but the radical narrowing of focus, the elevation of a minor activity into an end-in-itself. We become "humans" when we get caught into a closed, self-propelling loop of repeating the same gesture and finding satisfaction in it. We all recall one of the archetypal scenes from cartoons. While dancing, the cat jumps up into the air and turns around its own axis; however, instead of falling back down toward the earth's surface in accordance with the normal laws of gravity, it remains for some time suspended in the air, turning around in the levitated position as if caught in a loop of time, repeating the same circular movement on and on. (One also finds the same shot in some musical comedies that make use of the elements of slapstick. When a dancer turns around him- or herself in the air, he or she remains up there a little bit too long, as if, for a short period of time, he or she succeeded in suspending the law of gravity. And, effectively, is such an effect not the ultimate goal of the art of dancing?) In such moments, the "normal" run of things, the "normal" process of being caught in the imbecilic inertia of material reality, is for a brief moment suspended; we enter the magical domain of a suspended animation, of a kind of ethereal rotation that, as it were, sustains itself, hanging in the air like Baron Munchhausen, who raised himself from the swamp by grabbing his own hair and pulling himself up. This rotary movement, in which the linear progress of time is suspended in a repetitive loop, is *drive* at its most elementary. This, again, is "humanization" at its zero-level: this self-propelling loop that suspends/disrupts linear temporal enchainment.[41]

The lesson of spy novels and movies is relevant here: how does a perfect "operation" to entrap the enemy go wrong? The usual twist is that there is another even darker and more secret plot transpiring behind it—agents playing double or even triple games. However, there is a more tragic twist, namely, the unpredictable role of the "human factor." An agent whose task was to seduce, exploit, and then sacrifice a woman (or a man, for that matter) falls for her and is unable to betray and sacrifice her; so, he just pretends, for his spy masters, to manipulate his victim while effectively doing everything possible to save her. Much more than the multiple-levels deception, this is the specifically "human" complication: what was

---

[41] Opposed to this scene is the nightmarish fantasy of triggering by mistake a trickle that then never stops. In *Alice in Wonderland*, when she starts to cry, her tears gradually flood the entire room. Freud reports, in his *Interpretation of Dreams*, a scene of a small child who starts to urinate on the edge of a street—his flow grows into a river, and then into an ocean with a large ship. Closer to our ordinary daily experience, when witnessing a torrential rainfall, who among us does not feel the "irrational" fear that the rain will simply never stop?

planned to be just a means in a complex plot is suddenly elevated into the absolute End, into an object of ultimate fidelity—I am ready to stick to it even if everything falls apart.

The initial move of a human being is not thought, reflexive distance, but the "fetishization" of a partial moment into an autonomous goal: the elevation of pleasure into *jouissance*—a deadly excess of enjoyment as the goal-in-itself. Dennett approaches the same motif when, elaborating Dawkins's notion of "meme" in his *Darwin's Dangerous Idea,* he evokes the example of a vulgar tune that inexplicably pursues us, making us whistle it against our will and inclinations:

> The other day, I was embarrassed—dismayed—to catch myself walking along humming a melody to myself....I was energetically humming "It Takes Two to Tango"—a perfectly dismal and entirely unredeemed bit of chewing gum for the ears that was unaccountably popular sometime in the 1950s. I am sure I have never in my life chosen this melody, esteemed this melody, or in any way judged it to be better than silence, but there it was, a horrible musical virus, at least as robust in my meme pool as any melody I actually esteem.[42]

Is such an intrusive *sinthome,* a figment of obscene enjoyment spreading like a virus, really at the same level as, say, an intellectually stimulating theoretical insight that haunts us? Could it be maintained that such intrusive *sinthomes* provide the zero-level, the elementary matrix, of memes? Dennett is again right to emphasize the key significance of the fact that "children enjoy talking to themselves," not a full, articulated speech but a kind of "semi-understood self-commentary," repeating, through mimicry and imitation, bits of phrases overheard from their parents:

> The actual utterances would consist at the outset of large measures of "scribble"—nonsense talk composed of wordlike sounds—mixed with real words mouthed with much feeling but little or no appreciation of their meaning, and a few understood words.[43]

This babble provides "anchors of familiarity," knots of potential meaning identified/recognized as "the same," independently of their actual meaning: "A word can become familiar even without being understood."[44] This babble *has* to be devoid of meaning proper: *first,* signifiers have to be crystallized as identifiable entities; it is only *then* that they can acquire a proper meaning. And, is this babble not what Lacan called

[42] Daniel Dennett, *Darwin's Dangerous Idea* (NewYork: Simon and Schuster, 1995), p. 347.
[43] Daniel Dennett, *Kinds of Minds,* p. 197.
[44] Dennett, op. cit., p. 198.

lalangue ("llanguage"), preceding the articulated language: the succession of Ones, signifiers of *jouis-sense* ("enjoy-meant")? In other words, when Dennett writes that, "children *enjoy* talking to themselves," the "enjoyment" is to be taken here in a strict Lacanian sense. And such babble can also function as an excellent political intervention. Several decades ago, in Carinthia, Austria's southern province that borders on Slovenia, German nationalists organized a campaign against the alleged Slovene "threat" under the motto *Kärnten bleibt Deutsch!* (Carinthia will remain German!), to which Austrian Leftists found a perfect answer: instead of rational counterargumentation, they simply printed, in the main newspapers, an advertisement with obscene, disgusting sounding variations of the nationalists' motto: "Kärnten deibt bleutsch! Kärnten leibt beutsch! Kärnten beibt dleutsch!" Isn't this procedure worthy of the obscene, "anal," meaningless speech spoken by the Hitler figure in Chaplin's *The Great Dictator*? One should also establish here a link with Pinker's idea that humans can directly posit pleasure as the aim of their activity. Language is the supreme example here, that is to say, it is only through the enjoyment provided by the very act of speaking, through the speaker getting caught in the closed loop of pleasurable self-affection, that humans can detach themselves from their immersion in their environs and thus acquire a proper symbolic distance toward it.

Along these lines, when Dennett discusses the passage from "free-floating" intentionality to explicit intentionality (from a mind that acts intentionally without being aware of it to a mind that is "fully conscious," which explicitly sets its goals, which not only acts blindly in an intentional way but represents to itself its intentions—in short, the Hegelian passage from In-itself to For-itself, from implicit intentionality to intentionality posited as such), he introduces two interconnected features.[45] First, such a passage is embedded in (what will later become) "intersubjectivity": an agent is led to represent its goals to itself when it is compelled to probe into the enigma of other's (his competitors, his prey or predators) goals. Second, the capacity to explicitly communicate the goal of one's behavior to another agent (gestures that mean "Look, I am trying to catch a fish!" "Look, I am trying to escape!" etc.) is strictly correlative to the capacity to *cheat*, to keep a secret (to pretend not to know something—say, the location of a rich source of food—or, on the contrary, to pretend to know something one does not really know), to delude the other as to one's true intention. The capacity to explicate meaning *equals* the capacity to conceal what one really means—or, to refer to Talleyrand (quoted by Dennett): "Language was invented so that people could conceal their

---

[45] Dennett, op. cit., pp. 164–74.

thoughts from each other."[46] And, one might add, language helps people conceal their thoughts from themselves. Or, as Lacan put it, symbolic representation is strictly correlative to the emergence of the abyss of the Other's desire: "*Che vuoi?*" What do you *really* want from me? Dennett refers here to the case of a hare chased by a fox who, when it determines that this fox is unlikely to succeed in its chase,

> does a strange and wonderful thing. It stands up on its hind legs, most conspicuously, and stares back the fox down! Why? Because it is announcing to the fox that the fox ought to give up. "I've already seen you, and I'm not afraid. Don't waste your precious time and even more precious energy chasing me. Give it up!" And the fox typically draws just this conclusion, turning elsewhere for its supper.[47]

Dennett is right to insist that, in spite of appearances, we are not yet dealing here with the case of proper communication, in which the speaker declares to the addressee its intention-to-signify—the hare does not yet fulfill the four levels which, according to the classical analysis of Paul Grice, have to be present in a full act of signification.[48] So, what should we add? It is not enough to impute to the hare the capacity to cheat (say, adopting this stance even if it "knows very well" that he *is* close enough to the fox for the fox to catch it). One should here follow Lacan and affirm that, in order for the hare's gesture to count as symbolic communication, the hare should display the capacity of *cheating in the guise of truth:* for instance, it should adopt this stance, counting on the fact that the fox will think that the hare is trying to deceive it and nonetheless start to run after it, thereby achieving it true aim (say, of diverting the fox's attention from another hare, the first hare's beloved mating partner, which effectively *is* close enough to the fox to be caught by it).

When, in Seattle, Bill Clinton deftly referred to the protesters on the streets outside the heavily guarded palace, reminding the gathered leaders inside the palace that they should learn to hear the message of the demonstrators (the message which, of course, Clinton interpreted, depriving it of its subversive sting by attributing this sting to the dangerous extremists who introduce chaos and violence into the majority of peaceful protesters), he resorted to the same strategy of lying in the guise of truth. Consequently, one cannot but recall here the old Freudian joke of the Jew lying to his friend about the true destination of his voyage in the guise of truth itself. "Why did Clinton say that they should listen to the protesters, when they should effectively listen to the protesters?"

---

[46] Dennett, op. cit., p. 168.
[47] Dennett, op. cit., p. 162.
[48] See Paul Grice, "Meaning," in *Studies in the Way of Words* (Cambridge, Mass.: Harvard University Press, 1989).

And, since Clinton is known for his sexual proclivities, one should not be surprised to learn about the libidinal roots of this kind of cheating. William Rice came to the disturbing conclusion that human intelligence developed as an instrument of sexual antagonism. Its main impetus was *not,* as we were usually taught, the fabrication of tools that enabled our ancestors to survive in unfriendly natural environs:

> [T]he more social and communicative a species is, the more likely it is to suffer from sexually antagonistic genes, because communication between the sexes provides the medium in which sexually antagonistic genes thrive. The most social and communicative species on the planet is humankind. Suddenly it begins to make sense why relations between the human sexes are such a minefield, and why men have such vastly different interpretations of what constitutes sexual harassment from women. . . . The notion that our brains grew big to help us make tools or start fires on the savannah has long since lost favor.[49]

The basic idea here is that, with humans, sexual antagonism (the tension between seduction and resistance to it) exploded into "interlocus contest evolution (ICE)": in a kind of vicious cycle resembling the self-propelling spiral of the arms race, the relative advantage gained by one sex propelled the other sex to invent an effective countermeasure. After males develop new and more efficient courtship and seduction techniques, females evolve so that they are turned off, not on, by the displays of males, which propels males to invent another technique. And, insofar as the passage from sexed animals to humans involves a qualitative leap marked by the emergence of the symbolic order, one is tempted to establish here the connection with Lacan's *il n'y a pas de rapport sexuel:* the passage to language, *the* medium of communication, far from bringing about the pacification of the antagonism, the reconciliation of the opposed sexes in the universal symbolic medium, raises antagonism itself to the level of the absolute. With humans, what was before (in the animal kingdom) a struggle of two opposed forces within the same field, is raised into the absolute antagonism that cuts from within the universal medium itself. The access to universality is paid for by a total impossibility of communication, of common measure, between the sexes: *the price paid for the universalization-symbolization of sexuality is the sexuation of symbolic universality itself.* Instead of the reconciliation of the sexual opposition in the universality of language, universality itself gets split, caught in the antagonism. With regard to deception, this means that the imaginary lure characteristic of animal courtship is raised (*aufgehoben*) to the level of properly human deception (deception in the guise of truth itself). One

[49] Ridley, *Genome*, pp. 115–16.

should conceive of this link between universality and (human) sexuality in all its strength. It is not only symbolization that is the "active" element, raising sexual polarity to the level of radical antagonism once sexuality gets caught in the symbolic order; the opposite direction is even more crucial—there is no (symbolic) universality outside sexual antagonism (Universality becomes "for itself," it gets "posited as such," only through sexual antagonism—or, to put it in more biological-evolutionary terms, the symbolic order emerges as a medium of deception that pertains to sexual antagonism).

2

ART: THE TALKING HEADS

How do art and science relate to sublimation? While they both engage in sublimation (i.e., they both generate a distance toward our immersion into the direct lived experience of reality), each of the two relies on a different mode of it.[1] Science accomplishes the process of sublimating abstraction. It totally evacuates the lived reality of the sexualized body, reducing reality to pure extension, to matter distributed in abstract space. For science, mathematizable abstraction is therefore the only contact with the Real. In it, reality and the Real are opposed as the concrete lived experience of bodies and abstract (ultimately senseless) numerical formulas. In contrast to it, art remains within lived reality. It cuts out from it a fragment, an object, elevating it to the "level of the Thing." (Recall, as the zero-level of this procedure, Duchamp's ready-made art: by displaying a urinal as an object of art, it "transubstantiated" its materiality into the mode of appearance of the Thing.)[2] Science and art thus relate to the Thing in a totally different way: art directly evokes it (i.e., artistic

---

[1] I rely here on Darian Leader, *Stealing the Mona Lisa: What Art Stops Us from Seeing* (London: Faber and Faber, 2002), pp. 103–105.

[2] In what sense does Duchamp's urinal stand for an act of creativity? At the level of its immediate material content, there is, of course, nothing creative about it; Duchamp just took an ordinary, vulgar object and displayed it as a work of art. His true act of creativity happened prior to this: in implicitly redefining the space of the work of art, the rules determining this space, in such a way that the displaying of a urinal can count as a work of art (or, rather, in forcing us, the spectators, to redefine the space of art in such a way that we are able to perceive the urinal as a work of art). What this means, of course, is that we become aware of the role of the (empty) space *as such*: being an object of art is not an immediate property of an object but its "reflexive determination" (Hegel). Along the same lines, Marx said that people do not treat a person as a king because he is a king in himself, but he is a king because people treat him like one. People do not treat an object as a work of art because it is in itself a work of art; it is a work of art because people treat it as one.

beauty is the last veil that conceals/announces the dimension of the Thing), while,

> rather than evoking it, science doesn't want to know anything about it. Which is why, perhaps, the Thing will habitually return through science in its most terrifying, catastrophic forms: the nuclear bomb, biological warfare, certain consequences of genetic engineering, and so on.[3]

What do all these examples enumerated by Leader have in common? They designate new "unnatural" (previously unknown) objects that emerged in our bodily reality as the result of scientific knowledge—they are, in a way, scientific knowledge materialized. As such, they undermine, violate even, our most elementary "sense of reality": what is so monstrous about the atomic bomb is not simply the amount of destruction but the more radical and unsettling fact that the very texture of our reality seems to disintegrate. Mutatis mutandis, the same goes for monsters that may emerge as the result of biogenetic engineering: in a sense, they are not a part of our "ordinary" reality.

Which, then, is more "radical," art or science? The alternative is properly undecidable. Science goes to the end in sublimating, in excluding "pathological" experiential reality; but, for that very reason, it also excludes the Thing. In art, sublimating is incomplete—the artist clings to (a piece of) experiential reality, but this very incompleteness of sublimating enables him or her to generate the effect of the Sublime by way of elevating this "pathological" remainder to the "dignity of the Thing." One encounters here the ambiguity of the Hegelian formula of art as "the sensitive manifestation of the Idea." As Schelling already knew, this formula is not to be read as if a preexisting notional truth is to be dressed in sensitive clothes—the structure is more paradoxical. The key term here is "Idea," which (in Kant) is precisely an index of the unknowable. So the point is that art manifests what *resists* the grasp of knowledge: the artistic "Beautiful" is the mask in the guise of which the abyss of the Real Thing, the Thing resisting symbolization, appears.[4] One thing is sure: the worst approach is to aim at a kind of "synthesis" of science and art—the only result of such endeavors is some kind of New Age monster of aestheticized knowledge.

So, sublimation in art. And, since cinema is the Deleuzian art par excellence, is not the first association here Hitchcock's *Vertigo*, arguably *the* film about the captivating force of a sublime image? As the last *Sight and Sound* opinion poll among critics and directors in 2002 showed, there

---

[3] Leader, op. cit., p. 105.
[4] Does this not hold even for Brecht, who appears to assert the opposite, the didacticism of art? Is the strength of *The Measure Taken* not that this piece articulates an excess (the dynamics of revolutionary political subjectivization) that eludes the Teaching staged in the play?

are, if we discount degenerate eccentrics, ultimately two basic groups of cinema lovers: those who think *Citizen Kane* is the greatest film ever made and those who think *Vertigo* deserves this title. (One should nonetheless note that the two films share the same composer, Bernard Hermann.) The author of the present lines belongs to those who think that, after the epoch of *The Battleship Potemkin* and the epoch of *Citizen Kane,* the next decades will be known as the epoch of *Vertigo,* that *Vertigo* will assert itself as the film which directly stands for cinema as such, *tout court* (more precisely, the only competition one can imagine is the one between Hitchcock's own two masterpieces, *Vertigo* and *Psycho*).

Hitchcock occupies a key place in Deleuze's cinema theory, that of the intermediary figure in the passage from movement-image to time-image. At a certain historical point, the subject is excessively overwhelmed by the shock of the Real; this intrusion of the Real disturbs the unity of action/reaction, the subject's direct insertion into a reality in which he can simply (re)act as an engaged agent. Overwhelmed by the Real, the subject is transformed into a powerless spectator of himself and his world. So, as Deleuze emphasizes, it is not enough to claim that, in modern cinema, the spectator is drawn into the action, turning into one of the agents: this feature is doubled by a more fundamental one, that of turning the agents themselves (screen personae, actors) into spectators of their own acts. For this reason, Deleuze considers Hitchcock's *Rear Window* as pointing toward the properly modern time-image. In it, James Stewart, the main agent, is reduced to a passive/impotent observer.

Kino-Eye

One of the most instructive things to do about Hitchcock's two master-pieces is to play the game of mental experiments. What if things were to take a different path (as they almost did)? Say, what if Bernard Hermann were to write for *Psycho* the planned score in free jazz style with heavy saxophone sound? *Vertigo* has three such "what ifs": what if Vera Miles had not gotten pregnant and had been able to play Madeleine-Judy, would it still be the same movie? What if, and this option cannot but strike us as ridiculous, Hitchcock had bowed to Paramount studio's pressure and accepted for the credit sequence the song "Vertigo," already written by the standard couple Livingstone-Evans? And, what if the film had been released with the extended ending, the additional short scene in Midge's apartment, with Scottie and Midge listening to the radio that announces that Elster was arrested abroad for the murder of his wife?

These mental experiments are often realized in what is one of the most revealing, although apparently trivial, aspects of Hitchcock studies: the extraordinary amount of factual mistakes, much greater than the (already low) cinema studies standard. Suffice it to recall one of the truly great Hitchcockians, Raymond Durgnat, who, in his *The Strange Case of Alfred Hitchcock,* in the course of a 40-page analysis of *Vertigo* (one should see it to believe it), while narrating the story in detail, continuously locates it in Los Angeles, not San Francisco, although the San Francisco background is so overwhelmingly present in *Vertigo* that one finds it very strange how someone could forget it. However, the very excess of these mistakes in the case of Hitchcock is symptomatic. If anything, then, far from simply devaluing the analyses in question, it rather bears witness to the excessive subjective engagement of the theorists in Hitchcock's films. As is the case with a Hitchcockian hero, they often blur the line that separates what effectively happens on the screen with their libidinal investment in it, an investment that finds its outlet in hallucinatory supplements or distortions. So, perhaps, in a true Freudian spirit, we need a theory of such misrepresentations. Stanley Cavell was right when, in a reply to his critics (who pointed out numerous mistakes in his retelling the story of films), he retorted that he fully stands by his mistakes.

These misrepresentations are most pertinent when they sustain a close formal analysis: how often, when a point is being made through a detailed description of the exchange of subjective (point-of-view) and objective shots and the cuts between them, when we take care to check it on video or DVD, we discover with surprise that the description is simply false. And, since the theoretical point of the analysis is often very perspicuous, we are tempted to adopt the attitude (falsely) attributed to Hegel: "If facts do not fit theory, so much worse for the facts!" One of the outstanding cases of such persisting misrepresentations concerns one of the most famous scenes in *Vertigo:* the magic moment when, in Ernie's restaurant, Scottie sees Madeleine for the first time.[5] More precisely, the misrepresentation concerns the status of two shots.

After seeing the entrance to Ernie's from the outside, there is a cut to Scottie sitting at the bar counter in the front room of the restaurant and looking through a partition into the large room with tables and guests. A long panning shot (without a cut) then takes us back and to the left, giving us an overview of the entire crowded room, the soundtrack reproducing the chatter and clatter of a busy restaurant—we should bear in mind that this, clearly, is *not* Scottie's point-of-view. All of a sudden, our (or, rather, the camera's) attention is caught by a focal point of attraction, a *fascinum* that fixes our gaze, a bright dazzling stain which we soon identify as the naked back of a beautiful woman. The background sound is then drowned out by Hermann's passionate music, which accompanies the

<hr>

5 I rely here extensively on Jean-Pierre Esquenazi, *Hitchcock et l'aventure de* Vertigo (Paris: CNRS Editions, 2001), pp. 123–26.

camera in its gradual approach to the *fascinum*—we first recognize Elster facing us, and from it we deduce that the woman must be Madeleine. After this long shot, there is a cut back to Scottie peeping at Madeleine's table from a perspective different from the previous long shot approaching her, and then another cut to Scottie's point-of-view and what he sees (Madeleine covering her back with her jacket and getting ready to leave). After Madeleine and Elster leave their table and approach Scottie on their way out, we get another famous shot. Scottie sees that the couple is getting close and, in order not to betray his mission, he looks away toward the glass across the partition of the bar, just barely peeping over his back. When Madeleine comes close to him and has to stop for a moment (while her husband is settling things with the waiter), we see her mysterious profile (and, the profile is always mysterious—we see only the half, while the other half can be a disgusting, disfigured face—or, as a matter of fact, the "true," common face of Judy). This fascinating shot is thus again *not* Scottie's point-of-view shot. It is only after Elster rejoins Madeleine, with the couple moving away from Scottie and approaching the exit from the restaurant, that we get, as a countershot to the shot of Scottie behind the bar, his point-of-view shot of Madeleine and Elster.

Here, again, the ambiguity of subjective and objective is crucial. Precisely insofar as Madeleine's profile is *not* Scottie's point-of-view, the shot of her profile is *totally* subjectivized, depicting, in a way, not what Scottie effectively sees but what he imagines, that is, his hallucinatory inner vision (recall how, while we see Madeleine's profile, the red background of the restaurant wall seems to get even more intense, almost threatening to explode in red heat turning into a yellow blaze—as if his passion is directly inscribed into the background). No wonder, then, that, although Scottie does not see Madeleine's profile, he acts as if he is mysteriously captivated by it, deeply affected by it. In these two excessive shots, we encounter the "kino-eye" at its purest: as the shot that is somehow "subjectivized," without the subject being given. The eye functions here as the "organ-without-body," directly registering the passion of an intensity that cannot be assumed by the (diegetic) subject.[6] So, what we get in these two shots that are subjectivized without being attributed to a subject is precisely the *pure, pre-subjective phenomenon*. Is the profile of Madeleine not such a pure appearance, permeated with an excessive libidinal investment—in a way, precisely too "*subjective*," too intense, to

[6] Another such example of an uncanny point-of-view shot without a bearer within the diegetic space are the two mysterious shots from above the sea water in the scene of Madeleine's jump below the Golden Gate Bridge. After we see Madeleine throwing petals from a bouquet of flowers into the sea, we see, from above, the petals floating on the waves; a little bit later, after she jumps into the sea, we see her from the same standpoint floating in the water. In both cases, the shot is somehow subjectivized, although there is no diegetic subject who can adopt that point-of-view.

be assumed by the subject? Or, to put it in Lacan's terms, this shot of the profile of Madeleine appears on the Other Scene, inaccessible to the subject precisely insofar as it is located in its very core.

We thus get, twice, the same movement from the excess of "subjectivity without subject-agent" to the standard procedure of "suture" (the exchange of objective and subjective shots—we are first shown the person looking and then what he sees). The excess is thus "domesticated," captivated in being caught within the subject-object mirror relationship as exemplified by the exchange of objective shot and point-of-view countershot. And, it is in order to erase the intensity of this subjectless "subjective" shot, displaying a kind of acephalous passion, that the large majority of interpreters, from Donald Spoto and Robin Wood onward, strangely insist, in their detailed description of the scene at Ernie's, that the two excessive shots render Scottie's point-of-view. In this way, the excess is contained within the suture-logic, reduced to the level of the standard exchange of objective and subjective shots. What we encounter in this excess is the gaze as object, free from the strings that attach it to a particular subject—no wonder that *Kino-Eye (Kino-glaz)*, Dziga Vertov's Soviet silent classic from 1924 (one of the highpoints of revolutionary cinema), takes as its emblem precisely the eye (of the camera) as an "autonomous organ" that wanders around in the early 1920s, giving us snippets of the NEP ("new economic politics") reality of the Soviet Union. Recall the common expression "to cast an eye over something," with its literal implication of picking the eye out of its socket and throwing it around. Martin, the legendary idiot from French fairy tales, did exactly this when his mother, worried that he will never find a wife, told him to go to church and cast an eye over the girls there. What he does is go to the butcher first, purchase a pig eye, and then, in the church, throw this eye around over the girls at prayer—no wonder he later reports to his mother that the girls were not too impressed by his behavior. This, precisely, is what revolutionary cinema should be doing: using the camera as a partial object, as an "eye" torn from the subject and freely thrown around—or, to quote Vertov himself:

> *The film camera drags the eyes of the audience* from the hands to the feet, from the feet to the eyes and so on in the most profitable order, and it organises the details into a regular montage exercise.[7]

We all know the uncanny moments in our everyday lives when we catch sight of our own image and this image is *not* looking back at us. I remember once trying to inspect a strange growth on the side of my head

---

[7] Quoted from Richard Taylor and Ian Christie, eds., *The Film Factory* (London: Routledge, 1988), p. 92.

using a double mirror, when, all of a sudden, I caught a glimpse of my face from the profile. The image replicated all my gestures, but in a weird uncoordinated way. In such a situation, "our specular image is torn away from us and, crucially, our look is no longer looking at ourselves."[8] It is in such weird experiences that one catches what Lacan called gaze as *objet petit a*, the part of our image that eludes the mirrorlike symmetrical relationship. When we see ourselves "from outside," from this impossible point, the traumatic feature is not that I am objectivized, reduced to an external object for the gaze, but, rather, that *it is my gaze itself that is objectivized*, which observes me from the outside, which, precisely, means that my gaze is no longer mine, that it is stolen from me.

A weird, real-life incident, which recently occurred to a friend of mine, renders palpable another aspect of this uncanny constellation. While he was driving a car with his wife sitting at his side, his cellular phone rang; he looked on the screen to see who was calling and saw his wife's name on display there. For a brief moment, he did not know what was going on: how can someone who is sitting at his side and talking to him also phone him at the same time? Is there a mysterious redoubling at work here, as in the famous scene from Lynch's *Lost Highway* in which the hero calls home and the phone is picked up by the evil Mystery Man who is standing there in front of him? (The explanation was not a theft of her phone but a more complex accident: his wife had her phone turned on in her bag that she was nervously pressing with her fingers; by chance, she pressed the buttons that set in motion the automatic call to her husband, since his name and number were on the top of the list of pre-programmed numbers.) This short vacillation mobilized the fetishist split: as in the old joke, he knew very well that there are no ghosts, that his wife does not have a ghostlike double calling him, but he was nonetheless, for a brief moment, seized by panic that this might be happening. Along the same lines, Fritz Lang wrote, apropos the release of his *Nibelungs* in 1924:

> Today someone who hears of Siegfried's battle with the dragon should not have to take it on faith, but instead should see it and experience it fully by seeing it. The mystical magic of Brunhild's mountain that stands under the eternal Northern Lights in the middle of the fiery seas should appear visible before him. The magic power of the *Tarnhelm*, with which Siegfried wins the bride for Gunther, should be believable through the viewer's own eyes.[9]

Who effectively believes here? Of course, not the spectator's conscious ego: we all know that what we see on the screen is the result of well-crafted tricks. Who, then? Let us return to *Vertigo*, to a detail of the

---

8 Leader, op. cit., p. 142.
9 Fritz Lang, quoted in Tom Gunning, *The Films of Fritz Lang* (London: BFI Publishing, 2000), p. 38.

scene in Scottie's apartment after he saves Madeleine from the bay under the Golden Gate Bridge, that demonstrates how censorship works (i.e., how its true target is not the viewer itself but the Third innocent observer). When the camera pans Scottie's room, we (automatically assume that we) see, suspended on a rope above the kitchen sink, Madeleine's underwear—a proof that, upon bringing her home, he undressed her. However, the Legion of Decency insisted that no underwear should be displayed, since its display might suggest that Scottie saw Madeleine naked. They got their way. If one freezes the image on DVD or video and inspects it, one can see that suspended on the rope are just a gown, socks, and two or three unspecified bits of cloth, but *no underwear*. This detail bears witness to the "hypocrisy" of censorship. Inattentive to details, not even given time to properly inspect the image, we, spectators, automatically assume that we see underwear, since such is the inexorable narrative logic of the scene.[10] *Who*, then, is effectively deceived here? *Who* should be assured that there is no feminine underwear hanging? The only candidate, of course, is the "big Other" itself, in the sense of the all-seeing, but innocent and stupid, observer. Censorship does not care if *we*, spectators, activate our dirty minds; the point is just that *the big Other should not notice it*.

The gaze *to which* it should be made clear that there is no underwear hanging above the sink is thus the nameless object-gaze, not the gaze attributed to any subject.[11] This same agency is also at work in a totally different kind of self-imposed censorship. Let us take a feature of the official discourse from today's North Korea, the only country that still practices the noble art of the Stalinist rewriting of history. The recent ruler, Kim Yong Il, was born in 1945 to his father, who was then in exile in a Siberian village. When, in the late 1950s, relations between North Korea and the USSR took a turn for the worse, the distance toward the USSR was signaled by a change of birthplace. All of a sudden and without explanations, the books were rewritten and it was claimed that Kim Yong Il was born at the top of the highest mountain of Korea. Before we all too quickly dismiss this as a sort of coded message to be properly deciphered

[10] And is this presumption not confirmed by what we see a couple of minutes later? When, after the phone call, Scottie returns to the drawing room and notices that Madeleine disappeared, he casts a quick glance at the kitchen sink and sees that the laundry previously hanging there also disappeared—why would Madeleine have taken it with her if it was not her underwear?

[11] Several years ago, when Deng Hsiao-Ping was still alive, although already retired from the post of the general secretary of the Chinese Communist Party, one of the top nomenklatura members was purged, and the official reason given to the press was that, in an interview with a foreign journalist, he divulged a state secret, namely, that Deng is still the supreme authority who makes effective decisions. The irony of it is that this fact was common knowledge. Everybody knew that Deng was still pulling the strings; it was in all the media all the time. The difference was just with regard to the big Other—this fact was never officially stated.

("It is not really about the birthplace, but just a signal about the changed relationship with the USSR!"), we should ask a more naive question: *why this strange censorship in the first place?* Why did the North Korean regime not simply and directly state that it is growing apart from the "revisionist" USSR? Why did it experience the need to formulate this change in its political alliances in the guise of a change of a simple, positive, historical fact?

Hitchcock as Anti-Plato

At this point, the probable reaction of the reader will be: of course, the opposition is simply the Platonic one, that between the limited view of us, mortals, and the view of the big Other which sees everything! And, effectively, as early as the late 1950s, immediately after *Vertigo*'s release, Eric Rohmer noted that the film is deeply immersed in the Platonic problematic.[12] However, this link is a negative one: *Vertigo* is, in a sense, the ultimate anti-Platonic film, a systematic materialist undermining of the Platonic project, akin to what Deleuze does in the appendix to *The Logic of Sense*. The murderous fury that seizes Scottie when he finally discovers that Judy, whom he tried to make into Madeleine, *is* (the woman he knew as) Madeleine, is the fury of the deceived Platonist when he perceives that the original he wants to remake in a perfect copy is already, in itself, a copy. The shock here is not that the original turns out to be merely a copy—a standard deception against which Platonism warns us all the time—but that (what we took to be) *the copy turns out to be the original.* Perhaps one should read *Vertigo* together with *General della Rovere*, Rossellini's late masterpiece, the story of a small thief and swindler (superbly played by Vittorio de Sica) who is arrested by the Germans in the winter of 1944–1945 in Genoa. The Germans propose a deal: in the prison, he will pass for the legendary General della Rovere, a Resistance hero, so that other political prisoners will tell him their secrets, especially the true identity of "Fabrizio," a key Resistance leader. However, the small thief gets so intensely caught up in the role that, at the end, he fully assumes it and prefers to be shot as General della Rovere. The anti-Platonic reversal to be accomplished apropos *General della Rovere* is the same as that of *Vertigo:* what if the "true" della Rovere was already a fake, in exactly the same way that the "true" Madeleine was already Judy faking to be Madeleine? That is to say, what if he was also, as a private person, a petty swindler acting as "General della Rovere," wearing this role as a mask? (The further, even more unsettling, question here is as follows: is such a pathetic identification with the fake role the ultimate

[12] See Eric Rohmer, "L'helice et l'idée," *Cahiers du cinéma* 93 (March 1959).

horizon of ethical experience?[13] Can we imagine the inverse situation: the "real" della Rovere is arrested, and the Resistance lets him know that he has to dirty his image, to die as a miserable traitor, in order to do one last great service to the Resistance?)

The shock of Scottie at the moment of recognition is also a Kafkaesque one. In the same way that, at the end of the parable on the Door of the Law in *The Trial*, the man from the country learns that the door was there only for him (that the spectacle of the magnificent Door was staged for his gaze, that the scene with regard to which he perceived himself as an accidental witness allowed to take a half-prohibited glimpse at it was entirely set up to fascinate him), in *Vertigo* also Scottie has to accept that the fascinating spectacle of Madeleine, which he was secretly following, was staged for his gaze only, that his gaze was included in it from the very beginning.[14]

When Scottie sees Madeleine's necklace on Judy, this object is a sign— of what? If Scottie were to be minimally open to Judy, he could have read it as the sign of Judy's love for him; she loved him so much that she wanted to keep a souvenir of her relationship with him. Instead, he opts for the Platonic reading: to put it abruptly, *the necklace demonstrates that Madeleine does not exist.*[15] Already, long before the final reversal (Scottie's insight into the identity of Judy and Madeleine), the famous fake portrait proposed to him by Midge, which reproduces the Carlotta portrait with Midge's spectacled head replacing the original head, is an affront to his Platonic sensitivity (no wonder he leaves the scene totally crushed). Again, what makes this scene so traumatic is not that it betrays/falsifies the original but that it undermines it from within. The key shot of this scene is the one in which we see (from Scottie's point-of-view) the Carlotta portrait with Midge's face side by side with the "real" Midge herself, in the same posture. One should reflect on the gap that separates this shot from the similar shot in Otto Preminger's *Laura*, with Laura side by side with her portrait. In *Laura,* the shock of the hero-investigator already in love with Laura (and, consequently, of us, spectators)—the hero thinks Laura is dead and is fascinated by her portrait—is to see the "real" Laura come to life and emerge side by side with her portrait. Here, the fascinating power of Laura is maintained, rather than being undermined.

---

[13] Is such an act of an "absolute ethics of alienation," brought to its extreme, not that of the rabbi in Auschwitz who, even there, obeyed the rule of fasting, and refused on those days even the meagre daily ration?

[14] Sometimes there is even less than a small step from the sublime to the ridiculous. *Vertigo* is definitely a sublime story, not meant to be laughed at. Yet, its twist could best be encapsulated as a variation of the old Marx brothers' joke: "this woman (Judy) looks like Madeleine and acts like Madeleine, but this should not deceive you—she *is* Madeleine!"

[15] Esquenazi, op. cit., p. 193.

If we are looking for a parallel anti-Platonic gesture, we find it in Billy Wilder's underrated *Fedora*, which, in a way, inverts the *Vertigo* story. The film's final surprise is not that the person who looks like X effectively *is* X but, on the contrary, that X *is not itself*. The movie tells the story of an elderly Hollywood star who mysteriously retains the beauty of her youthful appearance. A young actor who falls in love with her finally discovers the secret of her eternal youth: the woman who appeared as Fedora is actually her own look-alike daughter who replaced her at a certain point, whereas the true Fedora lives a secluded life in a lone villa. Fedora organized this replacement (which condemned her daughter to a total identification with the maternal image) so that her stardom will outlive her and continue to shine even after her physical decline. Both the mother and the daughter are thus thoroughly alienated: the mother is excluded from the public space, since her public Self is embodied in her daughter and the daughter is allowed to appear in the public space but is deprived of her symbolic identity. Is the very unpalatable, disturbing flavor of the film not due to the fact that it comes all too close to fantasy? Back to *Vertigo*. Crucial for the film's anti-Platonic thrust are the deceivingly "dead" ten minutes of the film after Scottie meets Judy and before he fully engages in her violent transformation into Madeleine (i.e., in-between Judy's famous flashback into the scene of her fake suicide and the visit to the exclusive fashion store that marks the beginning of the transformation). Three key scenes occurring here display the terms of how Scottie relates to Judy, and they stage a systematic undermining of the anti-feminist Platonic coordinates.

(1) First is the scene of their initial evening date (at Ernie's again), with the couple seated at a table opposite each other, obviously failing to engage in a meaningful conversation. All of a sudden, Scottie's gaze gets fixed on some point behind Judy, and we see that it is a woman vaguely similar to Madeleine, dressed in the same gray gown. When Judy notices what attracted Scottie's gaze, she is, of course, deeply hurt. The crucial moment here is when we see, from Scottie's point-of-view, the two of them in the same shot: Judy on the right side, close to him, the woman in gray to the left, in the background. Again, we get the vulgar reality side by side with the ethereal apparition of the ideal. The split from the shot of Midge and the portrait of Carlotta is here externalized onto two different persons: Judy right here and the momentary spectral apparition of Madeleine. The brief moment when Scottie is deluded into thinking that what he sees is Madeleine is the moment at which *the Absolute appears:* it appears "as such" in the very domain of appearances, in those sublime moments when a supra-sensible dimension "shines through" in our ordinary reality. When Plato dismisses art as the "copy of a copy," when he introduces three ontological levels (ideas, their material copies,

and copies of these copies), what gets lost is that the Idea can emerge only in the distance that separates our ordinary material reality (second level) from its copy. When we copy a material object, *what* we effectively copy, what our copy refers to, is never this particular object itself but its Idea. It is similar with a mask that engenders a third reality, a ghost in the mask that is not the face hidden beneath it. In this precise sense, the Idea is the appearance *as* appearance (as Hegel and Lacan put it): the Idea is something that *appears* when reality (the first-level copy/imitation of the Idea) is itself copied. It is that which is in the copy more than the original itself. No wonder that Plato reacted in such a panicky way against the threat of art. As Lacan pointed out in his *Séminar XI*, art (as the copy of a copy) does not compete with material objects as "direct," first-level copies of the Idea; rather, it competes with the supra-sensible Idea itself.[16]

(2) Second is the evening scene in Judy's room in the Empire Hotel, where the couple returns after diner at Ernie's. In this scene, the externalized split from the scene at Ernie's is, as it were, projected back into Judy. We see Judy's profile, which is completely dark (in contrast to Madeleine's dazzling profile at Ernie's). From this shot, we pass to the front shot of her face, the left half completely dark and the right half in a weird green (from the neon light outside the room). Instead of reading this shot as simply designating Judy's inner conflict, her inner split, one should confer on it its full ontological ambiguity. As in some versions of Gnosticism, Judy is depicted here as a protoentity, not yet ontologically constituted in full (a greenish plasm plus darkness). It is as if, to fully exist, her dark half waits to be filled in with the ethereal image of Madeleine. In other words, we get here literally the other side of the magnificent profile shot of Madeleine at Ernie's, its negative: the previously unseen dark half of Madeleine (the green anguished face of Judy) plus the dark half to be filled in by Madeleine's dazzling profile. And, at this very point at which Judy is reduced to less-than-object, to a formless pre-ontological stain, she is *subjectivized*—this anguished half-face, totally unsure of itself, designates the birth of the subject. Recall the proverbial imaginary resolution of Zeno's paradox of infinite divisibility: if we continue the division long enough, we will finally stumble on a point at which a part will no longer be divided into smaller parts but into a (smaller) part *and nothing*—this nothing "is" the subject.[17] And is

[16] See part 2 of Jacques Lacan, *The Four Fundamental Concepts of Psycho-Analysis* (New York: Norton, 1977).
[17] And, as to the reproach that such a conclusion of the work of division simply relies on our finitude, one should reply that therein resides the point of ontological difference: it is inextricably linked to human finitude.

this, exactly, not the division of Judy in the above-mentioned shot? We see half of her face while the other half is a dark void.

(3) Finally is the scene in a dancing bar, which perfectly renders Scottie's disgust at Judy's body, at her physical proximity (in contrast to the ethereal presence of Madeleine). While the couple is dancing, it is painfully obvious that Judy wants close contact with Scottie, whereas Scottie finds her bodily proximity repellent. How, then, do love and sexual *jouissance* relate? Although sexual *jouissance* is inherently masturbatory and idiotic, isolating me—the core of my subjectivity—from my partner, reducing the partner to an instrument (of my *jouissance*), it does *not* hold that, for this reason, I must renounce sexual *jouissance* to assert my love for the other. On the contrary, it is precisely such a renunciation that is, as a rule, a fake, a stratagem masking some unacknowledged *jouissance* (there is nothing more elementary than the *jouissance* provided by renouncing pleasures in sacrificing oneself for the other). For that reason, perhaps the ultimate proof of love for the other is that I am ready to share with the other the very heart of my masturbatory idiotic *jouissance*. Within this phallic masturbatory domain, the ironic quip of Karl Kraus, quoted by Freud, thus fully hits the mark: "*Koitus ist nur ein ungenügendes Surrogat für die Onanie!* (Coitus is only an insufficient substitute for masturbation!)" Scottie does not really want to make love to Judy-Madeleine; he literally wants to masturbate with the aid of her real body. And this phallic dimension also enables us to define, in a precise way, sexual possession. Its ultimate formula is not the exploitation of the partner as a sexual object but the renunciation of such use, the attitude of "I do not want anything from you, no sexual favors . . . on condition that you also do not have any sex with others!" This refusal to share sexual *jouissance is* absolute possession.

Do these three scenes not form a kind of Hegelian syllogism, with the first premise (Scottie is looking for Madeleine in Judy), the second premise (Judy herself is reduced to a proto-entity, an incomplete, formless slime, a kind of Platonic *chora,* a pure receptable for the sublime Idea of Madeleine), and the inevitable conclusion (Judy, in her bodily presence, can only be an object of disgust for Scottie)? Why, then, is Scottie's search for the mysterious truth about the beloved woman a fake? Apropos Antonioni's *Identification of a Woman*, Alain Badiou asked a simple, but crucial and difficult, question: how is the identification of a woman in love possible?[18] His answer is neither through her body (such a pornographic identification can end up only in the obscure indistinction of fornicating) nor through deep psychological knowledge of her persona,

---

[18] See Alain Badiou, *Petit manuel d'inésthétique* (Paris: Editions du Seuil, 1998).

which ends up in obscurantism. From this perspective, woman appears as a mystery. However, the mistake is to conceive of identification in love as epistemological, as an affair of knowledge (and, as we all know, the biblical term for fornication is "[carnal] knowledge"). Identification is a fact of *decision;* it relies on an abyssal decision to love a woman, a decision that cannot be grounded in her positive properties. The moment we formulate identification as knowing, the woman withdraws herself, appearing as mystery. The relationship is thus the opposite to what the standard male obscurantism claims. It is not that we cannot identify a woman because she is unknowable, an impenetrable mystery, but, on the contrary, the moment the male subject withdraws from the *act* of decision and adopts the stance of knowing, the woman emerges as a Mystery. (Is this not a kind of inversion of Otto Weininger? Woman as mystery is just an objectivization of the male ethical withdrawal, indecision.)

Vertigo is a movie in three parts (plus a prologue), each part lasting almost forty minutes, and with the closure marked by the suicidal jump of the heroine (first into San Francisco Bay, then twice from the tower at the Juan Batista mission). While each part focuses on the figure of Judy-Madeleine, it obeys an economy of its own; in each of them, Judy-Madeleine occupies a specific place. In part one, she is Phi, an imaginary presence at the site of the Real; in part two, she is S(a), the signifier of the barred Other (i.e., the signifier of a certain mystery); in part three, she is *a*, the excremental abject-remainder. All of these three figures are, of course, forms of defense against the central abyss threatening to swallow Scottie. *Vertigo* makes it clear that the phobia of heights is actually the phobia of depths: "It is the abyss, like *das Ding,* that is calling. The subject who suffers from vertigo perceives a call to which he or she is about to answer, throwing him- or herself into the void."[19] One should distinguish this Thing from the object-cause of desire. The Thing is this abyss that threatens to swallow Scottie, whereas the "object small a" is the pure *form* of a curve, this *sinthome* discernible in multiple guises that are echoed in each other—the uncanny curved shapes from the credits, the curve in Madeleine's hair (copied from the same curve in the hair of Carlotta Valdes from her portrait), the winding streets of San Francisco

---

[19] Roberto Harari, *Lacan's Seminar "On Anxiety": An Introduction* (New York: Other Press, 2001), p. 74. What one should bear in mind is that all three persons from the beginning of *Vertigo* who belong to the ordinary reality are frustrated, failed personalities. Scottie is disabled, his vertigo preventing him from pursuing his career, being left to dwell in a suspended space; Midge, his ex-fiancée (the spectacled "woman who knows too much"), even if she pretends to possess sexual enlightenment and maturity, dealing with the topic in an easy, mocking way (recall the discussion with Scottie about her drawing of a new bra model), is deeply sexually frustrated, unable to get over her infatuation with Scottie; Elster himself, the villain of the piece, is frustrated by the fact that he is not able to enjoy full "power and freedom" as the male inhabitants in old San Francisco were able to do.

where Scottie is tailing Madeleine, the spiral of the descending staircase in the tower of the Juan Batista mission, up to the full circle (360 degrees) movement of the camera around the embracing Madeleine and Scottie.

This is why *Vertigo* is not simply the movie about a contemporary case of courtly love but the movie that renders palpable the deadlock of courtly love, the terrible price that both partners have to pay for it. When, in his Seminar VII on the *Ethics of Psychoanalysis*, Lacan argues that, in courtly love poetry, the Lady is reduced to a void, that the predicates attributed to her (beauty, wisdom, etc.) are not to be read as actual descriptions, so that it appears as if all poets are addressing the same empty abstraction,[20] what is at stake here is not the claim that the poet loves the lady independently of her positive features, that he aims at the core of her being, the void of her subjectivity beyond all her positive characteristics.[21] Courtly love poetry effectively involves the *mortification* of the beloved Lady: what is missing in courtly love is the sign of imperfection, the minimal "pathological stain" that *causes* me to fall in love. Or, to put it in Badiou's terms, courtly love goes to the end in the passion of purification, abstracting all positive features of its object, reducing it to the Void. In contrast to it, true love follows the passion of subtraction—in suspending the weight of all positive features of the beloved, it does not merely reduce the beloved Other to a void; it also renders visible the "minimal difference" between the void and the pathological stain, the remainder of the Real, which sustains this void. However, to grasp properly the fatal attraction of the lady qua abyssal Thing, it is crucial to approach it through the topic of gaze. The gaze is not simply transfixed by the emergence of the excessive-unbearable Thing. Rather, it is, that the Thing (what we perceive as the traumatic-elusive point of attraction in the space of reality) is the very point at which the gaze inscribes itself into reality, the point at which the subject *encounters itself as gaze*.

The Cut of the Gaze

About one-third into Hitchcock's *Shadow of a Doubt,* there is a brief passage that fully bears witness to his genius: the young FBI detective investigating Uncle Charlie takes the latter's young niece Charlie out for a date; we see them in a couple of shots walking along the streets, laughing and talking vivaciously—then, unexpectedly, we get a fast fade out into

---

[20] See Jacques Lacan, *The Ethics of Psychoanalysis* (London: Routledge, 1992), p. 150.
[21] When a woman complains "I do not want you to love me just because of my body—I also want you to admire my brain!" this demand is a fake, a deceptive offer of another lure to avoid exposing the very heart of one's being.

the American shot of Charlie in a state of shock, gaping with a transfixed gaze at the detective off screen, blurting out nervously "I know what you are really! You are a detective!" Of course, we do expect the detective to use the opportunity and to acquaint Charlie with Uncle Charlie's dark side. However, what we expect is a gradual passage. The detective should first break the cheerful mood and address the serious issue, thus provoking Charlie's outburst when she realizes how she was being manipulated (the detective asked her for a date not because he liked her but as part of his professional work). Instead of this expected gradual passage, we are directly confronted with the traumatized Charlie. (One could argue that, with her shocked gaze, Charlie does not react to some previous detective's words: what happened is that, in the middle of the frivolous conversation, she all of a sudden grasps that there is something other than flirting going on. However, even in this case, the standard procedure to film the scene would have been to show the couple pleasantly talking; then, all of a sudden, Charlie would be struck by the fateful insight. The key Hitchcockian effect would thus be missing: the direct jump to the shocked gaze.) It is only *after* this shocking discontinuity that the detective voices his suspicions about Uncle Charlie's murderous past. To put it in temporal terms: it is as if, in this scene, the effect precedes its cause, that is, we are first shown the effect (the traumatized gaze) and then given the context responsible for this traumatic impact—or are we? Is the relationship between cause and effect really inverted here? What if the gaze is here not merely a recipient of the event? What if it somehow mysteriously generates the perceived incident? What if the conversation that follows is ultimately an attempt to symbolize/domesticate this traumatic incident? Such a cut in the continuous texture of reality, such a momentous inversion of the proper temporal order, signals the intervention of the Real. If the scene were to be short in the linear order (first the cause, then the effect), the texture of reality would have been left undamaged. That is to say, the Real is discernible in the gap between the true cause of the terrified gaze and what we are given to see later as its cause: the true cause of the terrified gaze is not what we are shown or told afterwards but the fantasized, traumatic excess "projected" by the gaze into the perceived reality.

A more complex example of the same procedure is one of the key recurring Hitchcockian motifs, that of a couple arguing on a small hill, half-barren, with a few trees and bushes, usually windy, just outside the scope of the public place populated by a group of ignorant observers. For Alain Bergala, this scene stages Adam and Eve in the Garden of Eden, just prior to being chased from it, in the process of tasting the forbidden knowledge.[22] If one discounts a couple of minor references and variations (from *Notorious* to *Topaz*), there are three main versions of it: *Suspicion, The Birds,* and *Torn Curtain.* In *Suspicion,* it is the brief shot of Grant and Fontaine struggling on a windy hill near the church, observed by Fontaine's friend from the entrance to the church. In *The Birds,* it is the scene, just prior to the first bird attack on the group of children, in which Mitch and Melanie withdraw to a small hill above the picnic place where children are celebrating a birthday party. Finally, in *Torn Curtain,* it is the scene in which Newman and Andrews withdraw to a small hill, out of earshot of the East German secret police officials who can only observe them—there, Newman explains to his fiancée the truth about his mission.

The key feature is that, in all three cases, the couple on the hill is observed by an innocent-threatening-ignorant observer below the hill (friends close to the church, Mitch's ex-lover and mother, East German secret policemen, respectively) who sees only the scene and is unable to discern the meaning of the intense exchange of the observed couple. The traumatic character of the scene, the excess of the Real that pertains to it, hinges on this gaze: it is only from the standpoint of this gaze that the scene is traumatic. When, later, the camera jumps closer to the couple, the situation is again "normalized." Bergala is right to emphasize how this scene reproduces the basic coordinates of the child's primordial sexual encounter: witnessing the parents' lovemaking, unable to decide what the scene he sees is (violence or love?). The problem of his account is simply that it appears all too close to the standard "archetypal" reading, trying to identify the kernel of the meaning of the scene instead of conceiving of it as a meaningless *sinthome.* The fundamental lesson of this procedure is that there is more truth in this misperception by the partial gaze than in the "objective," true state of things. This gap is rendered palpable by the fantasmatic opening scene of *Beau Geste* (William Wellman), the classic Hollywood adventure melodrama from 1939: the mysterious desert fortress in which there is no living person, only dead soldiers placed on its walls, a true desert counterpart to the specter of the ship floating around without any crew. Toward its end, *Beau Geste* renders the same sequence from within the fortress, namely, it depicts how this haunting image of the fortress with dead soldiers was generated. The key point here is the *excess* of this scene of illusory appearance: its libidinal force overpowers its later rational explanation.

---

[22] Alain Bergala, "Alfred, Adam and Eve," in *Hitchcock and Art: Fatal Coincidences* (accompanying volume to the Centre Pompidou exposition), edited by Dominique Paini and Guy Cogeval (Paris: Centre Pompidou and Mazotta, 2001), pp. 111–25.

The notion of sacrifice usually associated with Lacanian psychoanalysis is that of a gesture that enacts the disavowal of the impotence of the big Other: at its most elementary, the subject offers his sacrifice not to profit from it himself but to fill in the lack in the Other, to sustain the appearance of the Other's omnipotence or, at least, consistency. In *Beau Geste,* the elder of the three brothers (Gary Cooper) living with their benevolent aunt, in what seems to be a gesture of excessive, ungrateful cruelty, steals the enormously expensive diamond necklace that is the pride of the aunt's family. He disappears with it, knowing that his reputation is ruined, that he will be forever known as the ungracious embezzler of his benefactress. So, why did he do it? At the end of the film, we learn that he did it to prevent the embarrassing disclosure that the necklace was a fake. Unbeknownst to everyone else, he knew that, some time ago, the aunt had to sell the necklace to a rich maharaja to save the family from bankruptcy, and she replaced it with a worthless imitation. Just prior to his "theft," he learned that a distant uncle who co-owned the necklace wanted it sold for financial gain; if the necklace were to be sold, the fact that it is a fake would undoubtedly be discovered. Consequently, the only way to retain the aunt's (and, thus, the family's) honor is to stage its theft. This is the proper deception of the crime of stealing: to occlude the fact that, ultimately, *there is nothing to steal*—this way, the constitutive lack of the Other is concealed (i.e., the illusion is maintained that the Other possessed what was stolen from it). If, in love, one gives what one does not possess, in a crime of love, one steals from the beloved Other what the Other does not possess—the "beau geste" of the film's title alludes to precisely this. And therein also resides the meaning of sacrifice: one sacrifices oneself (one's honor and future in respectful society) to maintain the appearance of the Other's honor, to save the beloved Other from shame.

One cannot but take note of the strange echo between the two false appearances: the fortress with dead soldiers (i.e., with no one to defend it) and the other fortress, the English home with no real wealth sustaining it, the stone on which the family fortune rests being a fake. This brings us to the opposition of the two communities: the warm English upper-class family home dominated by a Woman versus the all-male Foreign Legion community dominated by the fascinating figure of the sadistic, but militarily very efficient, Russian sergeant Markoff (in the novel by Percival Christopher Wren, on which the movie is based, he is a Frenchman named Lejeune—in a displacement typical of the late 1930s, the evil character was Russified, although, in a politically interesting way, the film hints that Markoff must be a White Russian counterrevolutionary émigré). The two communities, of course, are equivalent, two sides of the same coin, of the suspended "normal" paternal authority. One is even tempted to claim that Sir Hector Brandon, the bad husband of the good Aunt Patricia (who is always away from home, looking for adventures in exotic countries) *is* libidinally equivalent to the evil Markoff.[23]

And does the same not also apply to Hitchcock's *Vertigo*? Like *Beau Geste*, the focus of *Vertigo* is on creating the perfect semblance, which is then explained away. Furthermore, the whole point is that, when we learn the "true story," the first part of the movie (until Madeleine's suicide) is *not* simply explained away as a fake—there is more truth in the appearance than in the true story behind it. Truth has the structure of a fiction, which is why we often pay the price for getting involved in a fake appearance in flesh, by death. Playing with appearances *is* playing with fire. This is why the crucial question of *Vertigo* is "But how real is Elster?" Like the Judge in Kieslowski's *Red*, is Elster not, as to his libidinal status, the fantasy product of the hero's imagination? This fits well into the reading of *Vertigo* as a film that plays on two registers:

> On the one hand, it is a carefully crafted "yarn," the story of the character, Scottie, of what happens to him, and of how he responds, located in a detailed and recognisable California environment. On the other hand, it is famously dreamlike both in its texture and in the way it introduces story and protagonist. Echoing Robin Wood, James Maxfield argues that "everything after the opening sequence is . . . dream or fantasy."[24]

In the second reading, the structure is the one of Ambrose Bierce's famous short story "An Occurrence at Owl Creek Bridge," in which everything that follows the hanging of a man at the story's outset is, at the end, revealed as the fantasy of the dying man. This structure is also recognizable in films like *Point Blank*, which is often read as depicting the fantasy of the mortally wounded Lee Marvin. The crucial point here is to identify what Deleuze would have called the "dark precursors," the nonrepeated, unique elements that, precisely insofar as they belong only to one level, serve as the bridge, mediator, or point of passage between the two. The point is not so much to identify the stand-in for reality within fantasy (like, in *Vanilla Sky*, the doctor from real life who appears within the hero's digitally generated universe to warn him) but, rather, to identify the stand-in for the "illusory" mental universe within "reality" itself. The gap and, simultaneously, link between the two levels is

---

[23] This brings us to the failed sexual relation. The novel concludes with George Lawrence, the army officer (its narrator), deeply in love with Aunt Patricia. He patiently waits for her for decades, finally marrying her. The balance is thus restored, and the source of evil (the twisted maternal desire, that is, the young Patricia choosing the wrong man for her husband) is undone.

[24] Charles Barr, *Vertigo* (London: BFI Classics, 2002), p. 77.

rendered palpable in the mysterious moments of the perfect timing of the interrupting intrusion of the third agency:

- in the pivotal and, perhaps, most beautiful scene of the film, that of Scottie and Madeleine in his apartment, after he saves her from drowning under the Golden Gate Bridge: "As their talk grows more intimate, Scottie offers to get her more coffee, and reaches for her cup; their hands touch, and we can see, within a two-shot, that for both of them this is a moment of erotic tension and possibility. Immediately, the phone rings, the tension is broken, and Scottie leaves the room to answer it. When he returns, she has gone. . . . The call is, of course, from Elster, and its timing is uncannily precise, to the second, allowing them to get so far but no further."[25]
- at the film's end, the nun appears in the tower at the very moment Scottie and Judy embrace in a reconciliation, with Scottie content to accept the reality of Judy: "What if the nun had not appeared, at the moment when, for the very first time, they are being completely open and honest with each other?"[26] Would they live happily ever after?[27]

When the Fantasy Falls Apart

One should here go a crucial step further into the disintegration of fantasy. David Lynch's *Mulholland Drive* perfectly depicts this gradual disintegration. The two main stages of this process are, first, the excessively intense acting in the test scene, and, then, when the autonomous partial object ("organ without a body") emerges in the scene in the nightclub *Silencio*. Here, the movement is from the excess, which is still contained in reality although already disturbing it, sticking out of it, to its full autonomization, which causes the disintegration of reality itself; say, from the pathological distortion of a mouth to the mouth leaving the body and

---

[25] Barr, op. cit., p. 59.

[26] Barr, op. cit., p. 76.

[27] In Irwin Shaw's *Rich Man, Poor Man,* a bestseller from the 1960s, there is a memorable scene in which the heroine is accidentally intercepted by her fiancé (and future husband) when she is on her way to a suburban house in which a group of young black men are waiting for her. She had accepted their offer of $400 if she comes to their apartment and is at their disposal to engage in repeated group sexual acts with them for an entire afternoon. The impact of this scene lies in its ambiguity. The heroine, of course, does not accept the offer only for financial reasons; rather, she succumbed to the lure of a kind of antiracist politicosexual utopia (the blacks, who are shy and respectful toward her—not the standard macho figures—dared to invite her because, in contrast to other of their common acquaintances from their workplace, she treated them in a friendly and warm way). This is yet another (and perhaps the ultimate) example of a chance encounter intervening at exactly the right moment, as an agent of established morality.

floating around as a spectral partial object (the same as in Syberberg's *Parsifal,* in which we pass from the wound on the body to the wound as autonomous organ without a body, outside it). This excess is what Lacan calls *lamella,* the infinitely plastic object that can transpose itself from one to another medium: from excessive (trans-semantic) scream to a stain (or anamorphic visual distortion). Is this not what takes place in Munch's *Scream*? The scream is silent, a bone stuck in the throat, a stop-page that cannot be vocalized and can express itself only in the guise of a silent visual distortion, curving the space around the screaming subject.

In *Silencio,* where Betty and Rita go after successfully making love, a singer sings Roy Orbison's "Crying" in Spanish. When the singer col-lapses, the song goes on. At this point, the fantasy collapses too—*not* in the sense that "the mist dissipates and we are back in sober reality" but, rather, in the sense that, from within, as it were, fantasy loses its mooring in reality and gets autonomized, as a pure spectral apparition of a bodi-less "undead" voice (a rendering of the Real of the Voice similar to that at the beginning of Sergio Leone's *Once upon a Time in America,* in which we see a phone ringing loudly, and, when a hand picks up the receiver, the ringing goes on). The shot of the voice continuing to sing even when its bodily support collapses is the inversion of the famous Balanchine ballet staging of a short piece by Webern: in this staging, the dancing goes on even after the music stops. We have thus, in one case, the voice that insists even when deprived of its bodily support, and, in the other case, the bodily movements that insist even when deprived of their vo-cal (musical) support. The effect is not simply symmetrical because, in the first case, we have the undead vocal drive, the immortal life, going on, whereas in the second case, the figures that continue to dance are "dead men dancing," shadows deprived of their life-substance. However, in both cases what we witness is the dissociation between reality and the real; in both cases the Real insists even when reality disintegrates. This real, of course, is the fantasmatic Real at its purest. And, to put it in Deleuzian terms, is this "autonomization" of the partial object not the very moment of the extraction of the virtual from the actual? The status of the "organ without the body" is that of the virtual—in other words, in the opposition between the virtual and the actual, the Lacanian Real is on the side of the virtual.

Of course, in all of these cases, the shock effect is followed by an explanation that relocates it back within ordinary reality. In the night club scene in *Mulholland Drive,* we are warned at the very outset that we are listening to prerecorded music, that the singers just mimic the act of singing; in the case from Leone, the phone we continue to hear ringing after the receiver is picked up is another phone, and so forth.

However, what is nonetheless crucial is that, for a short moment, part of reality was (mis)perceived as a nightmarish apparition—and, in a way, this apparition was "more real than reality itself," since, in it, the Real shone through. In short, one should discern which part of reality is "transfunctionalized" through fantasy, so that, although it is part of reality, it is perceived in a fictional mode. Much more difficult than to denounce/unmask (what appears as) reality as fiction is to recognize in "real" reality the part of fiction. Is this not what happens in transference, in which, while we relate to a "real person" in front of us, we effectively relate to the fiction of, say, our father? Recall also *Home Alone,* especially part two. In both parts, there is a cut two-thirds into the film; although the story seems to take place in a continuous diegetic place, it is clear that, with the final confrontation between the small kid and the two robbers, we enter a different ontological realm, a plastic cartoon-space in which there is no death, in which my head can explode, yet I go on as normal in the next scene. Again, part of reality is fictionalized.

It is such a fictionalized partial object that also serves as the support of voice. In his advice to young composers, Richard Wagner wrote that, after elaborating the contours of the musical piece one wants to compose, one should erase everything and just focus one's mind on a lone head floating freely in a dark void and wait for the moment when this white apparition starts to move its lips and sing. This music should be the germ of the work to be composed. Is this procedure not that of getting the partial object to sing? It is not a person (a subject)—the object itself should start to sing.

"I, the Truth, Am Speaking"

At the beginning of Monteverdi's *Orfeo,* the goddess of music introduces herself with the words "Io sono la musica . . ."—is this not something that soon afterward, when "psychological" subjects had invaded the stage, became unthinkable, or, rather, unrepresentable? One had to wait until the 1930s for such strange creatures to reappear on the stage. In Bertolt Brecht's "learning plays," an actor enters the stage and addresses the public: "I am a capitalist. I'll now approach a worker and try to deceive him with my talk of the equity of capitalism." The charm of this procedure resides in the psychologically "impossible" combination, in one and the same actor, of two distinct roles, as if a person from the play's diegetic reality can also, from time to time, step outside himself and utter "objective" comments about his acts and attitudes. This second role is the descendant of Prologue, a unique figure that often appears in Shakespeare but that later disappears with the advent of psychological-realist theater: an actor who, at the beginning, between the scenes or at the end, addresses the public directly with explanatory comments, didactic or ironic points about the play, and so forth. Prologue thus effectively functions as the Freudian *Vorstellungs-Repräsentanz* (representative of representing): an element that, on stage, within its diegetic reality of representation, holds the place of the mechanism of representing as such, thereby introducing the moment of distance, interpretation, ironic comment—and, for that reason, it had to disappear with the victory of psychological realism. Things are here even more complex than in a naive version of Brecht. The uncanny effect of Prologue does not hinge on the fact that he "disturbs the stage illusion" but, on the contrary, on the fact that he does *not* disturb it. Notwithstanding his comments and their effect of "extraneation," we, the spectators, are still able to participate in the stage illusion. And this is how one should also locate Lacan's "*c'est moi, la vérité, qui parle*" from his "*La Chose freudienne*,"[28] namely, as the same shocking emergence of a word where one would not expect it. Therein resides the traumatic impact of this shift: the distance between the Other and the Thing is momentarily suspended, and it is the Thing itself that starts to speak. One cannot help but recall here Marx's version of Lacan's "*c'est moi, la vérité, qui parle*," his famous "Let us imagine that a commodity would start to speak..." from *Capital:* here also, the key to the logic of commodity fetishism is provided by the fictive "magic" of an object starting to talk.[29]

This notion of the partial object that starts to talk is also the site of forceful ideological investments, especially with regard to the way the male gaze endeavors to counter the fundamental hystericity (lie, lack of a firm position of enunciation) of the feminine speech. In his extraordinary philosophical novel *Les Bijoux indiscrets* (1748), Denis Diderot renders the ultimate fantasmatic answer:[30] a woman speaks with *two* voices. The first one, that of her soul (mind and heart), is constitutively lying, deceiving, covering up her promiscuity; it is only the second voice, that of her *bijou* (the pearl which, of course, is vagina itself), which, by definition, *always* speaks the truth—a boring, repetitive, automatic, "mechanical" truth, but truth nonetheless, the truth about her unconstrained voluptuousness. This notion of the "talking vagina" is not meant as a metaphor but meant quite literally. Diderot provides the anatomical description of vagina as *instrument à corde et à vent* capable of emitting sounds. (He even reports on a medical experiment: after excising

---

[28] See Jacques Lacan, *Ecrits* (Paris: Editions du Seuil, 1966), p. 409.

[29] Of course, this scene of commodities talking to each other is a fiction—but a necessary one. What one should bear in mind is that, according to Lacan, truth has the structure of a fiction.

[30] Denis Diderot, *Les Bijoux indiscrets*, vol. 3, in *Oeuvres complètes* (Paris: Hermann, 1978). I rely here on Miran Božovič, "Diderot and l'âme-machine," *Filozofski vestnik* 3 (2001).

the entire vagina from the body, doctors tried to "make it talk" through blowing it and using it as a string.) This, then, would be one of the meanings of Lacan's *la femme n'existe pas:* there are no talking vaginas directly telling the truth; there is only the elusive, lying, hysterical subject.

Does, however, this mean that the concept of the talking vagina is a useless one, just a sexual-ideological fantasy? A closer reading of Diderot is necessary here. His thesis is not simply that the woman has two souls, one—superficial, deceiving—expressing itself through her mouth and the other through her vagina. What speaks through woman's mouth is her Soul that desperately tries to dominate her bodily organs. And, as Diderot makes clear, what speaks through her vagina is not the Body as such but precisely the vagina as *organ,* as a subjectless partial object. The speaking vagina thus has to be inserted into the same series as the autonomized hand in *Fight Club* and *Me, Myself and Irene.* It is in this sense that, in the case of the talking vagina, it is not the woman, the feminine subject, who compulsively tells the truth about herself. It is, rather, the truth itself that speaks when her vagina starts to talk: "It's me, the truth, which speaks here"—me, and not I. What speaks through the vagina is drive, this asubjective *moi.*

The ultimate *perverse* vision would have been that the entire human body, inclusive of the head, is nothing but a combination of such partial organs—the head itself is reduced to just another partial organ of *jouissance,* as in those unique utopian moments of hard-core pornography, when the very unity of the bodily self-experience is magically dissolved, so that the spectator perceives the bodies of the actors not as unified totalities but as a kind of vaguely coordinated agglomerate of partial objects: here the mouth, there a breast, over there the anus, close to it the vaginal opening. The effect of close-up shots and of the strangely twisted and contorted bodies of the actors is to deprive these bodies of their unity—somewhat like the body of a circus clown, which the clown himself perceives as a composite of partial organs that he fails to coordinate completely, so that some parts of his body seem to lead their own particular lives (suffice it to recall the standard stage number in which the clown raises his hand, but the upper part of the hand does not obey his will and continues to dangle loosely). This change of the body into a desubjectivized multitude of partial objects is accomplished when, for example, a woman is in bed with two men and does fellatio on one of them, not in the standard way, actively sucking his penis, but so that she lies flat on a bed and leans her head over its edge downward into the air. When the man is penetrating her, her mouth is above her eyes, the face is turned upside-down, and the effect is one of an uncanny transformation of the human face, the seat of subjectivity, into a kind of impersonal sucking machine being pumped by the man's penis. The other man is, meanwhile, working on her vagina, which is also elevated above her head and thus asserted as an autonomous center of *jouissance* not subordinated to the head. The woman's body is thus transformed into a multitude of "organs without a body," machines of *jouissance*, while the men working on it are also desubjectivized, instrumentalized, reduced to workers serving these different partial objects. Within such a scene, even when a vagina talks, it is just a "talking head" in the same way that any other organ just exerts its function of *jouissance*. (This perverse vision of body as a multitude of the sites of partial drives, however, is condemned to failure: it disavows castration.)

There is, of course, a vast contemporary literary and art tradition concerning the talking vagina—from the French cult film of 1975 *Le sexe qui parle—Pussy Talk* (Frederic Lansac and Francis Leroi) to Eve Ensler recent notorious monodrama *The Vagina Monologues*. However, what happens here is precisely the wrong step: the vagina is subjectivized, transformed into the site of woman's true subjectivity. In Ensler, sometimes ironic, sometimes desperate . . . it is *the* Woman who speaks through her vagina, not *vagina-truth itself that speaks*. It is for this precise reason that *The Vagina Monologues* remains caught in the logic of bourgeois subjectivity. If we are to look for a place where the subversive potential of an object starting to speak is unleashed, we have to look elsewhere.

In the middle of David Fincher's *Fight Club* (1999), there is an almost unbearably painful scene, worthy of the weirdest David Lynch moments, which serves as a kind of clue for the film's final surprising twist. To blackmail his boss into continuing to pay him even after he quits working, the hero throws himself around the man's office, beating himself bloody before the building's security officers arrive. In front of his embarrassed boss, the narrator thus enacts upon himself the boss's aggression toward him. The only similar case of self-beating is found in *Me, Myself and Irene,* in which Jim Carrey beats himself up—here, of course, in a comic (although painfully exaggerated) way, as one part of a split personality pounding the other part. In both films, the self-beating begins with the hero's hand acquiring a life of its own, escaping the hero's control—in short, turning into a partial object, or, to put it in Deleuze's terms, into *an organ without a body* (the obverse of the body without an organ). This provides the key to the figure of the double with whom, in both films, the hero is fighting. The double, the hero's Ideal-Ego, a spectral/invisible hallucinatory entity, is not simply external to the hero—its efficacy is inscribed within the hero's body itself as the autonomization of one of its organs (hand). The hand acting on its own is the drive ignoring the dialectic of the subject's desire: drive is fundamentally the insistence of an undead "organ without a body," standing, like Lacan's *lamella,* for that which the subject had to lose in order to subjectivize itself in the symbolic space of the sexual difference.[31]

What, then, does the self-beating in *Fight Club* stand for? If, following Fanon, we define political violence not as opposed to work but, precisely, as the ultimate political version of the "work of the negative," of the Hegelian process of *Bildung,* of the educational self-formation, then violence should primarily be conceived as self-violence, as a violent reformation of the very substance of the subject's being. Therein resides the lesson of *Fight Club:*

> First, one has the difficulty of emancipating oneself from one's chains; and, ultimately, one has to emancipate oneself from this emancipation too! Each of us has to suffer, though in greatly different ways, from the chain sickness, even after he has broken the chains.[32]

In many of the smaller American cities with a large unemployed working-class population, something that uncannily resembles "Fight Club" has recently emerged: "toughman-fights," in which only amateur men (and women also) engage in violent boxing matches, getting their faces bloody, testing their limits. The point is not to win (losers are often more popular than winners) but, rather, to persist, to continue standing on one's feet, not to remain lying on the floor. Although these fights stand under the sign of "God bless America!" and are perceived by (most of) the participants themselves as part of the "war on terror," one should not immediately dismiss them as symptomatic of a redneck "proto-Fascist" tendency: they are part of a potentially redemptive disciplinary drive. So when, in *Fight Club,* after a bloody fight, the hero comments "This was a near-life experience!" (thereby reversing the standard phrase "a near-death experience"), is this not an indication that fighting brings the participants close to the excess-of-life over and above the simple run of life—in the Paulinian sense, they are *alive*?

What, then, does it mean, exactly, that the (partial) object itself starts to speak? It is not that this object is subjectless but that this object is the correlate of the "pure" subject prior to subjectivization. Subjectivization refers to the "whole person" as the correlate of the body, whereas

---

[31] In today's popular women's journals, one often encounters the idea that sex with a vibrator is more "the real thing" than sex with a real man—why, precisely? Because the vibrator functions as the fantasmatic-undead "organ without a body."

[32] Friedrich Nietzsche, in a letter to a friend (from July 1882), quoted in Bryan Magge, *The Tristan Chord* (New York: Henry Holt, 2000), p. 333.

the "pure" subject refers to the partial object alone.[33] When the object starts to speak, what we hear is the voice of the monstrous, impersonal, empty-machinic subject that does not yet involve subjectivization (the assumption of an experienced universe of sense). One should bear in mind here that the two couples, subject-object and person-thing, form a Greimasian semiotic square. That is to say, if we take "subject" as the starting point, there are two opposites to it: its contrary (counterpart) is, of course, "object," but, its "contradiction" is a "person" (the "pathological" wealth of inner life as opposed to the void of pure subjectivity). In a symmetrical way, the opposite counterpart to a "person" is a "thing," and its "contradiction" is the subject. "Thing" is something embedded in a concrete life-world, in which the entire wealth of the meaning of the life-world echoes, while "object" is an "abstraction," something extracted from its embeddedness in the life-world.

The key point here is that the subject is not the correlate of "thing" (or, more precisely, a "body"). The *person* dwells in a body while the subject is the correlate of *a* (partial object), of an organ without a body. And, against the standard notion of person-thing as a life-world totality from which the subject-object couple is extrapolated, one should assert the couple subject-object (in Lacanese: $-a$, the barred subject coupled with the "object small a") as primordial—and the couple person-thing as its "domestication." What gets lost in the passage from subject-object to person-thing is the twisted relationship of the Moebius band: "persons" and "things" are part of the same reality, whereas the object is the impossible equivalent of the subject itself. We arrive at the object when we pursue the side of the subject (of its signifying representation) on the Moebius track to the end and find ourselves on the other side of the same place from where we started. One should thus reject the topic of the personality, a soul-body unity, as the organic Whole dismembered in the process of reification-alienation: the subject emerges out of the person as the product of the violent reduction of the person's body to a partial object.

One should bear in mind here how the Freudian notion of the "partial object" is not that of an element or constituent of the body but that of an organ that *resists* its inclusion within the Whole of a body. This object, which is the correlate of the subject, is the subject's stand-in within the order of objectivity. It is the proverbial "piece of flesh," the part of the subject that the subject had to renounce to subjectivize itself, to emerge as

[33] The organ without body as "partial object" is not the Kleinian partial object but what Lacan, in his *Seminar XI*, theorizes as the object of drive, the eroticized (libidinally invested) part of the body incommensurable with the Whole of the body, sticking out of it, resisting its integration into the bodily Whole.

subject. Was this not what Marx was aiming at when he wrote about the rise of the class consciousness of the proletariat? Does this also not mean that the commodity "working force," which, on the market, is reduced to an object to be exchanged, starts to speak? Here is the shortest Jacob and Wilhelm Grimm fairy tale, "The Willful Child":

> Once upon a time there was a child who was willful and did not do what his mother wanted. For this reason God was displeased with him and caused him to become ill, and no doctor could help him, and in a short time he lay on his deathbed. He was lowered into a grave and covered with earth, but his little arm suddenly came forth and reached up, and it didn't help when they put it back in and put fresh earth over it, for the little arm always came out again. So the mother herself had to go to the grave and beat the little arm with a switch, and as soon as she had done that, it withdrew, and the child finally came to rest beneath the earth.[34]

Is this obstinacy that persists even beyond death not freedom—death drive—at its most elementary? Instead of condemning it, should we not rather celebrate it as the ultimate resort of our resistance? The refrain of an old German Communist song from the 1930s is *Die Freiheit hat Soldaten!* (Freedom has its soldiers!). It may appear that such an identification of a particular unit as the military instrument of freedom itself is the very formula of the "totalitarian" temptation: we do not just fight for (our understanding of) freedom, we do not just serve freedom, it is freedom that immediately avails itself of us. The way seems open to terror: who would be allowed to oppose freedom itself? However, the identification of a revolutionary military unit as a direct organ of freedom cannot simply be dismissed as a fetishistic short circuit: in a pathetic way, this *is* true of the authentic revolutionary explosion. What happens in such an "ecstatic" experience is that the subject who acts is no longer a person but, precisely, an *object.*

It is only the "transcendental" Lacan (the Lacan of the symbolic Law that constitutes human desire by way of prohibiting access to the noumenal maternal Thing) who can be said to invoke a democratic politics that, in the same way that every positive object of desire falls short of the void of the absolute-impossible Thing, asserts that every positive political agent just fills in the void at the center of power. The moment we pass to the Lacan of the drives, an acephalous subject who assumes the position of the object—or, from another direction, the position of an object that starts to talk, that subjectivizes itself—can no longer be dismissed as the outcome of a perverse short circuit.

---

[34] The German title "Das eigensinnige Kind" is also translated as "The Stubborn Child," "The Wayward Child," or "The Naughty Child."

Beyond Morality

The collective that emerges at the level of such a fighting subjectivity is to be thoroughly opposed to the intersubjective topic of "how to reach the other," how to maintain the openness and respect toward Otherness. There are, *grosso modo*, three ways to reach out to the other that fit the triad of ISR: imaginary ("human touch"), symbolic ("politeness," "good manners"), real (shared obscenity). Each of the three has its own dangers. As to the "human touch" (the display of "human warmth" beneath the official role one is playing), suffice it to recall how, when, in January 2003, the Israeli Defense Forces demolished the house of the family of a suspected "terrorist," they did it with accentuated kindness, even to helping the family to move the furniture out before destroying the house with a bulldozer. A similar incident was reported in the Israeli press. When an Israeli soldier was searching a Palestinian house for suspects, the mother of the family called her daughter by her name to calm her down, and the surprised soldier learned that the frightened girl's name was the same as that of his own daughter; in a sentimental upsurge, he pulled out his wallet and showed her picture to the Palestinian mother. It is easy to discern the falsity of such a gesture of empathy: the notion that, in spite of political differences, we are all human beings with the same loves and worries, neutralizes the impact of what the soldier is effectively doing at that moment. So, the only proper reply of the mother should be, "If you really are human like me, *why are you doing what you are doing now*?" The soldier can then only take refuge only in reified duty: "I don't like it, but it is my duty . . ."—thus avoiding the subjective assumption of his duty.

As for human warmth, one of the most depressive motifs in Victor Klemperer's wartime diaries *To the Bitter End (1942–45)* [35] is the oft-repeated scene of a "good" ordinary German with sympathies for Jews, even helping them sometimes, who, in a moment of "human warmth," takes Klemperer, a Jew, into his confidence and explains to him his view of the war: it is difficult, but *you* should not worry, *we* (inclusive!) shall win! At the very moment of "opening up his heart," the "good" German tries to involve the Jew in the project responsible for his destruction. The price of his offer of "human sympathy" is that the Jew—the ultimate victim—should identify with the survival of the system bent on destroying him. As for good manners and elementary decency (the proper treatment of people at the security control or of the suspects at interrogation, etc.), it can also be a fake—it was already Adorno who emphasized how "good manners" (tactfulness) can be the ultimate shield that conceals

[35] See Victor Klemperer, *To the Bitter End (1942–45)* (London: Phoenix, 2000).

my cold distance toward the other. As to shared obscenity, the proposal of obscenity is also an extremely risky move. It can backfire and work as a brutal intrusion into the other's privacy—not to mention the fact that it can function as a fake solidarity masking underlying power relations.

However, the trap to be avoided here is the dismissal of appearances in the style of "better a true brutal power relation than a fake"—as if, in the West Bank, the choice is simply "either occupation with good manners *or* no occupation," as if there is not also the choice between minimal "kindness" and a brutal occupation. The dismissal of such "apparent" overtures as false has its limits too. If one goes to the end in this logic, one can easily dismiss the acts of the Israeli refuseniks as already "co-opted" by the Israeli official ideology: don't they "objectively" serve the Israeli state, enabling it to present Israel as a civilized, moral society, in contrast to Arab fanaticism? Furthermore, if the refuseniks act via selective refusal, do not they thereby admit and thus legitimate the *basic* right of the IDF to act? What one should retain here is trust in the potential power of appearances, even if they are subjectively false: the sad fact is that, in a tension between good manners and the call of one's conscience, the truth can be on the side of superficial manners. When, in Mark Twain's novel, Huck Finn is on the run with a black slave, he treats him in a friendly way because of his good manners, although his conscience makes him feel guilty for that, telling him that he should return the runaway slave to his legal owner.[36]

The truth is thus in no way automatically at the level of intimate conviction. In *Minima moralia,* Adorno refers to the example of a wife who, while holding the coat for her husband, gives an ironic smile to the others around her, saying "Let the poor guy think I am serving him, let him have his small pleasures, while I am the real boss." Is this not the fundamental feminine strategy, that of *faking* a submissive subjectivization? However, what if the truth is the opposite one? What if the wife's ironic distance is false? What if the patriarchal domination takes this distance into account and not only tolerates it but even solicits it as the way to subjectivize the feminine subject? Many Western academics cling to some humanitarian ritual (helping to educate poor children, etc.) as the proof that, at the core of their being, they are not just cynical career-oriented individuals but human beings naively and sincerely trying to help others. However, again, what if this humanitarian activity is a fetish, a false distance that allows them to pursue their power struggles and ambitions with the clear conscience that they are not really "that," that their heart is "elsewhere"? In other words, when a cynical Western academic refers to his or her humanitarian activity taking place elsewhere, one should simply retort that

---

[36] I owe this reference to Ishai Menuchin (Jerusalem), one of the Israeli refuseniks.

this "elsewhere" is of absolutely no significance to what goes on here: his or her activity here is in no way "redeemed" by this elsewhere, in the same way that, commendable as it is in itself, Bill Gates's charitable activity of gigantic proportions in no way redeems his economic pursuits. More generally, charity is, today, part of the game as a humanitarian mask hiding the underlying economic exploitation: in a superego-blackmail of gigantic proportions, the developed countries are constantly "helping" the undeveloped (with aid, credits, etc.), thereby avoiding the key issue, namely, their *complicity* in and coresponsibility for the miserable situation of the undeveloped.

One is tempted to conceive interpassivity as a way to avoid ideological interpellation. If I let a candle burn in the church for me instead of praying and spend the time I thus gain for more pleasurable activities, is it not that I thereby acquire a minimal distance toward the (recognition in) religious interpellation?[37] However, what if, far from avoiding interpellation, such a distance effectively sustains it? Is not the ideal religious subject the one who maintains a minimal distance toward his identity as a believer, instead of fully identifying with it (which cannot but end in a psychotic short circuit—to paraphrase Lacan, in this case, he is "a believer who thinks he really is a believer")? It is only within this distance that subjectivization proper can take place: what makes me a "human subject" is the very fact that I cannot be reduced to my symbolic identity, that I display a wealth of idiosyncratic features. Recall the short paragraph about the writer on a book cover, in which the brief description of his life and work is always supplemented by some private detail: "In his free time, X is an avid bird-watcher and active member of an amateur opera society." It is this supplement that subjectivizes the author, who would otherwise appear as a monstrous machine. There are, effectively, only two kinds of believers: the "Catholics" who maintain a distance toward a ritual and the "Protestants" who engage themselves completely in their belief and, for that very reason, have to sustain eternal existential doubt about who they are.

Graham Greene's *The Quiet American* fully deploys the paradoxes of this dialectical tension between public and private. The fate of the movie version from 2001 is the proof of why simple repression doesn't work, of how the repressed always returns. The movie was destined to open in the fall of 2001; its release was postponed because of September 11th. The main fear was probably that the central idea of the plot—namely, that the terrorist explosions that kill hundreds of innocent Vietnamese civilians, attributed to pro-communist forces, are really the work of mercenaries

---

[37] This idea was deployed by Robert Pfaller in his *Illusionen der Anderen* (Frankfurt: Suhrkamp Verlag, 2002).

paid and organized by the Americans themselves—would imply an unacceptable parallel notion regarding the causes of September 11th. However, when the film was finally released in early 2003, in the wake of the expected U.S. attack on Iraq, its message appeared even more timely: will the "liberating" intervention of George W. Bush, like that of the "quiet American" in the film, not unmask itself as a similar catastrophic miscalculation? Even the fact that the film's English hero embodies the tired and decadent "old Europe" seems to gain new, unexpected actuality after Donald Rumsfeld's notorious denunciation of "old Europe."

This does not mean that the film is ultimately not a failure, politically as well as artistically. The best way to locate this failure is to start with the difference between the film and Graham Greene's novel of the same name from 1955. In the film, the "quiet American," who poses as a naive, benevolent organizer of medical help for the Vietnamese, is gradually unmasked as what he truly is, namely, a ruthless real-politician who finances mass terror against civilians to prevent the communist seizure of power. In clear contrast to the film, the main point of the novel is that the "quiet American" effectively *is* a naive benevolent agent who sincerely wants to bring to the Vietnamese democracy and Western freedom—it is just that his intentions totally misfire: "I never knew a man who had better motives for all the trouble he caused." The shift from the novel to the film is thus the shift from tragedy proper (the subject intervenes with the best intentions and causes unforeseen catastrophe) to melodrama (the good guy is revealed as the ultimate evil).

The film tells the story of Fowler, a late-middle-aged, resigned, opium-addicted Englishman, correspondent of the *Times* in Saigon in 1952, who lives with Phuong, a beautiful young Vietnamese woman. Although he would like to marry her, he cannot do it, because his wife back in England will not give him a divorce. In a café where he takes his morning coffee, he meets Pyle, a young, idealistic American involved in medical help to cure eye diseases. At the same time, a new "Third Way" (neither pro-communist nor pro-French) opposition movement is formed, and mass slaughter is regularly reported, usually attributed to communists. Gradually, Fowler becomes aware of the truth behind Pyle, the "quiet American": his medical task is just a cover; it is Pyle who is behind the "Third Force" and who finances and coordinates mass bombings as part of a ruthless scheme to save Vietnam from communist victory. At the same time, while becoming friendly with Fowler, Pyle falls in love with Phuong and proposes to her. She leaves Fowler for Pyle, since she wants the security of a marriage to an American. At this point, the Vietnamese secretary of Fowler, a covert communist also aware of Pyle's role, asks Fowler to clearly take sides in the struggle by inviting Pyle to dinner in a certain restaurant, thus enabling the communists to liquidate him. Fowler does it, and, as a result, Phuong also returns to him.

The courage of the film is that, along the lines of old classics like Lillian Hellman's *Watch on the Rhine,* it violates the liberal taboo: in the political struggle, one cannot remain an observer, one has to take sides, which means not only general sympathy for one side but, much more unsettling, that one has to dirty one's hands with blood. In short, we find here the political version of what some Catholic critics were horrified to discern as the basic lesson of *The End of the Affair,* Greene's key "Catholic" novel about marriage and sexuality—that of Christ telling his disciples: "If you love me, break my commandments." How, then, are we to read the film's uncanny *double* "happy ending," in which the hero does the politically right thing and, by means of this very gesture, gets the beloved girl back? The spontaneous reaction of an "educated" viewer is, of course, that this is cheap kitsch at its worst, since a "serious" work of art should have rendered the hero's predicament as tragic, as that of a forced choice: doing the right thing and losing the girl are mutually exclusive. However, is such a notion of "tragedy" not too narrow, too "bourgeois" (if this term has any meaning today)?[38]

One way to read the film would have been to interpret its political dimension as the allegorical background for its interpersonal love dynamics: the hero finds himself in a rewarding situation in which, by betraying the American to the communists who slaughter him, he also gets back the beloved Vietnamese beauty, who left him for the American. Read this way, the film effectively participates in the worst opportunistic self-indulgence. However, what if one radically changes the perspective and, while wholly endorsing this hopelessly patriarchal-racist economy of the film's private love dynamics, simply shifts the focus onto the public political struggle as the crucial, decisive dimension? Instead of reading (in a Hollywood way) the public political level as merely a background allegory of the private as the true moral center, one should see the underlying insight of the film in the assertion of the ultimate *irrelevance* of the private—*so what* if, at the private level, the hero "cheats emotionally"; *so what* if, at the level of subjective self-experience, the American is sincere and naively enthusiastic? *What if,* at the personal level, the conflict is the one between the naive-honest American and the cynically hypocritical

---

[38] Furthermore, it is true that today, in 2003, one cannot but be shocked at how such a blatant reduction of the Third World beautiful young woman to an object of exchange between (white) men can still be found: with the (ambiguous) exception of the very end (when he assures the hero that there is nothing she has to forgive him for), she is not once subjectivized, presented as an agent with her own inner life. However, one may also read this very absence of subjectivization as more truthful, as an index of the girl's objective position, a position that does not allow for subjectivization.

Englishman? *What if,* as in Racine's Jansenist tragedies, in which intimate good and evil have no relationship with the fact of whether one is touched by grace, here also personal qualities have no direct bearing on the political, "objective-ethical" meaning of one's acts? *What if* the truth is at the level of the political meaning of the acts, not at the level of intimate sincerity or hypocrisy? *What if,* in this sense, one should reject thoroughly T. S. Eliot's famous line from his *Murder at the Cathedral,* according to which the highest form of treason is "to do the right deed for the wrong reason"? Unfortunately, by indulging in the melodramatic portrayal of the American as an evil manipulator beneath the benevolent mask, the film misses this opportunity. Such an image of the American cannot but arouse moral indignation in the spectators, thereby redeeming the hero's betrayal as a fully justified act, grounded in his moral indignation once he sees the American in his true colors.

And it is here that the film misses its chance: that of focusing on the properly Kierkegaardian dilemma of its hero whose predicament "is an ordeal such that, please note, the ethical is the temptation."[39] That is to say, the hero should have been *disturbed* by the terrifying prospect of "doing the right deed for the wrong reason," that is, of profiting from the denunciation of the American and thus opening up the suspicion that his difficult politicoethical decision was grounded in private motives. In this precise sense, for the hero, "the ethical is the temptation." The main dilemma is the political one (will he gather the courage to clearly take sides and help annihilate the American?), and the level of private ethics affects this dilemma precisely as a temptation—will he succumb to the temptation of virtue and refuse to betray the American or will he gather the strength to overcome his private sensibility and accomplish the act, *in spite of the fact that he will profit from it*?

[39] Søren Kierkegaard, *Fear and Trembling* (Princeton, N.J.: Princeton University Press, 1983), p. 115.

3

POLITICS: A PLEA FOR
CULTURAL REVOLUTION

A Yuppie Reading Deleuze

In his admirable "The Pedagogy of Philosophy," Jean-Jacques Lecercle described the scene of a yuppie on the Paris underground reading Deleuze and Guattari's *What Is Philosophy?*:

> The incongruity of the scene induces a smile—after all, this is a book explicitly written against yuppies. . . . Your smile turns into a grin as you imagine that this enlightenment-seeking yuppie bought the book because of its title. . . . Already you see the puzzled look on the yuppie's face, as he reads page after page of vintage Deleuze.[1]

What, however, if there is no puzzled look, but enthusiasm, when the yuppie reads about impersonal imitation of affects, about the communication of affective intensities beneath the level of meaning ("Yes, this is how I design my publicities!"), or when he reads about exploding the limits of self-contained subjectivity and directly coupling man to a machine ("This reminds me of my son's favorite toy, the action-man that can turn into a car!"), or about the need to reinvent oneself permanently, opening oneself up to a multitude of desires that push us to the limit ("Is this not the aim of the virtual sex video game I am working on now? It is no longer a question of reproducing sexual bodily contact but of exploding the confines of established reality and imagining new, unheard-of intensive modes of sexual pleasures!"). There are, effectively, features

[1] Jean-Jacques Lecercle, "The Pedagogy of Philosophy," *Radical Philosophy* 75 (January–February 1996): 44.

that justify calling Deleuze the ideologist of late capitalism. Is the much celebrated Spinozan *imitatio afecti,* the impersonal circulation of affects bypassing persons, not the very logic of publicity, of video clips, and so forth in which what matters is not the message about the product but the intensity of the transmitted affects and perceptions? Furthermore, recall again the hard-core pornography scenes in which the very unity of the bodily self-experience is magically dissolved, so that the spectator perceives the bodies as a kind of vaguely coordinated agglomerate of partial objects. Is this logic in which we are no longer dealing with persons interacting but just with the multiplicity of intensities, of places of enjoyment, plus bodies as a collective/impersonal desiring machine not eminently Deleuzian?

And, to go a step further, is the practice of fist-fucking not the exemplary case of what Deleuze called the "expansion of a concept"? The fist is put to a new use; the notion of penetration is expanded into the combination of the hand with sexual penetration, into the exploration of the inside of a body. No wonder Foucault, Deleuze's Other, was practicing fisting: is fist-fucking not *the* sexual invention of the twentieth century, the first model of postsexual eroticism and pleasure? It is no longer genitalized but focused just on the penetration of the surface, with the role of the phallus being taken over by the hand, the autonomized partial object par excellence. And, what about the so-called Transformer or Animorph toys, a car or a plane that can be transformed into a humanoid robot, an animal that can be morphed into a human or robot—is this not Deleuzian? There are no "metaphorics" here: the point is not that the machinic or animal form is revealed as a mask containing a human shape but, rather, as the "becoming-machine" or "becoming-animal" of the human, the flow of continuous morphing. What is blurred here is also the divide machine/living organism: a car transmutes into a humanoid/cyborg organism. And is the ultimate irony not that, for Deleuze, *the* sport was surfing, a Californian sport par excellence if there ever was one: no longer a sport of self-control and domination directed toward some goal but just a practice of inserting oneself into a wave and letting oneself be carried by it. Brian Massumi formulated clearly this deadlock, which is based on the fact that today's capitalism already overcame the logic of totalizing normality and adopted the logic of the erratic excess:

> [T]he more varied, and even erratic, the better. Normalcy starts to lose its hold. The regularities start to loosen. This loosening of normalcy is part of capitalism's dynamic. It's not a simple liberation. It's capitalism's own form of power. It's no longer disciplinary institutional power that defines everything, it's capitalism's power to produce variety—because markets get saturated. Produce variety and you produce a niche market. The oddest of affective

tendencies are okay—as long as they pay. Capitalism starts intensifying or diversifying affect, but only in order to extract surplus-value. It hijacks affect in order to intensify profit potential. It literally valorises affect. The capitalist logic of surplus-value production starts to take over the relational field that is also the domain of political ecology, the ethical field of resistance to identity and predictable paths. It's very troubling and confusing, because it seems to me that there's been a certain kind of convergence between the dynamic of capitalist power and the dynamic of resistance.[2]

So, when Naomi Klein writes that "[n]eo-liberal economics is biased at every level towards centralization, consolidation, homogenization. It is a war waged on diversity,"[3] is she not focusing on a figure of capitalism whose days are numbered? Would she not be applauded by contemporary capitalist modernizers? Is not the latest trend in corporate management itself "diversify, devolve power, try to mobilize local creativity and self-organization"? Is not anticentralization *the* topic of the "new" digitalized capitalism? The problem here is even more "troubling and confusing" than it may appear. As Lacan pointed out apropos his deployment of the structural homology between surplus-value and surplus-enjoyment, what if the surplus-value does not simply "hijack" a preexisting relational field of affects—what if what appears an obstacle is effectively a positive condition of possibility, the element that triggers and propels the explosion of affective productivity? What if, consequently, one should precisely "throw out the baby with the dirty bath water" and renounce the very notion of erratic affective productivity as the libidinal support of revolutionary activity?

More than ever, Capital is the "concrete universal" of our historical epoch. What this means is that, while it remains a particular formation, it overdetermines all alternative formations, as well as all noneconomic strata of social life. The twentieth-century communist movement emerged, defining itself as an opponent of capitalism, and was defeated by it; fascism emerged as an attempt to master capitalism's excesses, to build a kind of "capitalism without capitalism." For this reason, it is also much too simple, in a Heideggerian mood, to reduce capitalism to one of the ontic realizations of a more fundamental ontological attitude of "Will to Power" and technological domination (claiming that the alternatives to it remain caught within this same ontological horizon). Modern technological domination is inextricably intertwined with the social form of Capital; it can occur only within this form, and, insofar as

[2] Brian Massumi, "Navigating Movements," in *Hope*, edited by Mary Zournazi (New York: Routledge, 2002), p. 224.
[3] Naomi Klein, *Fences and Windows: Dispatches from the Frontlines of the Globalization Debate* (London: Flamingo, 2002), p. 245.

the alternative social formations display the same ontological attitude, this merely confirms that they are, in their innermost core, mediated by Capital as their concrete universality, as the particular formation that colors the entire scope of alternatives, that is, which functions as the encompassing totality mediating all other particular formations. In his new book on modernity, Fredric Jameson offers a concise critique of the recently fashionable theories of "alternate modernities":

> How then can the ideologues of "modernity" in its current sense manage to distinguish their product—the information revolution, and globalized, free-market modernity—from the detestable older kind, without getting themselves involved in asking the kinds of serious political and economic, systemic questions that the concept of a postmodernity makes unavoidable? The answer is simple: you talk about "alternate" or "alternative" modernities. Everyone knows the formula by now: this means that there can be a modernity for everybody which is different from the standard or hegemonic Anglo-Saxon model. Whatever you dislike about the latter, including the subaltern position it leaves you in, can be effaced by the reassuring and "cultural" notion that you can fashion your own modernity differently, so that there can be a Latin-American kind, or an Indian kind or an African kind, and so on. . . . But this is to overlook the other fundamental meaning of modernity which is that of a worldwide capitalism itself.[4]

As Jameson is well aware, the line goes on and on, up to those Muslims who dream about a specific Arab modernity that would magically bypass the destructive aspects of Western global capitalism. The significance of this critique reaches far beyond the case of modernity—it concerns the fundamental limitation of the nominalist historicizing. The recourse to multitude ("there is not one modernity with a fixed essence, there are multiple modernities, each of them irreducible to others . . .") is false not because it does not recognize a unique fixed "essence" of modernity but because multiplication functions as the disavowal of the antagonism that inheres to the notion of modernity as such: the falsity of multiplication resides in the fact that it frees the universal notion of modernity of its antagonism, of the way it is embedded in the capitalist system, by relegating this aspect just to one of its historical subspecies. And, insofar as this inherent antagonism could be designated as a "castrative" dimension, and, furthermore, insofar as, according to Freud, the disavowal of castration is represented as the multiplication of the phallus-representatives (a multitude of phalluses signals castration, the lack of the one), it is easy to conceive such a multiplication of modernities as a form of fetishist disavowal. This logic holds also for other ideological notions, especially, today, for democracy: do those who want to distinguish another

[4] Fredric Jameson, *A Singular Modernity* (London: Verso Books, 2002), p. 12.

("radical") democracy from its existing form and thereby cut off its links with capitalism, not commit the same categorial mistake?

Is the ultimate example of what Jean-Pierre Dupuy, following Ivan Illich, isolates as the vicious cycle of capitalist productivity, multiplying the very problems it pretends to solve,[5] not *cyberspace*? The more cyberspace brings us together, enabling us to communicate in "real time" with anyone on the globe, the more it isolates as, reducing us to individuals staring into computer screens. Furthermore, Dupuy asks the naive, but crucial, question: at what point does the justified critique of ideology, which elevates a contingent obstacle into a necessary form of suffering ("a woman must suffer at birth"), turn into a no less ideological perception of the very limits of our finitude (death, restriction to our body) as a contingent limitation to be vanquished? Here again, is the paradigmatic case not that of cyberspace, of its Gnostic dream of transforming ourselves into "software" or into virtual beings able to cut off the links to our natural body and freely float from one to another virtual embodiment? What gets lost in this gnostic vision is the fact that the obstacle to our fulfillment (our finitude) is a positive condition of (a limited) fulfillment: if we take away the obstacle to fulfillment, we lose fulfillment itself (or, in the terms of sense: if we take away the irreducible kernel of nonsense, we lose sense itself).

Micro-Fascisms

The inverted mirror-image or counterpart of this ambiguity of the Deleuzian attitude toward capitalism is the ambiguity of Deleuze's theory of fascism, a theory whose basic insight is that fascism does not take hold of subjects at the level of ideology, interests, and so forth but takes hold directly at the level of bodily investments, libidinal gestures, and so on. Fascism enacts a certain assemblage of bodies, so one should fight it (also) at *this* level, with impersonal counterstrategies. At the same time, there is the opposition of micro- and macro-, molecular and molar: fascism is a life-denying view, a view of renunciation, of the sacrificial subordination to Higher Goals; it relies on impersonal micro-strategies, manipulations of intensities, which work as life-denying. Here, however, things get complicated: is the fascist renunciation not—in the best Deleuzian way—a deceiving mask, a lure to distract us from the *positivity* of fascism's actual ideological functioning, which is one of superego obscene enjoyment? In short, is fascism not playing the old hypocritical game of a fake sacrifice here, of the superficial renunciation of enjoyment destined to deceive the big Other, to conceal from it the fact that we *do*

---

[5] See Jean-Pierre Dupuy, *Pour un catastrophisme éclairé* (Paris: Editions du Seuil, 2002), pp. 58–59.

enjoy, and enjoy even excessively? "God demands constant enjoyment, as the normal mode of existence for souls within the Order of the World. It is my duty to provide him with it"[6]—do these words of Daniel Paul Schreber not supply the best description of the superego in its extreme psychotic dimension?

Deleuze's account of fascism is that, although subjects as individuals can rationally perceive that it is against their interests to follow it, it seizes them precisely at the impersonal level of pure intensities: "abstract" bodily motions, libidinally invested collective rhythmic movements, affects of hatred and passion that cannot be attributed to any determinate individual. It is thus the impersonal level of pure affects that sustains fascism, not the level of represented and constituted reality. Perhaps the ultimate example here is provided by *The Sound of Music:* an antifascist film, as to its "official" storyline, whose texture of intensities generates the opposite message. That is to say, through closer examination, it becomes evident that the Austrians resisting the Nazi invasion are presented as "good Fascists" (displaying their rootedness in the local patriarchal life-world, enjoying the stupidity of the yodelling culture, etc.), while the film's portrait of the Nazis uncannily echoes the Nazi portrait of the Jews, uprooted political manipulators striving for global power. The struggle against fascism should be fought at this impersonal level of intensities—not (only) at the level of rational critique—by undermining the fascist libidinal economy with a more radical one.

Really Existing Socialism is often designated as a system that "functioned because it did not function" (incidentally, this is also an elegantly simple definition of the Freudian symptom): the system survived precisely through the exceptions violating its explicit rules (the black market, etc.). In short, what the regime perceived as a threat effectively enabled it to survive, which is why all big campaigns against the illegal economy, corruption, alcoholism, and so forth, were self-defeating—the system was undermining its own conditions of existence. And, does the same not go for *every* ideology that also has to rely on a set of unwritten rules violating its explicit rules? Today, one often evokes the "market of ideas" (to assert themselves, new ideas have to be tested in the marketlike competition of free discussion)—could one not say that this "market of ideas" is also necessarily accompanied by the *black market* of ideas, swarms of disavowed, obscene sexist and racist ideas (and other such ideas of a similar nature) that an ideological edifice has to rely on if it is to remain efficient?

---

[6] Daniel Paul Schreber, *Memoirs of My Nervous Illness* (New York: New York Review Books, 2000), p. 250.

In November 2002, George Bush came under attack by the right-wing members of his own party for what was perceived as too soft a stance on Islam: like Netanyahu and other hard-liners, he was reproached for repeating the mantra that terrorism has nothing to do with Islam, this great and tolerant religion. As a column in the *Wall Street Journal* put it, the true enemy of the United States is not terrorism but militant Islam. The idea of these critics is that one should gather the courage and proclaim the politically incorrect (but, nonetheless, obvious) fact that there is a deep strain of violence and intolerance in Islam—that, to put it bluntly, something in Islam resists the acceptance of the liberal-capitalist world order. It is here that a truly radical analysis should break with the standard liberal attitude: no, one should *not* defend Bush here—his attitude is ultimately no better than that of Cohen, Buchanan, Pat Robertson, and other anti-Islamists—both sides of this coin are equally wrong. It is against this background that one should approach Oriana Fallaci's *The Rage and the Pride*,[7] this passionate defense of the West against the Muslim threat, this open assertion of the superiority of the West, this denigration of Islam not even as a different culture but as barbarism (entailing that we are not even dealing with a clash of cultures but with a clash of our culture and Muslim barbarism). The book is stricto sensu the obverse of Politically Correct tolerance: its lively passion is the truth of lifeless PC tolerance.

Recall the immigrant-bashing skinhead who, when interviewed, sneers back at the journalist and provides him with a perfect social psychologist's explanation of his own misdeeds (lack of paternal authority and maternal care, the crisis of values in our society, etc.), and whose unsurpassable model is still the song "Officer Krupke" from Leonard Bernstein's *West Side Story*. This figure cannot simply be dismissed as the supreme case of cynical reason, as the embodiment of the actual functioning of today's ideology. Since he speaks from the position of the *explanandum,* his remarks also effectively denounce the fakeness and falsity of the way the ruling ideology and its knowledge account for his acts: "This is what you think I am, this is how, in your learned interventions and reports, you will characterize and dismiss me, but you see, I can also play that game, and it doesn't touch me at all!" Is this not an act of denouncing the hidden cynicism of the humanist "all-understanding" social workers and psychologists themselves? What if *they* are the true cynics in this affair?

Another example of the same tension, in October 2002, Washington, D.C., was in the grip of a panic: an unknown sniper shot a dozen

---

[7] See Oriana Fallaci, *The Rage and the Pride* (New York: Rizzoli, 2002).

(randomly selected) individuals in less than two weeks, thereby mimicking cinema examples like the one from Louis Bunuel's *The Phantom of Freedom,* in which a guy goes to the top of a Paris skyscraper and shoots unsuspecting pedestrians. One could make a wager that there will soon be a video game allowing the player to assume the role of the sniper—why? Although the sniper's acts were reinscribed into the field of "terrorism," even with hints that al-Qaeda may have been directly behind them, the subjective logic of his acts is exclusively late capitalist: the lone psychopathic individual, asocial but well disciplined and perfectly trained, with a grudge against "society." The proposed video game, which would rely on the player's identification with the sniper, thus articulates a fundamental feature of today's subjectivity: the rise of the "asocial," solipsist individual—again, the excluded outsider is unmasked as the hidden model of the "normal" insider.

Two important, interconnected conclusions are to be drawn from such Deleuzian analyses. First, there is the limitation plaguing attempts to undermine the hold of any ideological edifice by means of reference to facts, that is, by rendering all the hidden data public. According to Deleuze, "Syberberg's powerful idea in his *Hitler. A Film from Germany* is that no information, whatever it might be, is sufficent to defeat Hitler. All the documents could be known, all the testimonies could be heard, but in vain."[8] This serves as a profound insight against people like Chomsky, whose wager is precisely the opposite one (one only needs to be told all the facts). The second, complementary conclusion is that the struggle for liberation is *not* reducible to a struggle for the "right to narrate," to the struggle of deprived marginal groups to freely articulate their position, or, as Deleuze puts it when answering an interviewer's question, "You are asking if societies of control and information will not give rise to forms of resistance capable of again giving a chance to communism conceived as a 'transversal organization of free individuals.' I don't know, perhaps. But this will not be insofar as minorities will be able to acquire speech. Perhaps, speech and communication are rotten.... To create was always something else than to communicate."[9]

And yet, productive as this Deleuzian approach is, it is time to problematize it, and, with it, the general tendency popular among (especially Western) Marxists and post-Marxists of relying on a set of simplistic clues for the triumph of fascism (or, nowadays, for the crisis of the Left), as if the result would have been entirely different if only the Left were to fight fascism at the level of libidinal micro-politics, or, today, if only the

---

[8] Gilles Deleuze, *The Time-Image* (Minneapolis: University of Minnesota Press, 1989), p. 268.
[9] Gilles Deleuze, *Pourparlers* (Paris: Editions de Minuit, 1990), p. 237.

Left were to abandon "class essentialism" and accept the multitude of "post-political" struggles as the proper terrain of its activity. If ever there was *the* case of the Leftist arrogant intellectual stupidity, this is the one.

There are two problems with Deleuze's and Guattari's theory of fascism. The notion that fascism could have been defeated earlier if only the Left would have countered it with its own "politics of passions," an old idea defended already by Ernst Bloch and Wilhelm Reich, seems naive enough. Furthermore, was what Deleuze proposes as his big insight not—albeit in a different mode—claimed already by the most traditional marxism, which often repeated that Fascists disdain rational argumentation and play on people's base irrational instincts? More generally, this Deleuzian approach is all too abstract—all "bad" politics is declared "fascist," so that "fascism" is elevated into a global container, a catch all, an all-encompassing term for everything that opposes the free flow of Becoming. It is

> inseparable from a proliferation of molecular focuses in interaction, which skip from point to point, *before* beginning to resonate together in the National Socialist State. Rural fascism and city or neighbourhood fascism, youth fascism and war veteran's fascism, fascism of the Left and fascism of the Right, fascism of the couple, family, school, and office.[10]

One is almost tempted to add the following: and the fascism of the irrationalist vitalism of Deleuze himself (in an early polemic, Badiou effectively accused Deleuze of harboring fascist tendencies!). Deleuze and Guattari (especially Guattari) often indulge here in a true interpretive delirium of hasty generalizations: in one great arc, they draw the line of continuity from the early Christian procedure of confessions through the self-probing of Romantic subjectivity and the psychoanalytic treatment (confessing one's secret, perverse desires) up to the forced confessions of the Stalinist show trials (Guattari once directly characterized these trials as an exercice in collective psychoanalysis to which one is tempted to respond by pointing out how the Stalinist trials were evidently "productive": their actual goal was not to discover the truth but to create new truth, to construct/generate it). It is here, against such generalizations, that one should evoke the lesson of Laclau's notion of hegemonic articulation: fascism emerges *only* when the disperse elements start to "resonate together." In fact, it *is* only a specific mode of this resonance of elements (elements that can also be inserted into totally different hegemonic chains of articulation).[11] At this precise point, one should also

---

[10] Gilles Deleuze and Felix Guattari, *A Thousand Plateaus* (Minneapolis: University of Minnesota Press, 1987), p. 214.
[11] See Ernesto Laclau, *Politics and Ideology in Marxist Theory* (London: Verso Books, 1977).

emphasize the problematic nature of Deleuze's sympathy for Wilhelm Reich: is not Reich's thesis on the nuclear bourgeois family as the elementary cell generating the fascist authoritarian personality blatantly wrong (as it was demonstrated already by the analyses of Adorno and Horkheimer in the 1930s)?

Netocracy?

The "pro-capitalist" aspect of Deleuze and Guattari was fully developed by Alexander Bard and Jan Soderqvist in their *Netocracy,*[12] a supreme example of what one is tempted to call—not cyber-Communism—*cyber-Stalinism.* While cruelly dismissing marxism as outdated, as part of the old industrial society, it takes from Stalinist marxism a whole series of key features, from primitive economic determinism and linear historical evolutionism (the development of the forces of production—the shift of accent from industry to management of information—necessitates new social relations, the replacement of the class antagonism of capitalist and proletariat with the new class antagonism of "netocrats" and "consumtariat") to the extremely rude notion of ideology (in the best naive Enlightened way, ideology, from traditional religion to bourgeois humanism, is repeatedly dismissed as the instrument of the ruling classes and their paid intellectuals, destined to keep in check the lower classes). Here, then, is the basic vision of "netocracy" as a new mode of production (the term is inadequate because, in it, production precisely loses its key role). Whereas in feudalism the key to social power was the ownership of land (legitimized by religious ideology) and in capitalism the key to power is the ownership of capital (with money as the measure of social status), with private property as the fundamental legal category and the market as the dominant field of social exchange (all of this legitimized by the humanist ideology of Man as an autonomous free agent), in the newly emerging "netocracy" the measure of power and social status is the access to key pieces of information. Money and material possessions are relegated to a secondary role. The dominated class is no longer the working class but the class of consumerists ("consumtariat"), those condemned to consume the information prepared and manipulated by the netocratic elite. This shift in power generates an entirely new social logic and ideology. Since information circulates and changes all the time, there is no longer a stable, long-term hierarchy but a permanently changing network of power relations. Individuals are "nomadic," "dividuals," constantly reinventing themselves, adopting different roles; society

[12] See Alexander Bard and Jan Soderqvist, *Netocracy: The New Power Elite and Life after Capitalism* (London: Reuters, 2002).

itself is no longer a hierarchic Whole but a complex, open network of networks.

Netocracy presents the local groups of the new informational elite almost as islands of nonalienated, utopian communities. It describes the life of the new "symbolic class," for which lifestyle, access to exclusive information, and social circles matter more than money (top academics, journalists, designers, programmers, etc. do indeed live this way). The first problem here is that of *recognition:* do netocrats *really* not care about others, or is their ignorance feigned, a way to assert their elitism in the eyes of others? (Obviously, they do not care for money, because they have enough of it.) Plus, to what extent and in what more precise sense are they "in power," independently of their wealth? Are the authors of *Netocracy* fully aware of the ultimate irony of their notion of "nomadic" subjects and thought as opposed to traditional, hierarchic thought? What they are actually claiming is that the netocrats, today's elite, realize the dream of yesterday's marginal philosophers and outcast artists (from Spinoza to Nietzsche and Deleuze). In short, and stated even more pointedly, the thought of Foucault, Deleuze, and Guattari, the ultimate philosophers of resistance, of marginal positions crushed by the hegemonic power network, is effectively the ideology of the newly emerging ruling class.[13]

The problem of *Netocracy* is that it moves simultaneously too fast and not fast enough. As such, it shares the mistake of all those other attempts that much too quickly elevated a new entity into the successor of capitalism and other candidates: the postindustrial society, the informational society. Against such temptations, one should insist that the "informational society" is simply *not* a concept at the same level as "feudalism" or "capitalism." The picture of the accomplished rule of the netocracy is therefore, in spite of the authors' stress on new class antagonisms, a utopia: an inconsistent composite that cannot survive and reproduce itself on its own terms. All too many of the features of the new

---

[13] However, was Hegel ever really a state philosopher against the "marginal" nomadic series of Spinoza-Nietzsche? There are two brief periods when he may have qualified for this role. He himself in his last decade, and the conservative British Hegelians (Bradley, et al.), with their ridiculous misreading of Hegel. But what about the numerous explosive, revolutionary appropriations of Hegel, starting with Bakunin? What about Friedrich Wilhelm IV calling the late Schelling to Berlin in 1840 to fight Hegel's revolutionary influence ten years after Hegel's death? And what about Nietzsche as a German state philosopher? In the Germany of the late nineteenth century, it was, rather, Nietzsche who was a proto-state-philosopher against Hegel—not to mention Spinoza himself as the philosopher of the de Witt brothers faction of the Dutch state. The philosopher whose watered-down version effectively can function as a "state philosophy" is Kant: from neo-Kantians a century ago to Luc Ferry, now a minister of education in France, and, up to a point, Habermas in Germany. The reason is that Kant ideally unites respect for the positive sciences with the limitation of the scope of scientific knowledge (thus making space for religion and morality)—this being exactly what a state ideology needs.

netocratic class are sustainable only within a capitalist regime. Therein resides the weakness of *Netocracy:* following the elementary logic of ideological mystification, it dismisses as "remainders of the (capitalist and statist) past" what are, effectively, positive conditions of the functioning of the informational society.

The key problem is that of capitalism, the way "netocracy" relates to capitalism. On one side, we have patents, copyrights, and so forth—all the different modalities in which information itself is offered and sold on the market as "intellectual property," as another commodity. (And when the authors claim that the true elite of netocracy is beyond patents, and so forth, because its privilege is no longer based on possessing the information but on being able to discern, in the confusingly massive quantity of information, the relevant material, they strangely miss the point: why should this ability to discern what really matters, the ability to discard the irrelevant ballast, not be another—perhaps crucial—information to be sold? In other words, they seem to forget the basic lesson of today's cognitive sciences, namely that, already, at the most elementary level of consciousness, information *is* the ability to "abstract," to discern the relevant aspects in the confusing multitude with which we are constantly bombarded.) On the other side, there is the prospect of the exchange of information *beyond* the property relations characterizing capitalism. This inner antagonism is realized in the basic tension within the new netocratic class between procapitalists (types like Bill Gates) and those advocating a postcapitalist utopia (and, the authors are right in emphasizing that the future "class struggle" will be decided with regard to the possible coalition between the postcapitalist netocrats and the underprivileged "consumtariat"). Without this coalition and support from within netocracy, the "consumtariat" alone can only articulate its protest in violent negative actions lacking any positive, future-oriented program. The key point is thus that there is no "neutral" netocracy: there is either a procapitalist netocracy, itself part of late capitalism, or the postcapitalist netocracy, part of a different mode of production. To complicate things further, this postcapitalist perspective is, in itself, ambiguous: it can mean a more open "democratic" system or the emergence of a new hierarchy, a kind of informational/biogenetic neofeudalism.

This struggle is already taking place. In 2001, the Microsoft Corporation announced that it is working on Palladium, a radically new version of Windows with a separate security chip that would give users protection and control of their information: "Nothing leaves your PC without your permission." Palladium ensures, through encryption, that no one eavesdrops on you, all ingoing mail is filtered, your outgoing messages can be opened only by those you authorize, you can track who opened them, and so forth—it is a "plan to remake the personal computer to ensure security, privacy and intellectual property."[14] Is this not *the* big attempt to inscribe the informational universe into the capitalist logic of private property? Opposed to this tendency are attempts to develop a new cyberspace language, an alternative to Windows, that would be not only freely accessible to everyone but also developed through free social interaction (preliminary versions are not kept hidden, awaiting the magic moment when the new product is revealed to the market; on the contrary, these versions already freely circulate in order to elicit feedback from the users). The fact that AOL supports such an alternative in order to strike at its competitor is telltale: why should progressive forces not strategically use this support?[15]

Blows against the Empire

Today's global capitalism can no longer be combined with democratic representation: the key economic decisions of bodies like the International Monetary Fund (IMF) or World Trade Organization (WTO) are not legitimized by any democratic process, and this lack of democratic representation is structural, not empirical. For this reason, the call for a global (representative) democracy that would submit the IMF, WTO, and other agencies to some kind of democratic control (voiced, in Germany, by Habermas, Beck, Lafontaine, and others) is illusory. Can one really even imagine a worldwide vote for the board of the IMF? We are dealing with more than the usual complaint that parliamentary democracy is "formal"—here, even the form is absent.

---

[14] See the report "The Big Secret" in *Newsweek,* July 8, 2002, pp. 50–52.

[15] There is more than one story to be told about Bill Gates. First, there is the American success story: a young boy starting a company in his garage a mere quarter of a century ago, borrowing ridiculously small amounts of money from his neighbors and relatives, who is now the richest man in the world—the latest proof of the infinite opportunities of America, the American dream at its purest. Then there is the story of Bill Gates the evil monopolist, the ominous master with his weird smile whom we love to hate—the obverse of the American dream, one of the ideal figures of American paranoia. In spite of its apparent anticapitalist stance, this second story is no less ideological than the first. It is sustained by another myth, that of American freedom, of a freedom fighter destroying the bad Institution (from the Watergate journalists to Noam Chomsky). In short, what these two stories share is the fetishized personification of social struggles: the belief in the key role of the heroic individual. Finally, there is the Bill Gates of "frictionless capitalism," the emblem of a postindustrial society in which we witness the "end of labor," in which software is winning over hardware and the young nerd over the old top manager in a black suit. In the new company headquarters, there is little external discipline: (ex)hackers, who dominate the scene, work long hours, enjoying free drinks in green surroundings. How, then, do these three stories relate? To get the complete picture, one should add a *fourth* story, the one that would supplement the third one (the ideology of "frictionless capitalism") in the same way the ominous figure of Gates-the-evil-monopolist supplements the figure of the boy next door who made it and became the richest man in the world: the (Marxist) narrative of the inherent antagonisms and destructive potentials of capitalism.

Hardt and Negri's *Empire*[16] aims at providing a solution to this predicament. Their wager is to repeat Marx. For Marx, highly organized corporate capitalism was already a form of socialism within capitalism (a kind of socialization of capitalism, with the absent owners becoming superfluous), so that one need only cut the nominal head off and we get socialism. In an identical fashion, Hardt and Negri see the same potential in the emerging hegemonic role of immaterial labor. Today, immaterial labor is "hegemonic" in the precise sense in which Marx proclaimed that, in nineteenth-century capitalism, large industrial production was hegemonic as the specific color giving its tone to the totality—not quantitatively but playing the key, emblematic structural role. This, then, far from posing a mortal threat to democracy (as conservative cultural critics want us to believe), opens up a unique chance of "absolute democracy"—why?

In immaterial production, the products are no longer material objects but new social (interpersonal) relations themselves. It was already Marx who emphasized how material production is always also the (re)production of the social relations within which it occurs; with today's capitalism, however, the production of social relations is the immediate end/goal of production. The wager of Hardt and Negri is that this directly socialized, immaterial production not only renders owners progressively superfluous (who needs them when production is directly social, formally and as to its content?); the producers also master the regulation of social space, since social relations (politics) *is* the stuff of their work. The way is thus open for "absolute democracy," for the producers directly regulating their social relations without even the detour of democratic representation.

The problem here is, at a minimum, triple. First, can one really interpret this move toward the hegemonic role of immaterial labor as the move from production to communication, to social interaction (i.e., in Aristotelian terms, from *techne* as *poiesis* to *praxis*?) Does it really indicate the overcoming of the Arendtian distinction between production and *vis activa*, or of the Habermasian distinction between instrumental and communicational reason? Second, how does this "politicization" of production, in which production directly produces (new) social relations, affect the very notion of politics? Is such an "administration of people" (subordinated to the logic of profit) still politics, or is it the most radical sort of depoliticization, the entry into "post-politics"? And last but not least, is democracy not by necessity, with regard to its very notion, nonabsolute? There is no democracy without a hidden, presupposed

---

[16] Michael Hardt and Toni Negri, *Empire* (Cambridge, Mass.: Harvard University Press, 2000).

elitism. Democracy is, by definition, not "global"; it *has* to be based on values or truths that one cannot select "democratically." In democracy one can fight for truth but not decide what *is* truth. As Claude Lefort and others amply demonstrated, democracy is never simply representative in the sense of adequately re-presenting (expressing) a preexisting set of interests, opinions, and so forth since these interests and opinions are constituted only through such representation. In other words, the democratic articulation of an interest is always minimally performative: through their democratic representatives people establish what their interests and opinions are. As Hegel already knew, "absolute democracy" could actualize itself only in the guise of its "oppositional determination," as *terror*. There is, thus, a choice to be made here: do we accept democracy's structural, not just accidental, imperfection, or do we also endorse its terroristic dimension?

Hardt and Negri's slogan—multitude as the site of resistance against the Empire—opens up a further series of problems, the primary one among them being the level at which a multitude functions—what a given field of multitudes excludes, what it *has* to exclude to function. There is, hence, always a nonmultiple excess over multitudes. Take multiculturalist identity politics. Yes, a thriving multitude of identities—religious, ethnic, sexual, cultural—asserted against the specter of antiquated "class reductionism and essentialism." However it was noted long ago by many a perspicacious observer, in the mantra of "class, gender, race," "class" sticks out, never properly thematized. Another case of such a homogenization of multitudes is capital itself: capitalism is multiplicity in principle (totally monopolistic capital is conceptual nonsense), but, precisely as such, it needs a universal medium as the sole domain within which its multitude can thrive, the medium of a legally regulated market in which contracts are respected and their breach punished, and so on. In what I would call a properly dialectical move, Ernesto Laclau points out how "it was only when [the] process of centralization [in the early modernity] had advanced beyond a certain point that something resembling a unitary multitude could emerge through the transference of sovereignty from the king to the people."[17] In other words, one cannot simply oppose the subversive immanent multitude to the centralizing transcendent State Power: it was the very establishment of a centralized state power in the seventeenth and eighteenth centuries that created the space for the emergence of the modern political multitude in the first place.

So, to ask a naive question, what would "multitude in power" (not only as resistance) be? How would it *function*? Hardt and Negri distinguish

[17] Ernesto Laclau, "Can immanence explain social struggles?" unpublished manuscript.

two ways to oppose the global capitalist Empire: either the "protection-ist" advocacy of the return to the strong nation-state or the deployment of even more flexible forms of multitude. Along these lines, in his analy-sis of the Porto Allegro antiglobalist meeting, Hardt emphasizes the new logic of political space at work there. It was no longer the old "us versus them" binary logic, with the Leninist call for a firm, singular party line but the coexistence of a multitude of political agencies and positions that are incompatible with each other as far as their ideological and program-matic accents are concerned (from "conservative" farmers and ecologists worried about the fate of their local tradition and patrimony to human rights groups and agents standing for the interests of immigrants, ad-vocating global mobility). It is, effectively, today's opposition to global capital that seems to provide a kind of negative mirror-image in relation to Deleuze's claim about the inherently antagonistic nature of capitalist dynamics (a strong machine of deterritorialization that generates new modes of reterritorialization): today's resistance to capitalism reproduces the same antagonism. Calls for the defense of particular (cultural, ethnic) identities being threatened by global dynamics coexist with the demands for more global mobility (against the new barriers imposed by capital-ism, which concern, above all, the free movement of individuals). Is it, then, true that these tendencies (these *lignes de fuite,* as Deleuze would have put it) can coexist in a nonantagonistic way, as parts of the same global network of resistance? One is tempted to answer this claim by applying to it Laclau's notion of the chain of equivalences: of course, this logic of multitude functions, because we are still dealing with *resistance.* However, what about when—if this really is the desire and will of these movements—"we take it over"? What would the "multitude in power" look like?

There was a similar constellation in the last years of the decaying Really-Existing Socialism: the nonantagonistic coexistence, within the oppositional field, of a multitude of ideologicopolitical tendencies, from liberal human rights groups to "liberal" business-oriented groups, con-servative religious groups and leftist workers' demands. This multitude functioned well as long as it was united in the opposition to "them," the Party hegemony. Once they found *themselves* in power, the game was over. Another case of acting multitude is the crowd that brought back into power Hugo Chávez in Venezuela. However, can we forget the obvi-ous fact that Chávez functions as a Latino-American *caudillo,* the unique Leader whose function is to magically resolve the conflicting interests of those who support him? "Multitude in power" thus necessarily actu-alizes itself in the guise of an authoritarian leader whose charisma can serve as the "empty signifier" able to contain the multitude of interests (it was already Perón who was a militaristic patriot to the army, a devout Christian to the church, a supporter of the poor against oligarchy on behalf of workers, etc.). The favored example of the supporters (and practitioners) of the new, dispersed counterpower of the multitude is, of course, the Zapatista movement in Chiapas, Mexico. Here is Naomi Klein's description of how its leading figure, subcommandante Marcos, functions:

> [H]e wasn't a commander barking orders, but a subcommandante, a conduit for the will of the councils. His first words, in his new persona, were "Through me speaks the will of the Zapatista National Liberation Army." Further subjugating himself, Marcos says to those who seek him out that he is not a leader, but that his black mask is a mirror, reflecting each of their own struggles; that a Zapatista is anyone anywhere fighting injustice, that "We are you." Most famously, he once told a reporter that "Marcos is gay in San Francisco, black in South Africa, an Asian in Europe, a Chicano in San Ysidro, an anarchist in Spain, a Palestinian in Israel, . . . a single woman on the Metro at 10 P.M., a peasant without land, a gang member in the slums. . . . Meanwhile, Marcos himself—the supposed non-self, the conduit, the mirror—writes in a tone so personal and poetic, so completely and unmistakably his own.[18]

It is clear that such a structure can function only as the ethicopoetic shadowy double of the existing positive state power structure. No wonder Marcos cannot show his face; no wonder his idea is to throw off his mask and disappear back into anonymity if and when the movement reaches its goals. If the Zapatistas were to effectively take power, statements like "Through me speaks the will of . . ." would immediately acquire a much more ominous dimension—their apparent modesty would reveal itself as extreme arrogance, as the presumption of one particular individual that his subjectivity serves as a direct medium of expression for the universal will. Do we still remember how phrases like "I am nothing in myself, my entire strength is yours, I am just an expression of your will!" was the standard cliché of "totalitarian" leaders, who also knew very well how to manipulate their dark implication—". . . so anyone who attacks me personally is effectively attacking you all, the entire people, your love for freedom and justice!" The greater the poetic potential of Marcos in opposition, as a critical voice of *virtual* protest, the greater would be the terror of Marcos as an *actual* leader. As to the political effects of the Zapatista movement, one should note the final irony here: when Klein lists as the main Zapatista political achievement that this movement "helped topple the corrupt seventy-one-year reign of the Institutional

[18] Naomi Klein, *Fences and Windows* (London: Flamingo, 2002), pp. 211–12.

Revolutionary Party,"[19] what this amounts to is that, with Zapatista help, Mexico got the first postrevolutionary government, a government that cut the last links with the historical heritage of Zapata and fully endorsed Mexico's integration into the neo-liberal New World Order (no wonder the two presidents, Fox—ex-boss of the Mexican branch of Coca-Cola—and Bush, are personal friends).

However, is it not that the Zapatistas *did* develop a minimal, positive political program, that of local self-determination, of moving in where state power failed and enabling people to constitute new spaces of local community democracy? "What sets the Zapatistas apart from your average Marxist guerrilla insurgents is that their goal is not to win control but to seize and build autonomous spaces where 'democracy, liberty and justice' can thrive. . . . Marcos is convinced that these free spaces, born of reclaimed land, communal agriculture, resistance to privatization, will eventually create counter-powers to the state simply by existing as alternatives."[20] And yet, we encounter here the same ambiguity: are these autonomous spaces germs of the organization-to-come of the entire society or just phenomena emerging in the crevices and gaps of the social order? Marcos's formulation that the Zapatistas are not interested in the Revolution but, rather, in "a revolution that makes revolution possible" is deeply true, but nonetheless profoundly ambiguous. Does this mean that the Zapatistas are a "Cultural Revolution" laying the foundation for the actual political revolution (what, way back in the 1960s, Marcuse called "freedom as the condition of liberation"), *or* does it mean that they should remain merely a "site of resistance," a corrective to the existing state power (not only without the aim to replace it but also without the aim to organize the conditions in which this power will disappear)?

When Marcos lists all those covered by the signifier "Zapatista," all those rendered invisible by neo-liberal globalization, its excluded ("the indigenous, youth, women, homosexuals, lesbians, people of color, immigrants, workers, peasants . . ."), this effectively sounds like Laclau's "chain of equivalences." However, with the twist that this chain clearly refers to a privileged central signifier, that of neo-liberal global capitalism. So, when Klein herself had to note how the Zapatista movement is "keenly aware of the power of words and symbols,"[21] when Marcos proclaims that *words* are his weapons, one should neither joyfully assert how we are dealing with a truly postmodern "politics of the signifier" nor should one indulge in cynical quips about how the Zapatistas are well

[19] Klein, op. cit., p. 214.
[20] Klein, op. cit., p. 228.
[21] Klein, op. cit., p. 213.

versed in mobilizing the fetishizing power of logos (the focus of Naomi's bestseller). One should, rather, reflect on how this use of mythical-poetic Master-Signifiers affects the actual political impact of the movement. If the defenders of the Zapatistas were to reply here that, in this case, the central Master-Signifier is not a totalizing-homogenizing force but just a kind of empty container, a designation that holds open the space for the thriving of the irreducible plurality, one should add to that this, precisely, is how Master-Signifiers already functioned in fascism and populism, in which the reference to a charismatic Leader serves to neutralize the inconsistent multitude of ideological references.

The response of the partisans of Negri and Hardt to this critique is, of course, that it continues to perceive the new situation from within the old framework. In the contemporary information society, the question of "taking power" is more and more irrelevant since there is no longer any central Power agency that plays a de facto decisive role—power itself is shifting, decentered, "Protean . . ." Perhaps, then, today, in the epoch of *homo sacer,* one of the options is to pursue the trend of self-organized collectives in areas outside the law.[22] Recall life in today's *favelas* in Latin American megalopolises: are they, in some sense, not the first "liberated territories," the cells of futural self-organized societies? Are institutions like community kitchens not a model of "socialized" communal local life? (And, perhaps, from this standpoint, one can also approach, in a new way, the "politics of drugs." Was it really an accident that, at every moment that a strong self-organized collective of those outside the law emerged, it was soon corrupted by hard drugs—from African American ghettos after the rebellions in the 1960s and Italian cities after the workers' unrests of the 1970s up to today's *favelas*? And the same holds even for Poland after Jaruzelski's coup in 1980. All of a sudden, drugs were easily available, together with pornography, alcohol, and Eastern Wisdom manuals, in order to ruin the self-organized civil society. Those in power knew full well when to use drugs as a weapon against self-organized resistance.)

However, what about the complex network of material, legal, institutional, and other conditions that must be maintained for the informational "multitude" to be able to function? Naomi Klein writes, "Decentralizing power doesn't mean abandoning strong national and international standards—and stable, equitable funding—for health care,

---

[22] Perhaps the greatest literary monument to such a utopia comes from an unexpected source— Mario Vargas Llosa's *The War of the End of the World* (1981), the novel about Canudos, an outlaw community deep in the Brazilian backlands that was a home to prostitutes, freaks, beggars, bandits, and the most wretched of the poor. Canudos, led by an apocalyptic prophet, was a utopian space without money, property, taxes, and marriage. In 1987, it was destroyed by the military forces of the Brazilian government.

education, affordable housing and environmental protection. But it does mean that the mantra of the left needs to change from 'increase funding' to 'empower the grassroots' "[23]—and so one should ask the naive question: *how?* How are these strong standards and funding—in short, the main ingredients of the welfare state—to be maintained? No wonder that, in a kind of ironic twist proper to the "cunning of reason," Hardt and Negri end their *Empire* with a minimal positive political program of three points: the demand for global citizenship (so that the mobility of the working force under the present capitalist conditions is recognized); the right to a social wage (a minimal income guaranteed to everybody); the right to reappropriation (so that the key means of production, especially those of new informational media, are socially owned). The irony here is not only the content of these demands (with which, *in abstractu,* every radical liberal or social democrat would agree) but their very form—*rights, demands*—which unexpectedly brings back into the picture what the entire book was fighting against: political agents all of a sudden appear as subjects of universal rights, demanding their realization (from whom, if not some universal form of legal state power?). In short (psychoanalytic terms), from the nomadic schizo outside the Law we pass to the hysterical subject trying to provoke the Master by way of bombarding him with impossible demands. Brian Massumi writes

> [T]he way that a concept like hope can be made useful is when it is *not* connected to an expected success—when it starts to be something different from optimism—because when you start trying to think ahead into the future from the present point, rationally there really isn't much room for hope. Globally it's a very pessimistic affair, with economic inequalities increasing in many regions, with the global effects of environmental deterioration already being felt, with conflicts among nations and peoples apparently only getting more intractable, leading to mass displacements of workers and refugees... it seems such a mess that I think it can be paralysing.... On the other hand, if hope is separated from concepts of optimism and pessimism, from a wishful projection of success or even some kind of rational calculation of outcomes, then I think it starts to be interesting—because it places it in the *present.*[24]

One should bear in mind the radical ambiguity of this position: the suspension of the teleological dimension, the immersion into the "now," the fact that the process of liberation already has to practice freedom, all this remains tainted by the suspicion that the focus on the "now" constitutes a desperate strategic retreat from the hopelessness of any approach based on the more global "cognitive mapping" of the situation.

[23] Klein, op. cit., p. 223.
[24] Brian Massumi, in *Hope*, op. cit., p. 211.

On the Permanent Actuality for Revolutionary Cultural Politics of President Mao Ze Dong's Slogan "Long Live the Great Proletarian Cultural Revolution"

A revolutionary process is not a well-planned strategic activity with no place in it for a full immersion into the Now without regard to long-term consequences. Quite the contrary: the suspension of all strategic considerations based on hope for a better future, the stance of *on attaque, et puis, on le verra* (Lenin often referred to this slogan of Napoleon), is a key part of any revolutionary process. Recall the staged performance of "Storming the Winter Palace" in Petrograd on the third anniversary of the October Revolution (November 7, 1920).[25] Thousands of workers, soldiers, students, and artists worked round the clock, living on *kasha* (tasteless wheat porridge), tea, and frozen apples, preparing the performance at the very place where the event "really took place" three years earlier. Their work was coordinated by army officers as well as by avant-garde artists, musicians, and directors, from Malevich to Meyerhold. Although this was acting and not "reality," the soldiers and sailors were playing themselves—many of them not only actually participated in the event of 1917 but were also simultaneously involved in the real battles of the Civil War that were raging in the nearby vicinity of Petrograd, a city under siege and suffering from severe shortages of food. A contemporary commented on the performance: "The future historian will record how, throughout one of the bloodiest and most brutal revolutions, all of Russia was acting."[26] And the formalist theoretician Viktor Shklovski noted that "some kind of elemental process is taking place where the living fabric of life is being transformed into the theatrical."[27] We all remember the infamous, self-celebratory First of May parades that were one of the supreme signs of recognition of the Stalinist regimes. If one needs proof of how Leninism functioned in an entirely different way, are such performances not the supreme proof that the October Revolution was definitely *not* a simple coup d'état by the small group of Bolsheviks but an event that unleashed a tremendous emancipatory potential? Does the "Storming of the Winter Palace" staging not display the force of a

---

[25] This event (directed by Nikolai Evreinov who, in 1925, emigrated to France) involved 8,000 direct participants and an audience of 100,000 (a quarter of the city's population, in spite of heavy rain). The underlying idea was formulated by Anatoli Lunacharsky, people's commissar for enlightenment, in the spring of 1920: "In order to acquire a sense of self the masses must outwardly manifest themselves, and this is possible only when, in Robespierre's words, they become a spectacle unto themselves" (quoted in Richard Taylor, *October* [London: BFI, 2002]).

[26] Quoted from Susan Buck-Morss, *Dreamworld and Catastrophe* (Cambridge, Mass.: Harvard University Press, 2001), p. 144.

[27] Quoted from Buck-Morss, op. cit., p. 144.

sacred (pagan?) pageant, of the magic act of founding a new community? It is *here* that Heidegger should look when he wrote about founding a state as the event of truth (and not to the Nazi rituals); it is, perhaps, *here* that there occurred the only meaningful "return of the sacred." In short, it is here that, perhaps, one should look for the realization of Wagner's *Gesamtkunstwerk*, of what he aimed at with the designation of his *Parsifal* as *Bühnenweihfestspiel* (sacred festival drama): if ever, then, it was in Petrograd of 1919, much more than in ancient Greece, that, "in intimate connection with its history, the people itself that stood facing itself in the work of art, becoming conscious of itself, and, in the space of a few hours, rapturously devouring, as it were, its own essence." This aestheticization, in which the people quite literally "plays itself," certainly does not fall under Benjamin's indictment of the Fascist "aestheticization of the political." Instead of abandoning this aestheticization to the political Right, instead of a blanket dismissal of every mass political spectacle as "proto-Fascist," one should perceive, in this minimal, purely formal, difference of the people from itself, the unique case of "real life" differentiated from art by nothing more than an invisible, formal gap. The very fact that, in historical documentaries, movie shots from this reconstruction (as well as from Eisenstein's 1927 *October*) of the storming of the Winter Palace are often presented as documentary shots is to be taken as an indication of this deeper identity of people playing themselves.

The archetypal Eisensteinian cinematic scene rendering the exuberant orgy of revolutionary destructive violence (what Eisenstein himself called "a veritable bacchanalia of destruction") belongs to the same series. When, in *October*, the victorious revolutionaries penetrate the wine cellars of the Winter Palace, they indulge in the ecstatic orgy of smashing thousands of the expensive wine bottles. In *Bezhin Meadow*, the village Pioneers force their way into the local church and desecrate it, robbing it of its relics, squabbling over an icon, sacrilegiously trying on vestments, heretically laughing at the statuary. In this suspension of goal-oriented instrumental activity, we effectively get a kind of Bataillean "unrestrained expenditure"—the pious desire to deprive the revolution of this excess is simply the desire to have a revolution without revolution. However, this "unrestrained expenditure" is not enough. In a revolution proper, such a display of what Hegel would have called "abstract negativity" merely, as it were, wipes the slate clean for the second act, the imposition of a New Order.

What this means is that, in a truly radical political act, the opposition between a "crazy" destructive gesture and a strategic political decision momentarily breaks down. This is why it is theoretically and politically wrong to oppose strategic political acts, as risky as they might be, to radical "suicidal" gestures à la Antigone, gestures of pure self-destructive ethical insistence with, apparently, no political goal. The point is not simply that, once we are thoroughly engaged in a political project, we are ready to risk everything for it, inclusive of our lives, but, more precisely, that only such an "impossible" gesture of pure expenditure can change the very coordinates of what is strategically possible within a historical constellation. Another expression of this excess is an unexpected feature of all outbursts of revolt. Several years ago, there was a rebellion of Cuban refugees detained at the Guantánamo base. Its direct cause was that one group of refugees received lower quality orange juice than another group. The very trifling character of what triggered the violent uprising is indicative: not a big injustice or large-scale suffering but a minimal, ridiculous difference, especially for people who just came from Cuba, a country with severe food shortages. Does this not make it clear that the cause immediately triggering a rebellion is, by definition, trifling, a pseudo cause signalling that what is at stake is the relationship to the Other?

According to the standard Leftist periodization (first proposed by Trotsky), the "Thermidor" of the October Revolution occurred in the mid-1920s—in short, when Trotsky lost power, when the revolutionary élan changed into the rule of the new nomenklatura bent on constructing "socialism in one country." To this, one is tempted to oppose two alternatives: either the claim (advocated by Alain Badiou and Sylvain Lazarus in France) that the proper revolutionary sequence ended precisely in October 1917, when the Bolsheviks took over state power and thereby started to function as a *state* party, or the claim (articulated and defended in detail by Sheila Fitzpatrick) that the collectivization and rapid industrialization of the late 1920s was part of the inherent dynamic of the October Revolution, so that the revolutionary sequence proper ended only in 1937—the true "Thermidor" occurred only when the big purges were cut short to prevent what Getty and Naumov called the complete "suicide of the party,"[28] and the party nomenklatura stabilized itself into a "new class." And, effectively, it was only during the terrible events of 1928–1933 that the very body of Russian society effectively underwent a radical transformation. In the difficult but enthusiastic years of 1917–1921, the entire society was in a state of emergency; the period of New Economic Politics (NEP) marked a step backward, a consolidation of

---

[28] See J. Arch Getty and Oleg V. Naumov's outstanding *The Road to Terror: Stalin and the Self-Destruction of the Bolsheviks, 1932–39* (New Haven, Conn.: Yale University Press, 1999).

the Soviet state power leaving basically intact the texture of the social body (the large majority of peasants, artisans, intellectuals, etc.). It was only the thrust of 1928 that directly and brutally aimed at transforming the very composure of the social body, liquidating peasants as a class of individual owners, replacing the old intelligentsia (teachers, doctors, scientists, engineers, and technicians) with a new one. As Sheila Fitzpatrick puts it in plastic terms, if an emigrant who left Moscow in 1914 were to return in 1924, he would still recognize the same city, with the same array of shops, offices, theaters, and, in most cases, the same people in charge. If, however, he were to return another ten years later, in 1934, he would no longer recognize the city, so much was the entire texture of social life different.[29] The difficult thing to grasp about the terrible years after 1929, the years of the great push forward, was that, in all the horrors beyond recognition, one can discern a ruthless, but sincere and enthusiastic, will to a total revolutionary upheaval of the social body, to create a new state, intelligentsia, legal system, and so forth.[30] In the domain of historiography, the "Thermidor" occurred with the forceful reassertion of Russian nationalism, the reinterpretation of the great figures of the Russian past as "progressive" (including the tsars Ivan the Terrible and Peter the Great and conservative composers like Tschaikovsky), the ordered refocusing of history writing from anonymous mass trends toward great individuals and their heroic acts. In literary ideology and practice, the "Thermidor" coincides with the imposition of "Socialist Realism"—and here, precisely, one should not miss the mode of this imposition. It was *not* that the doctrine of Socialist Realism repressed the thriving plurality of styles and schools; on the contrary, Socialist Realism was imposed against the predominance of the "proletarian-sectarian" RAPP (the acronym for the "revolutionary association of proletarian writers"), which, in the epoch of the "second revolution" (1928–1932), became "a sort of monster that seemed to be swallowing the small independent writers' organizations one by one."[31] This is why the elevation of Socialist Realism into the "official" doctrine was greeted by the majority of writers with a sigh of relief: if was perceived (and also intended!) as the defeat of "proletarian sectarianism," as the assertion of the right of writers to refer to the large corpus of the "progressive" figures of the past and of the primacy of wide "humanism" over class sectarianism.

[29] Sheila Fitzpatrick, *The Russian Revolution* (Oxford: Oxford University Press, 1994), p. 148.
[30] If one is to experience the proper tragedy of the October Revolution, one only has to imagine it as a three-act drama, structured like J. B. Priestley's *Time and the Conways:* in Act I, we get the staged performance of 1920; in Act II, we get the Stalinist parade twenty years later; and, in Act III, we return to the performance of 1920 and see it to the end, with the unbearable awareness of what the October Revolution turned into two decades later.
[31] Katerina Clark, *The Soviet Novel* (Chicago: University of Chicago Press, 1981), p. 32.

The lack of a systematic and thorough confrontation with the phe-nomenon of Stalinism is the absolute *scandal* of the Frankfurt School.[32] How could a Marxist thought that claimed to focus on the conditions of the failure of the Marxist emancipatory project abstain from analyzing the nightmare of "really existing socialism"? Was not its focus on fascism *also* a displacement, a silent admission of the failure to confront the true trauma? To put it in a slightly simplified way, Nazism was enacted by a group of people who wanted to do very bad things, and they did them; Stalinism, on the contrary, emerged as the result of a radical emancipa-tory attempt. If one is looking for the historic moment when the Stalinist state started to acquire its clear contours, it was not the war communism of 1918–1920 but the epoch of the relaxation of NEP, which started in 1921, when, as a countermeasure to the retreat in the sphere of economy and culture, the Bolsheviks wanted to fortify their political power. Or, as Lenin himself expressed it in his unsurpassable style,

> When an army is in retreat, a hundred times more discipline is required than when the army is advancing.... When a Menshevik says, "You are now retreating; I have been advocating retreat all the time; I agree with you, I am your man, let us retreat together," we say in reply, "For public manifestation of Menshevism our revolutionary courts must pass the death sentence, otherwise they are not our courts, but God knows what."[33]

It was the unique greatness of Eisenstein that, in his *Ivan the Terrible,* he rendered the libidinal economy of the "Thermidor." In the second part of the film, the only colorized reel (the penultimate one) is limited to the hall in which the carnivalesque orgy takes place. It stands for the Bakhtinian fantasmatic space in which "normal" power relations are turned around, in which the tsar is the slave of the idiot whom he proclaims a new tsar; Ivan provides the imbecile Vladimir with all the imperial insignias, then humbly prostrates himself in front of him and kisses his hand. The scene in the hall begins with the obscene chorus and dance of the Oprichniki (Ivan's private army), staged in an entirely "unrealistic" way: a weird mixture of Hollywood and Japanese theater, a musical number whose words tell a weird story (they celebrate the axe that cuts off the heads of

---

[32] The very exceptions to this rule are telltale: Franz Neumann's *Behemoth,* a study of National Socialism, which, in the typical fashionable style of the late 1930s and 1940s, suggests that the three great world systems—the emerging New Deal capitalism, fascism, and Stalinism—tend toward the same bureaucratic, globally organized, "administered" society; Herbert Marcuse's *Soviet Marxism,* his least passionate and arguably worst book, a strangely neutral analysis of the Soviet ideology with no clear commitments; and, finally, in the 1980s, attempts by some Habermasians who, reflecting upon the emerging dissident phenomena, endeavored to elaborate the notion of civil society as the site of resistance to the communist regime—interesting politically but far from offering a satisfactory global theory of the specificity of the Stalinist "totalitarianism."

[33] V. I. Lenin, *Collected Works*, vol. 33 (Moscow: Progress Publishers, 1966), p. 282.

Ivan's enemies). The song first describes a group of boyars having a rich meal: *"Down the middle . . . the golden goblets pass . . . from hand to hand."* The chorus then asks with pleasurable nervous expectation: *"Come along. Come along. What happens next? Come on, tell us more!"* And the solo Oprichnik, bending forward and whistling, shouts the answer: *"Strike with the axes!"* Here we are at the obscene site where musical enjoyment meets political liquidation. And, taking into account the fact that the film was shot in 1944, does this not confirm the carnivalesque character of the Stalinist purges? We encounter a similar nocturnal orgy in the third part of *Ivan* (which was not shot—see the scenario),[34] in which the sacrilegious obscenity is explicit: Ivan and his Oprichniks perform their nightly drinking feast as a black mass, with black monastic robes over their normal clothing. Therein resides the true greatness of Eisenstein, namely, that he detected (and depicted) the fundamental shift in the status of political violence, from the "Leninist" liberating outburst of destructive energy to the "Stalinist" obscene underside of the Law.

Interestingly, the main opponent of Ivan in both parts of the film is not a man but a woman: the old powerful Euphrosyna Staritskaya, Ivan's aunt, who wants to replace Ivan with her imbecilic son Vladimir and thus effectively reign herself. In contrast to Ivan, who wants total power but perceives it as a "heavy load" in exercising it as a means to an end (the creation of a great and powerful Russian state), Euphrosyna is the subject of a morbid passion. For her, power is an end in itself. In his *Phenomenology of Spirit,* Hegel introduces his notorious notion of womankind as "the everlasting irony of the community." Womankind "changes by intrigue the universal end of the government into a private end, transforms its universal activity into a work of some particular individual, and perverts the universal property of the state into a possession and ornament for the family."[35] These lines fit perfectly the figure of Ortrud in Wagner's *Lohengrin:* for Wagner, there is nothing more horrible and disgusting than a woman who intervenes in political life, driven by the desire for power. In contrast to male ambition, a woman wants power to promote her own narrow family interests or, even worse, her personal caprice, incapable as she is of perceiving the universal dimension of state politics. How are we not to recall F. W. J. Schelling's claim that "the same principle carries and holds us in its ineffectiveness which would consume and destroy us in its effectiveness?"[36] A power that, when it is kept in its proper place, can be benign and pacifying that turns into its radical opposite, into the most destructive fury, the moment it intervenes at a higher level,

---

[34] See Sergei Eisenstein, *Ivan the Terrible* (London: Faber and Faber, 1989), pp. 225–64.

[35] G. W. F. Hegel, *Phenomenology of Spirit* (Oxford: Oxford University Press, 1977), p. 288.

[36] F. W. J. Schelling, ed. Manfred Schroeter *Die Weltalter. Fragmente. In den Urfassungen von 1811 und 1813* (Munich: Biederstein, 1946), p. 13.

the level that is not its own. The *same* femininity that, within the close circle of family life, is the very power of protective love that then turns into obscene frenzy when displayed at the level of public and state affairs. And does the same not hold for *Ivan the Terrible*? Is Euphrosyna not the necessary counterpoint of the poisoned Ivan's bride, a gentle woman totally dedicated and submissive to her husband?

Ivan's paradigmatic gesture is the following one: he puts on a show of horror and repentance at the bloodshed he had to order, and then, in a sudden reflective gesture, he fully endorses his cruelty, demanding even more. In a typical moment in Part II, inspecting the bodies of the boyars killed by his Oprichniks, he humbly crosses himself. Suddenly, he stops and points at the ground, a gleam of mad fury in his eyes, saying hoarsely: "Too few!" This sudden shift is best exemplified by the elementary cell in his acting. Repeatedly, we see Ivan staring up forward, with a pathetic expression on his face, as if passionately engrossed in a noble mission; then, all of a sudden, he withdraws his head and looks around himself with a suspicion bordering on paranoiac madness. A variation of this shift is the famous shot when, during his illness in Part I, the priests already and all too eagerly start to perform the appropriate rituals for a dying man. They cover his head with a gigantic sacred book; holding a burning candle on his breast, Ivan participates in the ritual, murmuring prayers; all of a sudden, however, he struggles to raise his head from under the Bible, glances around the room as if trying desperately to get the view of the situation, and then, exhausted, drops back on the pillow beneath the book.

This brings us to a scene that was planned as what Eisenstein called the *donnée* (the pivotal dramatic and emotional point) of the entire trilogy. In the middle of Part III, after the siege and destruction of Novgorod, a city that rebelled against his rule, Ivan, torn by inner doubts and qualms, asks for a priest and wants to confess. While the confessor's cross hangs by him, Ivan enumerates to the priest the horrible deeds he was forced to accomplish for the Motherland. All of a sudden, Eustace, the confessor, gets all too interested in the names of those killed (a fact nicely signaled by the trembling of his cross), and he eagerly asks about whether other names are also among the dead: "Phillip? And … Timothy? And Michael?" After reassuring him ("We will catch him!"), Ivan is suddenly taken aback. He seizes Eustace's cross and drags it down until he is face to face with his confessor. Then, his hands raise the chain to the confessor's throat, and he starts to accuse him menacingly: "Can it be that you too belong to this accursed line?" Finally, he explodes: "Arrest him! Interrogate him! Make him talk!"[37]

---

[37] Eisenstein, op. cit., pp. 240–41.

In a further climactic moment in Part III, Ivan involves God himself in this dialectic. While, in the church, a monk slowly reads the names of all those killed in Novgorod, Ivan lies prostrate in the dust beneath the large painting of the Last Judgment, from which sparks shoot out of the eyes of the celestial judge, whose grim face is full of rage. Ivan reflects on his bloodthirsty actions, trying to excuse them: "It's not wickedness. Not anger. Not cruelty. It is to punish treason. Treason against the common cause." Then, in anguish, he directly addresses God:

> "You say nothing, Celestial Tsar?"
> *He waits. There is no reply. Angrily, as though hurling a challenge, the earthly Tsar repeats menacingly to the Celestial Tsar:*
> "You say nothing, Celestial Tsar?"
> *The earthly Tsar, with a sudden, violent gesture, hurls his bejeweled sceptre at the Celestial Tsar. The sceptre smashes against the flat wall.*[38]

In what, exactly, resides the libidinal economy of this strange twist? It is not that Ivan is simply torn by an inner conflict between his personal ethical qualms and the duty of the ruler who has to perform cruel acts for the sake of his country; it is also not that Ivan is simply bluffing, just hypocritically feigning moral torment. While his will to repent is *absolutely sincere,* he does not subjectively identify with it. He is lodged within the subjective split introduced by the symbolic order. He wants the ritual of confession performed as a proper externalized ritual, and he plays the game of confession in a totally sincere way while, at the same time, retaining the position of a suspicious external observer of the entire spectacle, constantly vigilant, watching for a sudden stab in the back. All he wants is that the agent whom he is addressing, and from whom he expects pardon, will do his job properly, not meddling with politics. In short, Ivan's paranoia is that he cannot trust the agent to whom he is ready to confess his sins—he suspects that this agent (ultimately, God Himself) also harbors a hidden political agenda of his own running counter to Ivan's.

Many a commentator has made ironic remarks about the apparent stylistic clumsiness of the titles of Soviet Communist books and articles, such as their tautological character, in the sense of the repeated use of the same word (such as "revolutionary dynamics in the early stages of the Russian revolution" or "economic contradictions in the development of the Soviet economy"). However, what if this tautology points toward the awareness of the logic of betrayal best rendered by the classic reproach of Robespierre to the Dantonist opportunists: "What you want is a revolution without revolution?" The tautological repetition thus signals the

---

[38] Eisenstein, op. cit., p. 237.

urge to repeat the negation, to relate it to itself—the true revolution is "revolution with revolution," a revolution that, in its course, revolutionizes its own starting presuppositions. Hegel had a presentiment of this necessity when he wrote, "It is a modern folly to alter a corrupt ethical system, its constitution and legislation, without changing the religion, to have a revolution without a reformation."[39] He thereby announced the necessity of what Mao Ze Dong called the "Cultural Revolution" as the condition of the successful social revolution. What, exactly, does this mean? The problem with hitherto revolutionary attempts was not that they were "too extreme" but that they were *not radical enough,* that they did not question their own presuppositions. In a wonderful essay on *Chevengur,* Platonov's great peasant Utopia written in 1927 and 1928 (just prior to forced collectivization), Fredric Jameson describes the two moments of the revolutionary process. It begins with the gesture of radical negativity:

> [T]his first moment of world-reduction, of the destruction of the idols and the sweeping away of an old world in violence and pain, is itself the precondition for the reconstruction of something else. A first moment of absolute immanence is necessary, the blank slate of absolute peasant immanence or ignorance, before new and undreamed-of-sensations and feelings can come into being.[40]

Then follows the second stage, the invention of a new life—not only the construction of the new social reality in which our utopian dreams would be realized but also the (re)construction of these dreams themselves:

> [A] process that it would be too simple and misleading to call reconstruction or Utopian construction, since in effect it involves the very effort to find a way to begin imagining Utopia to begin with. Perhaps in a more Western kind of psychoanalytic language . . . we might think of the new onset of the Utopian process as a kind of desiring to desire, a learning to desire, the invention of the desire called Utopia in the first place, along with new rules for the fantasizing or daydreaming of such a thing—a set of narrative protocols with no precedent in our previous literary institutions.[41]

The reference to psychoanalysis is crucial and very precise: in a radical revolution, people not only "realize their old (emancipatory, etc.) dreams"; rather, they have to reinvent their very modes of dreaming. Is this not the exact formula of the link between death drive and sublimation? It is *only* this reference to what happens *after* the revolution, to the "morning after," that allows us to distinguish between libertarian

[39] G. W. F. Hegel, *Enzyklopaedie der philosophischen Wissenschaften* (Hamburg: 1959), p. 436.
[40] Fredric Jameson, *The Seeds of Time* (New York: Columbia University Press, 1994), p. 89.
[41] Jameson, op. cit., p. 90.

pathetic outbursts and true revolutionary upheavals. These upheavals lose their energy when one has to approach the prosaic work of social reconstruction—at this point, lethargy sets in. In contrast to it, recall the immense creativity of the Jacobins just prior to their fall, the numerous proposals about new civic religion, about how to sustain the dignity of old people, and so on. Therein also resides the interest in reading the reports about daily life in the Soviet Union in the early 1920s, with the enthusiastic urge to invent new rules for quotidian existence: how does one get married? What are the new rules of courting? How does one celebrate a birthday? How does one get buried?...[42] It is precisely with regard to this dimension that revolution proper is to be opposed to the carnivalesque reversal as a temporary respite, the exception stabilizing the hold of power:

> In the European Middle Ages it was customary for great households to choose a "Lord of Misrule." The person chosen was expected to preside over the revels that briefly reversed or parodied the conventional social and economic hierarchies.... When the brief reign of misrule was over, the customary order of things would be restored: the Lords of Misrule would go back to their menial occupations, while their social superiors resumed their wonted status.... Sometimes the idea of Lord of Misrule would spill over from the realm of revel to the realm of politics.... The apprentices took over from their guild masters for a reckless day or two, ... gender roles were reversed for a day as the women took over the tasks and airs normally associated only with men. Chinese philosophers also loved the paradoxes of status reversed, the ways that wit or shame could deflate pretension and lead to sudden shifts of insight.... It was Mao's terrible accomplishment to seize on such insights from earlier Chinese philosophers, combine them with elements drawn from Western socialist thought, and to use both in tandem to prolong the limited concept of misrule into a long-drawn-out adventure in upheaval. To Mao, the former lords and masters should never be allowed to return; he felt they were not his betters, and that society was liberated by their removal. He also thought the customary order of things should never be restored.[43]

[42] Was Che Guevara's withdrawal from all official functions, even from Cuban citizenship, in 1965 to dedicate himself to world revolution—this suicidal gesture of cutting the links with the institutional universe—really an *act*? Or, was it an escape from the impossible task of the positive construction of socialism, from remaining faithful to the *consequences* of the revolution, namely, an implicit admission of failure?

[43] Jonathan Spence, *Mao* (London: Weidenfeld and Nicolson, 1999), pp. xii–xiv. Was not Christ himself such a "Lord of Misrule?"—the abject beggar-king, laughed at in the ceremony of crucifixion, which (as one tends to forget) was not only a tragic event but, for the sneering crowd of spectators, a true *carnival* in the course of which the false pretender to the throne ("here is a man who calls himself the King of Israel") was mockingly crowned with a tiara of thorns. Did he also not preach the suspension or reversal of social hierarchies? Furthermore, is "the Lord of Misrule," also perhaps not one of the appropriate names for the psychoanalyst?

Is, however, such a "terrible accomplishment" not the elementary gesture of every true revolutionary? Why revolution at all, if we do not think that, "the customary order of things should never be restored." What Mao does is to deprive the transgression of its ritualized, ludic character by way of taking it seriously: revolution is not just a temporary safety valve, a carnivalesque explosion destined to be followed by a sobering morning after—*it is here to stay.* Furthermore, this logic of carnivalesque suspension is limited to traditional hierarchical societies. With the full deployment of capitalism, especially today's "late capitalism," it is the predominant "normal" life itself that, in a way, gets "carnivalized," with its constant self-revolutionizing, its reversals, crises, reinventions, so that it is the critique of capitalism, from a "stable" ethical position, that more and more appears today as an exception.

How, then, are we to revolutionize an order whose very principle is constant self-revolutionizing? Perhaps, this is *the* question today.

INDEX